"Jack Shaw's book, *Little by Little*, is a must-read. In the vein of Will Rogers, it is a book full of wit, wisdom, and sage advice for all who would follow God's design for a godly life, a successful life, and a joyful life. In this book, you will find a large number of wise and practical lessons that help people avoid some of the pitfalls of life while at the same time enjoying some aspects of life that others find mundane. I commend this book to you without hesitation. It is one of those books that is truly refreshing, and at the same time smacks of 'I wish I had said it that way' bits of advice. Because of my personal knowledge of the author, I can attest to the authenticity of this writing. I believe it will touch many lives in the days ahead."

Dr. Frank S. Page, Pastor
Taylors First Baptist Church
Taylors, South Carolina
Former President, Southern Baptist Convention

"Jack Shaw has written a book that is a must-read. Chronicling his life and the many things he has done in the business world over the years, he has given diamonds of principles that can challenge and bless everyone who reads it. It is filled with wit and inspiration. I found myself intrigued, charmed, and enlightened. The principles of life and business are priceless. He is uniquely qualified by experience and passion to set before the reader a wealth of knowledge and counsel. You will find it hard to put down when you start reading it. This is one of the best books I have read in years!"

Dr. Jimmy Draper, President Emeritus
LifeWay Christian Resources

"This book will nourish your soul, nurture your heart, and guide you on a significant journey founded in spiritual truth. Jack Shaw is a disciple extraordinaire and servant leader of the highest order. His life experience is a testimony that witnesses to us all."

Nido R. Qubein, President
High Point University

"Many have attempted to describe their journey *of* life, but Jack Shaw has drawn on his unique, intriguing, and inspiring experiences to explain how to journey *for* life. As a successful businessman, Jack has proven the wisdom for successful living he writes about. As an inspirational role model, he is not preachy but practical, although you will be moved and challenged to discover an intimate walk towards your destiny. Whether describing familial influences, leaps of faith, or the joy of giving to others, you'll be captivated by the nuggets of wisdom contained in this easy-reading book. A great life is indeed built 'little by little,' and Jack Shaw's book and life are living proof."

Tommy Barnett, Pastor
Phoenix First Assembly of God
Co-Pastor, Los Angeles Dream Center

"*Little by Little* is one man's account of life as he traveled the road from poverty to success using his own spiritual compass, coupled with his God-given talents and gifts. Jack Shaw has succeeded in giving us many valuable tools and pearls of wisdom in *Little by Little*, whether you aspire to the boardroom or the classroom. In this folksy yet penetrating exposé, you will find hardship and human failure walking hand-in-hand with honor and success—all to the glory of God. Enjoy the journey!"

James M. Ford, M.D.

"Jack Shaw is God-endowed with a can-do spirit. To him, there is no mountain too high to climb or ocean too wide to swim. Early in life he set goals, and I have observed him surpass those goals "little by little."

William F. "Bill" Shivers
Retired general contractor and former associate

"This is a book full of wisdom and inspiration based on the powerful Word of God and valuable life experiences. My only regret is not being able to read this book as a young married adult thirty-two years ago. A chapter that I need to review on at least a weekly basis is the chapter on listening."

Jo Weathers, RN-ONC

LITTLE *by* LITTLE

LITTLE
by LITTLE

A Journey
TO SUCCESS AND SIGNIFICANCE FOR LIFE

JACK E. SHAW

B&H
PUBLISHING GROUP
NASHVILLE, TENNESSEE

978-08054-4876-4

Published by B&H Publishing Group

Nashville, Tennessee

Dewey Decimal Classification: 248.84

Subject Heading: CHRISTIAN LIFE / SELF-IMPROVEMENT

1 2 3 4 5 6 7 8 • 13 12 11 10 09 08

DEDICATION

Without hesitation or reservation, I dedicate *Little by Little*
to my father, William Erby Shaw, and my father-in-law,
Waldo Norman Leslie, men who greatly influenced my life
and my career. But most of all I dedicate it to God, my
heavenly Father, who has guided me "little by little"
on the journey FOR life.

*I will not drive them out ahead of you in a
single year; otherwise, the land would become desolate,
and wild animals would multiply against you. I will drive
them out little by little ahead of you until you have become
numerous and take possession of the land.*

EXODUS 23:29–30

*If that's how God clothes the grass of the field, which is
here today and thrown into the furnace tomorrow, won't
He do much more for you—you of little faith?*

MATTHEW 6:30

CONTENTS: *Points of Interest*

FOREWORD

$\mathcal{S}$ome years ago, at the invitation of a friend, my wife and I were on a Mediterranean cruise. Although some of the momentary thrills of it are long gone, it was a memorable trip. But what I gained most out of that trip was a wonderful and lasting friendship with Jack Shaw. We shared many a meal, many a laugh, and many profound conversations at the table. What I saw in him then and what I have learned about him over these years has made me a better person. In a world where heroes are manufactured for all of the wrong reasons, Jack is a true hero for all of the *right* reasons. His love of God, country, family, and friends is never in question for anyone who watches his life closely. He has also proven the foundational truths of life in living them, in the successes he has enjoyed as a businessman, and in transferring them to those who know and love him. That is why I think this book is a gold mine of lessons learned and truths embodied.

As I read each short chapter, I could hear his voice speaking the words, and I know the heart from which they have come. Jack is an avid golfer and also, as you will read, a certified pilot. I would like to borrow from these two loves of his to drive home a couple of points and lift your sights to higher ground.

A professor held up before his class a jar filled with golf balls. "Is it full?" he asked the class. Hearing a resounding, "Yes," he dipped into his briefcase and emptied some small stone chips into the jar. "Is it full, now?" he asked. "Yes, for sure," came the answer. Once more he dipped into his bag and bringing out a small packet of sand, filled in all the little gaps that were still in the bottle. The class just chuckled and surrendered a grudging, "Oh boy! We were too quick on that. But it's full now without doubt." The professor then slowly emptied his thermos of coffee into the jar. Laughter was heard throughout the classroom.

But then he began his application. "The golf balls are representative of the most important big issues with which you must fill your life—God, family, your values, and so on. The little stones represent your calling, your profession, your social responsibilities. The sand is the hobbies and the recreational side of your life that must be there to fill in the gaps. And finally, no matter how busy you are or how demanding your life, always take time to sip a cup of coffee with a friend or neighbor and take time to unwind from the demands upon you."

Little by Little is a splendid example of this hierarchy of a distributed life. I am certain, and I say it with a smile, that Jack will be pleased to see the metaphor of the golf ball serving as the top priorities in life.

I come now to the second of Jack's loves and an analogy from flying. I had a friend who was a flight instructor at a university. He was talking to me once about the Five C's of flying in times of poor visibility and high risk for landing.

- CONFESS your situation and resist the temptation of a false sense of overconfidence.
- Keep CALM and keep your wits about you.
- CLIMB higher so you can get a better feel of the cloud and fog cover around. This will also buy you some time to think, reflect, and plan.
- Maintain COMMUNICATION with the ground authorities and with those who are going to help you to find your way back safely.
- COMPLY with the instructions they give you rather than depending on your own instincts.

How instructive these Five C's are for life itself.

This book helps you to climb higher to gain the right perspective on life, then leaves you with guidelines for making decisions. If you wish to navigate through the storms and uncertainties that life brings, here is a book to take on your journey, a book that will help bring you in to a safe landing.

Many of life's challenges demand a commitment to the fundamentals that hold true no matter what and a plan of action that has been established well before the urgency comes. That's what I call having a worldview that is set in place on the basis of which the particulars are addressed. Too often we go through life making "ad hoc" decisions—decisions that are made on the spur of the moment and often for momentary reasons.

That is not a wise way to live. The basic ground rules must be drawn before the forks in the road or the attractive seductions come.

This book helps you understand those rules in practical and simple anecdotes. There is nothing complex in these pages. But there is much sublimity that makes the simple attractive and that is worthy of embracing in everyday life. I am certain that every reader will find him or herself at times nodding with approval and putting the book down to contemplate the truths being read.

So let me return to my earlier lines. When we boarded the cruise ship, we were forewarned about the pounds the average person would likely gain during the next days and, at the same time, urged to anticipate the feasts that lay ahead of us. Yes, those pounds came and, thankfully, have gone. Yes, there was a feast at every meal. But my wife and I disembarked with a lasting enrichment from coming to know Jack and Jane Shaw. I have watched him live these truths, and I wish so much that I can be the person of stature that he is because of his wisdom and winsome spirit. That is why I am so delighted to write the foreword or the appetizer portion of this book. The main course is well seasoned and nourishing, and the weight you will gain is the kind you will never want to lose.

—Ravi Zacharias

INTRODUCTION

*T*he message of this book was prompted by three words: "little by little."

In my private devotions, I was reading the Bible—Exodus, chapter 23—when in verse 30, the words "little by little" appeared highlighted in what seemed to be boxcar-size letters. As these words became alive within me, my immediate thought was that this is the plan for the totality of life. I began to understand life as a journey.

The message of this book will be illustrated by meaningful, life-shaping events from my life experiences and personal encounters with others. I write about significant events that have happened to me—events that have helped shape my life, influencing me to experience success on the journey *for* life.

I share with you one ordinary life, extraordinarily blessed.

You may ask, "Why another success book?"

Little by Little is not a self-help, motivational challenge to join other volumes on your bookshelves. It is a truth so powerful that

I dare not keep silent about it. I sense an urgency to shout it from the rooftops.

Throughout time man has been confronted and confounded by many conflicting philosophies assessing life from multiple vantage points without ever reaching consensus as to the purpose and meaning of life. This book is an interim report on my journey, illustrated by significant, life-shaping events from my life experiences. It is my personal attempt to describe the difference between the journey *of* life—which each of us undertakes from birth—and the journey *for* life, which is far more important, even though not all pursue it.

Many individuals, voices, books, and events have helped mold my life. Not all thoughts expressed in *Little by Little* are original. Where possible, I have endeavored to give credit to the source; however, I have lived long enough by now that many truths and ideas I have heard and read have simply become a part of me.

As you search for purpose and meaning in your life, I hope this testimony of how I transitioned from the journey *of* life to the journey *for* life is helpful. My prayer is that through the sharing of these experiences, a dormant ember of curiosity and desire might be ignited within you, leading you to a personal and honest inquiry and consideration of your own journey.

It is not my desire or purpose to impose my views on you. This is not dogma. I share my real-life experiences so that you will see some of the options available to you as you travel life's road. I pray that you will receive it without bias or prejudice as a meaningful alternative to your journey *of* life.

Life is not idealistic. We are not residing in the Garden of Eden. In this book, I write about life outside the Garden of Eden. The garden's protective shield is gone. Paradise is lost. Created life continues where Satan operates as prince and power of the air. How can what is lost be regained?

What you read at times will be personal, entertaining, and (I hope) inspirational. My purpose in writing, however, is to challenge you to listen and hear God's voice. He can be heard in your mind and your spirit, as well as through interaction with others, but most clearly and authoritatively in the Bible.

My desire is for you to experience what happens when on the journey *for* life, a person becomes energized by God's Holy Spirit to "dream dreams" and "see visions," as the prophet Joel said (Acts 2:17)—and then to do them and live them!

Even though I often write in the first person, the focus of this book is not Jack Shaw. If it is, I will have failed in this endeavor. My passion is to introduce you to Jesus Christ, who is responsible for all the meaningful happenings in my life. The most searching question I pray you will be prompted to ask is, "Who is Jack Shaw's God?" Unless you have honestly inquired and put the claims of the Bible to the test of faith and personal experience, you cannot know, and there will always be the wonder, the uncertainty, the gnawing question: "What would my life—my journey—have been like had I only sought to know?"

Don't chance it!

The wonder, the emptiness, the void will remain and never be satisfied until you are unreservedly engaged in the pursuit of truth—wherever it leads. God spoke His invitation through Isaiah to everyone who will hear: "Come . . . let us reason together" (Isa. 1:18 KJV).

It is not my purpose to convince you. I rest the outcome of your inquiry on God. But my prayer is that He will cause you to consider the message of these pages so that when you face Him, you will be "without excuse" (Rom. 1:20), eternally assured of His reality.

┌─────────┐
│   1   │
└─────────┘

LITTLE BY LITTLE

How Life Began, How Life Continues

Little by little I will drive them out before you, until you have increased enough to take possession of the land.

Exodus 23:30 NIV

*W*hen I first observed these words—"little by little"—they became alive in my spirit, and my immediate thought was that this plan could be adapted to the totality of man's life. I began to see life as a journey, not an instantaneous happening. "Little by little" is how life develops. "Little by little" is how life is lived.

Someone once asked Will Rogers, the cowboy philosopher, "If you had only forty-eight hours to live, how would you spend them?" Will Rogers replied, "One at a time."

A Look Backward to Thrust Forward

Studying the history of the children of Israel in the Bible is not always encouraging. Disobedience was characteristic of much of their journey that evolved into many years. It may be easy for us to become instant critics of them; however, before we criticize them too much, let's mentally walk in their shoes.

Through Moses they had received God's promise of a better land, a better life. They could see the goal but could not grasp the journey. Much time had passed and they complained to Moses: "Is it because there are no graves in Egypt that you took us to die in the wilderness?" (Exod. 14:11). In harsh words of personal rebuke, they expressed their fickle desire to go back to the land of their slavery.

Is this different from those of us who now travel on the journey *for* life in its difficult moments? Surely their story reminds us of ourselves when we have had thoughts of turning back. Don't we often line up with their way of seeing things?

Move now to New Testament times, and contrast the apostle Paul's assessment of the path that lay before him. He saw the goal but knew there would be a journey, so he planned for it. In Philippians 3:13–14, he wrote: "One thing I do: forgetting what is behind and reaching forward to what is ahead, I pursue as my goal the prize promised by God's heavenly call in Christ Jesus." The goal should be the motivation for us to make the journey.

Moses reminded the people of God's promise as well as their own limitations. Likewise, in the difficult and uncertain times we experience, reflection is good for us. Sometimes we need to pause, take a deep spiritual breath, contemplate God's goodness that never changes, and then just trust that God knows best. In that reflective moment we move beyond our limitations and are prepared to believe God's promise and accept His way.

Don't worry and become overwhelmed. Worry will rob you of your most productive self. Worry is like a rocking chair: it gives you something to do but it gets you nowhere. The difficult things in life are not impossible; they are just accomplished "little by little," one step at a time.

"Little by little," step by step, test after test, encounter after encounter, the children of Israel crossed the Jordan River on their way to the Promised Land. We can learn many lessons from these illustrations. We learn:

1. The plan for life is for gradual, consistent growth.
2. There are periods in physical growth that must be allowed to occur.
3. Spiritual life is a developing, growing process.

Patience and Readiness

Physical life begins in a mother's womb and is a developing process over a determined period of time. What a marvel!—what a mystery!—the miracle of life developing. Birth occurs and a child begins to develop and grow outside his mother's body—"little by little."

Even Jesus, the Creator God, entered time and space this way. Luke tells us that when the event took place, an angel announced it in these words: "Today in the town of David a Savior has been born to you; he is Christ the Lord" (Luke 2:11 NIV). Jesus was ready when His time came.

"Little by little" speaks to my impatience. By nature, I'm not a patient person; however, God is not through with me yet. He knows what He is doing. There is a reason for the way He allows circumstances and events to happen. God knows me—and knows that "little by little" is for my good, even when it's accompanied with what seems like unanswered prayers.

Abraham's nephew Lot wanted all of life *now!* Given the option by Uncle Abraham to choose the land he preferred, Lot chose the obvious: the well-watered plains. His desire was for instant gratification. Money, possessions, and ambition are a blessing or a curse according to the character of those who possess them. It is not beneficial for a person to grow rich faster than he grows good. Lot's greed and avarice cost him everything meaningful in life.

Similarly, God's process for His people to possess the land was conditioned upon their *readiness*, and He would not lead them beyond it. Readiness qualifies a person for the task. God had said He would not drive out the inhabitants "in a single year" because this would exceed Israel's readiness capability. Possessing the land would be a developing process—"little by little"—over time.

The history of Israel is an example of the process through which mankind develops. A few but increasing number of faithful ones "keep on keeping on," striving to lift the world one by one, to a higher calling. Life can be a long, slow labor against immense difficulties; nevertheless, this defined process—"little by little"—is God's way onward to success on the journey *for* life. The time will come when God says, "You've been here long enough. It's time to move on."

In His humanity, was Jesus ever impatient? When He was twelve years old, He knew His mission and purpose. When as a boy he had journeyed away from the crowd, when Mary and Joseph realized He was missing, they searched days for Him and found Him on mission in the temple. Relieved, Mary and Joseph expressed their concern in a mild rebuke. Respectfully, Jesus replied, "Didn't you know that I had to be in My Father's house?" (Luke 2:49). Patience had made him ready to pursue His mission and purpose.

The American Dream: Little by Little

The "little by little" plan extends beyond physical life. It is applicable to the growth and development of all of life:

National life. How was America built? America is not great just because the Pilgrims landed on these shores. The whole continent was not settled all at once. It happened east to west, strengthened by diversity. America is "one nation under God," known as the "land of opportunity." But without God, it is a land that is being dismantled "little by little." Where are our moorings? We must stop the hemorrhaging. We must get back to our roots. We must heed God's call to revival and renewal—a spiritual battle not to be won with bombs or propaganda but by spiritual warriors being committed and obedient to God's Word and God's purpose. Ezekiel 22:30 speaks of this void: "I searched for a man among them who would repair the wall and stand in the gap before Me on behalf of the land so that I might not destroy it, but I found no one."

Corporate life. Great businesses don't just happen. Most begin small. Some of America's great corporations began in a back room, a garage, a basement. Like all of life, corporate development is a process that involves time and commitment. Research, marketing, goals. Companies can only grow as they are prepared for growth, being able to deliver what they promise. "Dishonest money dwindles away, but he who gathers money *little by little* makes it grow" (Prov. 13:11 NIV, my emphasis). In business you must have a plan of controlled growth. "Little by little." Sometimes it will just be dogged perseverance that gets it done. By perseverance, they say, the snail reached the ark. Walt Disney, for example, went bankrupt prior to the success of Disney World and Epcot.

Don't give up.

Pay attention to details.

Pay the price.

Don't shortcut.

Don't circumvent.

Be thorough.

Sports. The dominating force that African-Americans have become in the world of sports developed "little by little," beginning with such pioneers as Jesse Owens and Jackie Robinson. Great sports teams are recruited one player at a time. Those who strive for Olympic gold achieve their moment in the arena only after they have trained for years, "little by little."

Education. Education is not an instantaneous process. It involves a lifetime of commitment. The process often begins because caring parents take time to plant the seed of learning in a child. Observe how a child will listen as long as someone will read to him and then requests, "Read it again." From the early beginning in kindergarten all they way through the university, learning is a process of planned, gradual achievement and advancement.

Construction. An architect or engineer begins by drafting the first line, then continues one line after another. Magnificent buildings rise one brick at a time. Great bridges take years to build. Major highways seem to take a lifetime to complete; nevertheless, it is a process that can only be accomplished "little by little."

Sales and marketing. Direct selling was always a challenge to me. When I was selling Watkins Products, a line of specialty foods and home care products, I could only knock on one door at a time, and I could only ask for the order one prospect at a time.

Later, I will share where my sales experience would lead—"little by little."

Investing in the Little Things

In His humanity, Jesus knew the power of one by one, of two by two. He did not despise little things or little beginnings. He chose a team of twelve, not thousands—one at a time. This was His way, even though He had legions of angels at His command. Success on the journey *for* life is contingent upon our being obedient to this plan: little by little, one by one.

Think people, not programs.

Begin with yourself, where you are.

The world will only be transformed one soul at a time. As we succeed in getting Christian character in the individual, we will have Christian character in the community, the nation, and the world. This encompasses the Great Commission: "Go, therefore, and make disciples of all nations, baptizing them in the name of the Father and of the Son and of the Holy Spirit, teaching them to observe everything I have commanded you. And remember, I am with you always, to the end of the age" (Matt. 28:19–20).

What Can One Person Accomplish?

Dr. Earl D. Crumpler shared this lesson in a church bulletin more than twenty-five years ago. It magnifies what "little by little" can ignite: A Sunday school teacher, a Mr. Kimball, led a Boston shoe clerk to give his life to Christ in 1858. The clerk, Dwight L. Moody, became an evangelist.

In England in 1879, Moody awakened evangelistic zeal in the heart of Frederick B. Meyer, pastor of a small church. F. B. Meyer, preaching to an American college campus, brought to Christ a student named Wilbur Chapman. Chapman, engaged in YMCA work, employed a former baseball player, Billy Sunday, to do evangelistic work. Billy Sunday held a revival in Charlotte, North Carolina. A group of local men were so enthusiastic afterward that they planned another evangelistic campaign, bringing Mordecai Hamm to preach. During Hamm's revival, a young man named Billy Graham heard the gospel and yielded his life to Christ.

Only eternity will reveal the impact of that one Sunday school teacher who invested his life in the lives of others. Will you invest your life—"little by little"—in the lives of others?

A commencement speaker challenged graduates with these following questions:

"When you arrive at where you are headed, *where will you be?* When you get what you want from life, *what will you possess?* When you achieve the goals you have set for yourself, *what will you have?*"

"Little by little," life goes on. Commencement day is long passed for many. But the ramifications of these same questions still apply:

> Where are you?
> Where is your journey taking you?
> Is it time for a course correction?

Perhaps you got off course because your ambition propelled you beyond the guidelines for a dedicated life of purpose. Why stay where you are? Remember the Prodigal Son? He came to himself and retraced his steps—little by little, one at a time—all the way to his father's house.

The Father is waiting for you!

2

IT PAYS TO DREAM

Nothing happens but first a dream.

CARL SANDBURG

*Y*oung boys dream. God births dreams and desires into the heart and imagination of everyone. Where would we be without a dream? Everything is possible in a dream. Imagination has no limitations, no boundaries. Dreams cost nothing in monetary terms. Share your dreams. It's like "hitching your wagon to a star."

An early dream of mine was scripted under a chinaberry tree on the sodless, broom-swept yard of a three-room mill village house on Cox Street in Honea Path, South Carolina. Let me tell you about it.

Most toys at our house were imagined, except for the small, molded rubber automobile that was all mine. Little boys played

13

cars in my day, even if all they had was a block of wood or a brick and an imagination.

On that dirt track in our front yard my mind was racing, dreaming, thinking—*someday!*

On my knees, car in hand, the sound of its roaring engine echoing from my throat, I could see beyond that yard, beyond the town limits. I could see places I could only dream about. The automobile of my childish dreams had never yet graced the streets of Honea Path, but . . . it would. Someday!

Oh, how I dreamed of that "someday" when I would drive into Honea Path to take my friend, Ray Cox, on the ride of his life and the ride of my dreams. If that day ever came, I would know I'd arrived. Dreams, like life, are best when they are shared.

This little rubber car will come into play later when I tell you about its successor—the Little Red Wagon in chapter 6—and tell you more of my dream. Yes, I dreamed of elaborate vehicles even though our family owned no mode of transportation. In my dreams I knew I would be successful, even though the reality of the moment spoke to me somberly: Can any good thing come out of Honea Path, South Carolina?

Keep your dreams alive. Nourish them—because dreams can come true!

God has allowed me to achieve material possessions beyond my fondest dreams. Indeed, I am greatly blessed, even envied by some. Enjoy your possessions, but don't join the crowd whose measure of success is "the one who has the most toys." Toys may be the measure of success on the journey *of* life, but never on the journey *for* life.

My mind is flooded with memories from my humble beginnings. I discovered the world in Honea Path, South Carolina. Honea Path (pronounced HUN-ee-uh) was at that time a small textile village community, saddled with the ravages of the Depression. My mother often reminded me that the process of my discovery was very enduring. She remembered it like this: "The only thing Jack ever did that he wasn't in a hurry about was being born."

Yes, I guess you could say I was in a hurry. Big dreams were calling me.

Affirmation

Innate in the spirit of man is the desire to succeed. Always be alert and sensitive to the actions of others. Be ready to recognize, acknowledge, and affirm others. Most people I have known yearn for the satisfaction that comes with personal accomplishments followed by their recognition and acknowledgment by others.

This desire begins early in life. Infants want to be acknowledged. They want praise and acceptance:

> "Watch me, Mom."
> "How did I do, Dad?"

These oft-repeated questions or expressions from a child—whatever his age—linger until the desired response is heard.

Around 1993, David Brinkley, the famed television journalist, had just published *David Brinkley: A Memoir.* During an interview with Brinkley on his CNBC show, journalist and ex-NBC copyboy Cal Thomas mentioned that David's late mother kept popping up in the book, and she seemed to withhold her approval from him. Thomas asked him if he and his mother had reconciled before her death."

"No, but not because I didn't try."

"David, she should have been proud of you," Thomas said.

"I thought so, too," Brinkley replied, as tears filled his eyes.

Those of us traveling the journey *for* life should feel the challenge to positively influence aspiring young dreamers along the journey, even those who are less visible than the David Brinkleys of the world. Those we interact with daily in our homes, at work, or in social settings need the encouragement of a consoling word, the assurance that a tender, compassionate touch brings. Be generous with your affirmation and approval to lonely hurting others who are on the journey *for* life. It just might be the encouragement and hope a person needs in a decisive moment.

Most young people today are active participants in whatever sport or competitive event is in season. Whatever their level of talent, their energy and enthusiasm is contagious, and they are eager for encouragement and loving acceptance from their peers and those persons most important to them.

Believe me this desire for recognition never ends! As long as our parents and our bigger-than-life idols live, there will be nothing more rewarding than expressions like:

> "That's good, son."
> "I'm proud of you."

My mom (now in heaven) and Dad (now in his nineties) always caused me to swell with pride by their recognition and acknowledgment of my accomplishments.

Being a parent and a grandparent, I am often challenged to be an encourager. Nothing is more important than my being there, observing, acknowledging, encouraging, and cheering the effort. Whatever the commitment required—regardless of the perceived sacrifice—it's important that I *be there!*

As observed in life, everyone may not be equal in talent; however, no matter the skill level, each person is equal in heart and desire. By being there, you can observe and be an encourager as skills are developed "little by little." The earlier in life that your support and encouragement occur, confidence is gained that will influence the challenges you will face throughout life.

Putting this into perspective, we know from personal experience that it's not always the results but the giving of your best that counts most. For many (not all) of us, home is where encouragement and teaching begins. Outside the home, the encouragement and praise of a gifted school teacher is often the seed of recognition that challenges an individual to excel. Why else do we commit to teach if not to challenge youth to succeed and live a fulfilled life? Nothing is more important or more rewarding than the gift and call to teach challenging, active minds. Dedicated teachers with purpose and passion are strong contributors in any measure of success on the journey *of* life. And for those so called, teaching leads them to personal success on the journey *for* life.

Thank God for dedicated teachers who are committed to making a difference in young lives.

This need for recognition and approval does not end, however, when a person leaves home and school. We should always be observant of our important relationships and associates, being quick to respond with a sincere, personal, heartfelt acknowledgment of an assignment or a project well done. This acknowledgment is a reward in itself and is important beyond any monetary compensation. Don't be too busy to notice. "Be there" with praise and repeat it often.

"Good job!"

"I'm proud of you!"

"Great!"

The value of a person knowing his or her purpose early in his career should be encouraged by everyone in a position to influence others. In doing so, don't be surprised at the joy you experience by planting good seed in good soil.

David Brinkley, who I mentioned earlier, was acclaimed as one of the greatest broadcast journalists to ever live, yet he took time to plant a seed of encouragement in a young life. I remember reading a column where Cal Thomas wrote: "As a kid, I looked for excuses to take him wire service copy just to stand in his presence so that something might rub off on this aspiring journalist. I guess something did, because he told me once, 'You write well.'"

No award could have meant more. What a seed David Brinkley planted in a young life that day!

Even when others fail to recognize or acknowledge that you have done your best—whatever the task—nothing can replace the deep inner sense of personal fulfillment gained by giving your best in the effort. This satisfaction is not without its personal reward. But no matter how great the personal satisfaction of accomplishments may be, it is greatly multiplied when acknowledged by others. Don't just sit in the grandstand or the bleachers. Move to the sidelines:

> Be an encourager.
> Be involved. *Stay* involved.
> Be there!

The proper function of everyone on the journey *for* life is to live life to the fullest, not just to exist. And as paradoxical as it may sound, fullness of life is only realized when you are pouring your life into another life. You are never so full and successful as when you are pouring yourself passionately into another individual and observing the difference it makes.

This is our challenge. It will be realized only as we squeeze the most we can out of life and begin the process of pouring ourselves into others. Life is important—your life and the lives of others you can influence. Don't neglect this challenge—remember, life is what happens while you are making other plans.

Jesus said, "I assure you: Whatever you did for one of the least of these brothers of Mine, you did for me" (Matt. 25:40). You have a choice concerning life, and your life's outcome is up to you! Walk along with me through these pages as we consider life as a journey, differentiating between the journey *of* life and the journey *for* life, putting yourself in a position to encourage and influence the transition.

Never Stop Dreaming

I have always been fascinated with the dream that I would someday pilot an airplane. I remember the excitement when our family would park near the runway of the local airport just to view the takeoffs and landings. I also vividly remember my first flight as a passenger in a small airplane. I was accompanying a minister pilot to a mutual friend's funeral. It was not scheduled to be a long flight, but it seemed like forever. I experienced motion sickness and became ashen white. I had never experienced anything so miserable before. Nevertheless, as sick as I was, the dream to pilot an airplane remained in me.

Years passed, but my dream did not. Already established in business, I was able to sign up for a series of flying lessons leading to my first solo flight. The process of becoming a pilot did not speak to my impatience. A student pilot doesn't solo after his first instructional flight until FAA certification is received. Becoming a pilot is a process, not an event. It happens much like life—"little by little."

Accepting the inevitable, I put in the instructional flight hours and, without my prior knowledge, my instructor determined I was ready to be released for my initial solo flight.

What an exciting event! Here's how it happened.

My instructor, who was somewhat overweight, taxied with me to the designated runway for what I thought would be another in the series of lessons. How surprised, elated, and nervous I became when my instructor momentarily opened the door, looked at me, and said, "You're ready; you're on your own." He then closed the door and walked away from the Cessna 172. I made radio contact with the tower and was cleared for takeoff.

What a difference this experience would be! I didn't realize how heavy my instructor was until the liftoff, which became more like a fast elevator ride than a takeoff run. Absent my instructor, I anxiously made the necessary trim adjustments and flew the flight traffic pattern flawlessly by myself.

At the appropriate time in the traffic pattern, I made contact with the control tower and the controller cleared me for landing. I continued in the pattern and, just as I was about to touch down, he suddenly radioed back that I should abort the landing because a group of stray dogs was crossing the runway. I thought the controller was kidding me—and this was no time to joke! Following the tower's instructions, I gained the proper altitude, flew the traffic pattern, and again radioed the tower for landing instructions. Following the checklist for landing, I finally received clearance for landing, which I executed flawlessly.

And "little by little," the process continued until I had logged the flight hours required in order to take the check ride for my private pilot's certificate.

I took the short, cross country flight from Greenville, South Carolina, to Augusta, Georgia, for my FAA check ride. After completing the process with flying colors—my certification now in hand—my instructor flew back to Greenville with an FAA certified Private Pilot: me.

Arriving back in Greenville, the first thing I did was drive home and quickly return to the airport with my wife, Jane, for my first flight as pilot in command with precious cargo. I was excited. Jane seemed excited and trusting; however, she may have been somewhat nervous.

The Cessna 172 was still on the ramp, so Jane and I got buckled in our seats and taxied out for this proud moment. We were cleared for takeoff and, soon after liftoff, a black liquid substance began to cover the windshield on the pilot's side. Already committed to the takeoff, I anxiously prepared for an emergency landing. These were tense moments as Jane prayed and I piloted the Cessna, looking out the passenger's side of the windshield because now, the pilot's side of the windshield was covered with thick, black oil. I made the necessary maneuvers and received tower clearance for a memorable landing. On the ground I taxied to the ramp with many emotions, much relieved.

This really surprised me. I had been with this airplane most of the day, had performed the walk around and engine check several times, but I did not do the preflight check before my flight with Jane. How could this have happened? But during the brief time I had left the airport to get Jane, a ramp attendant had routinely checked the engine oil and failed to properly secure the oil cap. What a valuable lesson I learned about flying and life that day: never, never, never ignore the preflight checklist. *Never!*

Instruction and training are never over for a pilot. Ground school is a part of flight training and, sharing life the way we do, I wanted Jane to take the classes with me. (In retrospect, it's hard for me to imagine wanting her for my navigator when she has trouble reading an atlas or a road map.) I continued the training sessions, including simulator flying and instrument flying, advancing my skills "little by little," and after the approved FAA check ride, I earned my multi-engine rating.

My flying did not begin as a business tool. As our business grew, however, I was able to utilize our Cessna 205, Beechcraft Baron, Aero Commander, and later a Beechcraft King-Air for business purposes.

But piloting requires undivided attention. For me, flying for pleasure and flying for business is different. Piloting is a profession, and I determined that for my business flying I would always have a qualified professional in charge so that he could give his complete attention to flying and I could give my attention to the business purposes of the day.

I am not an adventuresome pilot. So my instructions to the pilot in command were always to avoid extreme weather. If the weather conditions were questionable, flight planning must include an alternate destination point rather than gambling with weather conditions. The flight was for me and not for the pilot, so I expected my instructions to be followed.

On one trip from Greenville to Myrtle Beach, we were aware that the destination weather was marginal because a significant weather front was forecast for the coastal area later that day. The pilot anticipated a window for landing based upon our ETA and the weather report received just prior to takeoff. We decided to proceed toward Myrtle Beach with Wilmington, North Carolina, being the alternate site should the weather deteriorate while in route.

Without informing me, the pilot decided to enter an ILS (Instrument Landing System) approach for Myrtle Beach. I recognized the sound of the landing gear being lowered into place.

The three green lights appeared, confirming the wheels were in place for landing. The engines were throttled back indicating we were approaching touchdown.

Suddenly, that was not the case.

On the approach, we encountered what quickly became adverse weather conditions. The turbulence began to whip the airplane like a carnival ride. My worst fears were being realized. The pilot was wrestling with the controls on approach without being able to hold the ILS heading. The airplane dropped, tilting to the right, then to the left. At that moment, the pilot (and I) knew that the landing must be aborted. Quickly, the engines were again at full throttle, the landing gear was retracted, and we were climbing through conditions that remained turbulent as we transitioned. Soon we were on the other side of the weather front in ideal flying conditions.

We landed in Wilmington, rented a car, and continued to our appointment in Myrtle Beach. After the storm the pilot brought the plane to Myrtle Beach and—needless to say—he was immediately unemployed.

When finally on the ground, Paul Foster, my friend and attorney who had been traveling with me, described the airborne events like this: "Jack was talking with someone I did not see." Paul was right. I was talking with the Pilot who guides me on my journey *for* life.

It is in moments like these that your purpose surfaces and the journey *for* life becomes all that matters.

The Ultimate Journey: An Uncommon Way

Every life and journey has a beginning point and a destination. The journey *of* life begins at birth; and as long as you choose to travel it, life will continue aimlessly without significance and purpose. No effort is required for an individual to continue on the journey *of* life. In order for a change in direction to occur, you must make a conscious choice, a personal response to God's invitation to "come unto Me."

Jesus makes it plain and clear. He said, "No one comes to the Father except through Me" (John 14:6). You can only arrive at this point by a work of God's Spirit. Nevertheless, your individual choice is essential. Most people arrive at this point when they sense life has no meaning and purpose. What is your assessment of your life?

Are you where you thought you would be at this point in life? Have you realized your goals? Are you where you want to be? If not, you are not hopelessly and helplessly chained to an unfulfilled life. Change in the direction of life is controlled by choice—your choice!

Joshua said, "If it doesn't please you to worship the Lord, choose for yourselves today the one you will worship. . . . As for me and my family, we will worship the Lord" (Josh. 24:15).

As you travel there are two ways to consider. These two ways are contrasted by Jesus in Matthew 7:13–14: "Enter through the narrow gate. For the gate is wide and the road is broad that leads to destruction, and there are many who go through it [the journey *of* life]. How narrow is the gate and difficult the road that leads to life [the journey *for* life], and few find it."

My purpose is not to be insensitive to where you are on your personal journey. I just want to help you know your options, to point you to the claims of Jesus. Consider that Jesus was direct but He was not insensitive when He contrasted the different ways and declared "I am the way."

Your personal response to the way you choose to travel will

make all the difference in your life. Observe the exact words Jesus used to describe these two ways:

The broad way. Multitudes travel what is described as the "broad" way. It leads to disappointment, unfulfilled ambitions, misery, confusion, destruction, death, and separation from God. Proverbs 14:12 reads, "There is a way that seems right to a man, but its end is the way to death."

The narrow way. This is the way that defines purpose, gives meaning to life, and promises heaven. It is a way prepared for all, but Jesus said, "Few find it."

You will read more about the broad way and the narrow way in chapter 5, but for now, let me share with you what I know about discovering the narrow way. For me, as a traveler on the journey *for* life, I have a passion to do something about making this way of life known to others. *Nothing* is more important to me.

Remember, entrance on this road is by invitation only. It is not a toll road; it is a road of choice. Know its demands. Share its rewards.

Isaiah said, "Come, everyone who is thirsty, come to the waters; and you without money, come, buy, and eat! Come, buy wine and milk without money and without cost!" (Isa. 55:1). He is saying that provision for life has been made and is available for all.

Consider Jesus' admonition as you choose: "What does it benefit a man to gain the whole world yet lose his life?" (Mark 8:36). "The one who comes to Me I will never cast out" (John 6:37). Why risk it?

Remember, access to the journey *for* life can only be gained by personal choice—*your choice*—and regardless of where you are on the journey *of* life, your journey *for* life can begin.

You are never alone on this journey. Jesus said, "If anyone wants to come with Me, he must deny himself, take up his cross, and follow Me" (Matt. 16:24). "Remember, I am with you always, to the end of the age" (Matt. 28:20).

So where do you begin? As on any journey, you must begin where you are. The journey *for* life does not begin at conception. It does not begin at birth. It does not begin in kindergarten or when a child enrolls in the first grade. It does not begin when all the entrance requirements for college are met. It does not begin with marriage. It does not begin when your children are born. Some parents may consider the empty nest as the beginning of the journey *for* life, but not so! It certainly does not begin at death, although death is the forerunner of resurrection. The journey *for* life begins wherever you are—whenever an individual realizes he is separated from God and acknowledges that his only hope and help will come from being reconciled to God.

According to the apostle Paul, "If anyone is in Christ, there is a new creation; old things have passed away, and look, new things have come" (2 Cor. 5:17). In fact, it is impossible for a person's imagination to conceive of anything more fulfilling than becoming the person God created him to be. Paul wrote: "What no eye has seen and no ear has heard, and what has never come into a man's heart, is what God has prepared for those who love Him" (1 Cor. 2:9).

Robert Louis Stevenson wrote: "To travel may be better than to arrive." This may be an accurate assessment on the journey *of* life, but on the journey *for* life, you don't arrive. Instead, every milestone increases your vision, expands your knowledge, broadens your horizons, and encourages you to continue. When you choose to begin the journey *for* life, experiencing God's constant presence and blessing is solely dependent upon your obedience to God.

Through Moses, God provided us with the history of the children of Israel to consider as we travel. God made gracious promises of guidance and provision to the children of Israel on their journey to the Promised Land—conditional promises based only upon their obedience to His Word. Throughout history He had proved Himself faithful to His people, yet they had not always been faithful to Him. Over and over again their rebellion and disobedience caused them to experience His disfavor.

During this period in their history (called the Exodus), their murmuring and complaining about the way of travel had caused them to experience forty years of aimless wandering in the desert because they were too stubborn and rebellious to follow God's directions.

How much of life do we miss today because of our complaining, unbelief, and disobedience? Too often we resemble those people. We reject God's best only to experience the chastisement of God, when all the time it is His desire to guide us, fellowship with us, and provide abundantly for us. He desires by His Holy Spirit to be with us, to comfort us, to be our teacher and guide, and to commission and enable us to be His ambassadors wherever the journey *for* life may take us.

There is no better time than now to begin your journey *for* life.

3

EXPERIENCE LIFE TO
THE FULL

Following the Designer's Plan

*L*ife happens! Without choice or input from you, your life is determined by others. Therefore, not everyone is satisfied with life, because life doesn't have the same connotation for everyone. Consider the trivial advertisements propelled at us by the media.

For some, life relates to where a person lives. An exclusive community is promoted with the slogan: *"LIFE* . . . as it was meant to be."

But "life" is a gift from God. Living by God's guiding principles is our gift back to God.

Anna, one of my twin granddaughters, came over to the table where I was writing. "What are you doing, Granddaddy?"

"I'm writing about how to live."

"Don't you know you're alive?"

29

"I'm writing about how to live and please God," I said.

"Granddaddy, it's in the Bible. You read the Bible and pray every night."

"Just at night?"

"Well, every morning too. Granddaddy, do you know the word "joy"?

"I think so. What do you know about joy?"

"Well, it's 'Jesus, Others, You.'"

"That's right, sweetheart, and in that order: Jesus first, others second, you last."

"Granddaddy, 'others' would have to include Pixie" (Abbey and Anna's little Shih Tzu).

This dialogue with Anna prompted me to check the dictionary definition of "life." Life is the quality that distinguishes a vital and functional being from a dead body. It is the living that takes place between birth and dying.

Life is *now*. And life is to be lived *now!* Give the most *to* life, and you'll receive the most *from* life. Life is opportunity.

The dictionary defines "opportunity" as a favorable juncture, a good chance, a fit time. God's greatest gifts are not *things* but opportunities; nevertheless, opportunity must be seized. Missed opportunities may stay with you forever.

In the annual Turkey Bowl football game at Emmanuel College, time was running out. The football was coming in my direction with no one in view, an open field between me and the goal line. The opportunity to intercept an errant pass and win the game was mine. I took a quick look at the goal line, and the football fell off my fingers. That missed opportunity to be the hero of the game, I have never forgotten.

Another missed opportunity occurred at a member/guest golf tournament recently. Through the years, my partner Chuck

Ramsay and I had consistently placed first or second in our flights and occasionally participated in the "shoot-out." That's a playoff where all the flight winners play three designated holes in an "alternate shot" format.

Chuck and I had done well on the first two playoff holes. The moment had finally arrived for Chuck and me! A par on this five-par hole was all we needed to become overall champions.

Here's the play-by-play for hole number five at the Thornblade Club:

Chuck was designated to drive on the odd holes. Pressure was mounting, but Chuck was steady and got off a great drive.

The pressure immediately transferred to me for the second shot. I selected a five wood. A slow backswing was achieved with a textbook follow-through, and the ball stopped just sixty-four yards from the hole. (Boy, was I glad I had recently been to golf school.) Now for the approach shot.

All Chuck had to do was get the ball on the green. No problem. His short game was a real strength of his play. Chuck had often worked with his golf professional on this shot. The pro would tell him, "Chuck, you don't have to hit the perfect shot. Just get the ball on the green."

The championship was on the line and the crowd had gathered. Now the pressure was on Chuck again. He knew what he had to do: "Get the ball on the green." But standing over the ball, he failed to follow through with his swing and hit the ball fat. The creek just thirty yards away claimed the ball—and our championship. Another missed opportunity! "Wait 'til next year."

In the technology frenzy of the nineties, many opportunities were missed as markets exploded. Only the well-connected could purchase the IPOs, and then the herd of the well-connected would run the prices through the roof. Obviously, some lucky ones sold shares into the market, feeding the frenzy, while others held on for the ride.

History had never observed a market like this—a market with no top. But there *was* a top, and the bubble burst.

Those who would not sell but held on would see their entry point and paper profits eclipse in a downward spiral like an elevator in a free fall. Time-tested strategies for buying and selling securities were ignored while a historical market with no bottom developed.

At the time, Federal Reserve chairman Alan Greenspan described it as "irrational exuberance." The herd mentality was evidenced. Due diligence was passé.

What is the result of missed opportunity? Blessing or tragedy? Oh, the tragedy of "what might have been"!

An Opportunity to Seize

Now I will tell you about an opportunity that I did *not* miss— one that changed my life forever. I may have taken my eyes off the ball at other times, but not this time. This was the moment I began traveling on the journey *for* life. I'm going to tell you about it "little by little" as we travel through these pages together.

The importance of your life cannot be overstated. Job said: "A man will give up everything he owns in exchange for his life" (Job 2:4). This is not always true, however. Many on life's journey resort to various addictions and miss life. Others choose an early exit. But your life is the reason Jesus came to earth. He said, "I am come that they might have life, and that they might have it more abundantly" (John 10:10 KJV).

The poet captured the essence of life with these words: "I love life, and I want to live, to drink of life's fullness, take all it can give. I love life, every moment must count." However, these optimistic, energetic words do not summarize every person's outlook of life. As mentioned before, Jesus spoke of two ways of life in describing our journey:

The broad way is lined by failures without a personal relationship with God. It is a way that encompasses the journey *of* life and leads to death. On the journey *of* life, the majority plan for travel on their own as though they are only physical beings and this life is all there is. *Wrong!* Man is a composite of body, mind, and spirit, and you must prepare each one for the journey. Far too many travelers—some with good intentions—procrastinate. Don't be among them!

The narrow way is a way in which life depends on whom you follow, not where you are going. It is a life that embraces the journey *for* life, which leads to real life.

It is one thing to know *about* life. However, the knowledge of *how* to live life is quite different. C. S. Lewis once said, "He who plans for this life but fails to plan for the next is wise for a moment but a fool forever."

Your personal choice predetermines the way you will travel, as well as your life's ultimate destination. When a person transitions from the journey *of* life to the journey *for* life, every aspect is impacted: desires, motives, attitudes, words, actions.

Paul describes it in these words: "If anyone is in Christ, there is a new creation; old things have passed away, and look, new things have come" (2 Cor. 5:17).

One Life to Live

Life is a learning process, and sometimes we disregard the warnings of others only to learn that experience is a harsh teacher. Nevertheless, experience can be a great teacher.

Experience is profitable in life if we learn from it, and it should be shared. To be guided by those with personal knowledge of real-life experiences is to "know sooner" and to have that knowledge available to guide and sustain you on the journey *for* life.

Time has been called the dressing room for eternity. How many travelers have said along the way, "If I had my life to live over, I'd . . ." How would you complete that statement? What would you do if you had your life to live over?

It is often surmised that life would be better lived the second time around. Given the choice, there are many things I would do differently. However, you only get one pass at life.

> I shall not pass through this world but once. If, there-
> fore, there be any kindness I can show, or any good
> thing I can do, let me do it now; let me not defer it or
> neglect it, for I shall not pass this way again.

Some take this attitude about life: "I didn't have anything to do with getting here. I don't know why I am here or where I am going, so I will just accept what life doles out." Their motto is: "Take life easy; eat, drink and be merry" (Luke 12:19 NIV).

Success for some people is personal satisfaction. They say, "I never had it this good, and this is good enough for me." How limited a person can become by negative thinking.

We are the product of our thinking, as Proverbs 23:7 states (KJV): "For as he thinketh in his heart, so is he."

On your journey *of* life, how do you deal with life's emergencies? Who and what are your resources of last resort? Can you be certain they are readily available, that they will always be there, and that they will be adequate for life's needs? On what premise have you made your conclusion? Who is your ideal? Who are you following? To whom do you pay allegiance?

There will come times in life, wherever you are, that you will come to the end of yourself. You will be helpless with no sense of hope. On the journey *of* life, success is not assured. Closed doors are often encountered. Obstacles appear. Hopes are dashed. Disappointments come. Failure occurs. What do you do?

Don't despair.
Don't give up.

At the end of yourself is where God abides. Life results from the choice you make at the intersection of the journey *of* life with the journey *for* life.

John recorded these words of Jesus about life: "Anyone who hears My word and believes Him who sent Me has eternal life . . . [and] has passed from death to life" (John 5:24).

The Journey *of* Life: It Just Happens

The apostle Paul wrote: "If we have placed our hope in Christ for this life only, we should be pitied more than anyone" (1 Cor. 15:19).

In spiritual terms, the "journey *of* life" is a life of indulgence. Everyone does what is right in his own eyes, as Frank Sinatra's hit song expresses: "I Did It My Way." But three words best describe the journey *of* life: confusion, anxiety, and desperation.

Making a living is the primary goal of the journey *of* life. However, on the journey *of* life you can make a fortune and have nothing. Take away purpose, and the journey *of* life leads to stress, depression, hopelessness, and fear. It is a haphazard journey with no ultimate fulfillment.

The journey *of* life is about *me*—who *I* am, what *I* have, what *I* have done, how *I* am perceived by others. This brings to my mind the old fellow listening to a politician. When he was asked, "Who is that?" he replied, "I don't know, but he sure thinks highly of himself."

The journey *of* life begins at birth, and because of the circumstances at birth, life may begin in abject poverty or in a palace. Nevertheless, the place of birth does not make a person. Lofty beginnings often end in desperate circumstances because of a lack of moral character and the choices made. From humble beginnings on the journey *of* life, some have risen to lofty heights because of good fortune, ambition, and personal resolve.

Perceived success on the self-centered journey *of* life blinds a person to the awesome possibilities of selfless living. The course of life is determined by whether you choose to take *from* life or you choose to give *to* life.

The journey *of* life does not necessarily focus on purpose and meaning. The measuring scale of accomplishment on the journey *of* life is temporal, not eternal. It can begin with promise of success, yet end in dismal failure.

Consider the conclusion of Solomon in the second chapter of Ecclesiastes:

> I said to myself, "Go ahead, I will test you with pleasure and enjoy what is good." But it turned out to be futile. I said about laughter, "It is madness," and about pleasure, "What does this accomplish?" I explored with my mind how to let my body enjoy life with wine and how to grasp folly—my mind still guiding me with wisdom—until I could see what is good for people to do under heaven during the few days of their lives.
>
> I increased my achievements. I built houses and planted vineyards for myself. I made gardens and

parks for myself and planted every kind of fruit tree in them. I constructed reservoirs of water for myself from which to irrigate a grove of flourishing trees. I acquired male and female servants and had slaves who were born in my house. I also owned many herds of cattle and flocks, more than all who were before me in Jerusalem. I also amassed silver and gold for myself, and the treasure of kings and provinces. I gathered male and female singers for myself, and many concubines, the delights of men.

Thus, I became great and surpassed all who were before me in Jerusalem; my wisdom also remained with me. All that my eyes desired, I did not deny them. I did not refuse myself any pleasure, for I took pleasure in all my struggles. This was my reward for all my struggles.

When I considered all that I had accomplished and what I had labored to achieve, I found everything to be futile and a pursuit of the wind. There was nothing to be gained under the sun. (Eccles. 2:1–11)

Jesus tells about a rich man and a rich young ruler on the journey *of* life. Jesus concludes with a question, "What will it benefit a man if he gains the whole world yet loses his life? (Matt. 16:26). "For where your treasure is, there your heart will be also" (Luke 12:34).

My question is: "Am I doing it for God, or for self?"

Transitioning to the Journey *for* Life

The journey *of* life can lead to the journey *for* life if you are ready to fulfill your purpose. A startling example of such a transition is shared by Jim Cymbala, pastor of the Brooklyn Tabernacle and author of many volumes, including *The Promise of God's Power*. Jim's journey *for* life once led him to David Berkowitz, the Son of Sam. Jim wrote: "David has become a dear friend to Carol and me. Not only that, he is also my brother in Christ, for God has changed the very chief of sinners—a demon-controlled serial killer—into a precious child of God."[1]

Saul of Tarsus was a person of power and authority, a citizen of Rome. He had degrees, having studied "at the feet of Gamaliel" (Acts 22:3). He measured himself by his peers and, in most ways, he exceeded them all—a good measure on the journey *of* life. Nevertheless, consider who this hero of the Pharisees became: Paul the apostle.

The journey *for* life is a "rags to riches" story, where a nobody can become a somebody. On the journey *for* life, you can have nothing and yet have everything. Everyone is equal at the cross of Jesus Christ.

Obedience is the passport on the journey *for* life. Access is not gained by good works. However, travel on the journey is fueled by good works. The journey *for* life is a choice you make. Moses expressed it this way in Deuteronomy 30:19–20:

> I call heaven and earth as witnesses against you today that I have set before you life and death, blessing and curse. Choose life so that you and your descendants may live, love the Lord your God, obey Him, and remain faithful to Him. For He is your life, and He will prolong your life in the land the Lord swore to give to your fathers Abraham, Isaac, and Jacob.

The journey *for* life is "one-way"—there is no looking back. It is not for the moment, not for the short term. The journey *for* life is a blueprint for *all* of life. It embraces destiny and eternity. The journey *for* life is not about me. It is about Jesus—His way, His glory—and of abundant living for all who travel this way. Jesus said: "If anyone wants to come with Me, he must deny himself, take up his cross daily, and follow Me" (Luke 9:23).

On the journey *for* life, we must distinguish ourselves, sometimes even by what we say. I am reminded of the quote: "I can't hear what you are saying because what you are doing is ringing too loud in my ears."

Those we compete with on the journey *of* life are committed, knowledgeable, trained, and skilled. Their people skills are good, and the most qualified are being hired. Don't expect life's best to fall into your lap just because you are on the journey *for* life. Being "born again" is awesome, and the assurance of heaven is wonderful; however, being saved doesn't pay the bills.

Who are the highest paid in commerce? The high performers. On the journey *for* life, I must compete at the highest level, even though it is not always a level playing field. I don't ever want to turn a secular person off by my demeanor or actions. Most people who consider the Christian life are influenced to do so by the example of a Christian. Paul instructed young Timothy to "set an example for the believers in speech, in life, in love, in faith, and in purity" and to "watch your life and doctrine closely" (1 Tim. 4:12, 16 NIV).

You may be the only Christian some person knows!

Effective living on the journey *for* life depends upon the indwelling and empowering of the Holy Spirit. The Lord's work can only be accomplished through the Spirit. Never underestimate what you can do for God in the power of the Spirit. At times on the journey *for* life, there are too many "technicians" void of power. The prophet Zechariah wrote: "'Not by might nor by power, but by my Spirit,' says the Lord Almighty" (Zech. 4:6 NIV).

We meet opposition on the journey *for* life, but our response does not have to be confrontational. Our best presentation is not an argument but a life. Jesus' encounter with Nicodemus was a gentle, reasoned approach. He also reasoned compassionately with the rich young ruler.

In many places of the world, Christians are a persecuted minority. The only way to witness is heart to heart, not blow for blow. Too often we try to do what only God can do.

Often on the journey *for* life, you will meet with loneliness and isolation. Jesus experienced this in the Garden and in the wilderness. There will be obstacles and difficulties on the way. There will be disappointments, frustrations, and setbacks as you travel. Temptation will abound, and at times you will feel "I'll never make it."

Our adversary is powerful. Learn how to recognize, confront, and resist him, and experience God's promise that he will flee from you. Then you can go to sleep in peace. God is awake. God works the night shift.

Are We There Yet?

The Bible offers encouragement to everyone who travels the journey *for* life. In Psalm 16:11 we read, "You reveal the path of life to me; in Your presence is abundant joy; in Your right hand are eternal pleasures."

Even so, there continues a contest for the soul. Satan will not give up. The journey *of* life will not surrender you. The allurements and enticements to remain there are real. Even though the desire was compelling, the rich young ruler could not forsake them, and he left Jesus in sorrow to continue his journey.

You will be challenged on your journey. The temptations will be overwhelming. Most travelers on the journey *of* life are reluctant to deal with spiritual issues related to the journey *for* life until they have explored all the exciting pleasures on the journey *of* life. Like Felix in his encounter with Paul, they are looking for a more "convenient season" (Acts 24:25). They are interested—just not now, not right this moment.

Do You Know Where You're Going?

A journey is the act of traveling from one place to another. It is a trip. There is a beginning and an ending.

How Do You Prepare for This Journey?

An old Turkish Proverb speaks to this question: "No matter how far you have gone on a wrong road, turn back."

Don't pack for a short trip; nevertheless, pack lightly. Paul instructs us to "lay aside every weight" (Heb. 12:1). Travel as a pilgrim. "Lay not up for yourselves treasures upon earth" (Matt. 6:19 KJV). Do all the good you can do; you won't pass this way again.

The choice to continue on the journey *of* life or to transition to the journey *for* life is up to you. The journey *for* life is not promoted by highly compensated travel professionals. It is a journey by invitation only. The price has been prepaid.

Following the transition, you will be guided by studying the Bible. The directions for travel on the journey *for* life are in "Life's Travel Guide," referenced in chapter 8 as the "Manufacturer's Handbook."

By your choice, a course correction for all of the missteps on the journey *of* life can occur instantly. When the prodigal son was in the pigpen, the Holy Spirit caused him to come to himself. What a revelation! A wayward person is not himself. After a wasted life and a wasted fortune, the prodigal came to himself, changed courses, and resolved to go home!

Even on the journey *for* life, periodic course adjustments may become necessary. After all, life is a process.

Peter also had a course correction. After he had miserably failed Jesus—denying that he knew Him and that he was His disciple—Jesus did not forsake Peter. On His way to be crucified, struggling under the weight of His cross, Jesus had time for Peter. Luke shares this moment in his Gospel: "Then the Lord turned and looked at Peter. So Peter remembered the word of the Lord, how He had said to him, 'Before the rooster crows today, you will deny Me three times'" (Luke 22:61). Remembering these words and broken by Jesus' tender, compassionate, focused look into his eyes, Peter "went outside and wept bitterly" (Luke 22:62).

Understand that when a course adjustment is required, Jesus forgives, forgets, restores, and leads you afresh on the journey *for* life.

Given the opportunity, Abraham's nephew Lot chose to go down to Sodom to transact business. Some of the Sodomites assured Lot that he would succeed much more in Sodom than he could living out in the plains. Lot was convinced and became a citizen of Sodom.

Lot chose. He did not allow God to choose for him. The choice seemed obvious to him. But God knew what was going to take place in Sodom, and He would never have led Lot there.

Every traveler needs the guidance of Proverbs 3:5–6 when choosing life's directions: "Trust in the Lord with all your heart, and do not rely on your own understanding; think about Him in all your ways, and He will guide you on the right paths."

Roadblocks and Detours

As you travel, there are many forks in the road, as well as roadblocks and detours. Which way are you going to travel? You must decide.

The esteemed philosopher Yogi Berra, of New York Yankee baseball fame, said, "When you come to a fork in the road, take it." He also said, "If you don't know where you're going, you end up somewhere else."

As a person travels the journey *of* life, conflicting ideas about God can create confusion that divides and keeps individuals and cultures bound. Doubt about the direction to travel leads to frustration. On the journey *of* life you are on your own. So why risk it?

But what recourse do you have?

Don't be mesmerized by the claims of success on the journey *of* life. These claims are often overstated and overrated. It appears that on the journey *of* life, the primary concern is "what do others think of me?" Yet prestige, prosperity, power, promotions, accomplishments, degrees, vehicles, homes—success and all its trappings as perceived by the eyes of others—is empty and meaningless. In the words of King Solomon in Ecclesiastes 1:2 (NIV)—"'Meaningless! Meaningless!' says the Teacher. 'Utterly meaningless! Everything is meaningless.'"

Many ask even today, "Is this all there is to life?"

Success Is Not a Look Back

You can't relive the past. The past is over. I know what it is to be disappointed, to hurt, and to stare failure in the face. I also know what it is to make a course correction and to resolve a different outcome.

What do you want out of life? What are your goals? What will you have when you reach your goals?

In Luke 16, Jesus related a story about a rich man and a beggar named Lazarus. In time, each died and experienced a reversal of circumstances. The beggar was resting at Abraham's side while the rich man was in agony. Now, the rich man wanted to be comforted by Lazarus, but to no avail. The rich man pleaded with Abraham, but all Abraham could do was reply, "A great chasm has been fixed between us and you, so that those who want to pass over from here to you cannot; neither can those from there cross over to us" (Luke 16:26).

As reality somberly set in, the rich man, thinking of his five brothers, begged that Lazarus be allowed to go and warn them about the torment at the end of the journey *of* life so that they would not come to this place.

"But Abraham said, 'They have Moses and the prophets; they should listen to them.'

"'No, father Abraham,' he said. 'But if someone from the dead goes to them, they will repent.'

"But he told him, 'If they do not listen to Moses and the prophets, they will not be persuaded if someone rises from the dead'" (Luke 16:29–31).

Where are *you* on your journey? You have today. You are not promised tomorrow. If you continue as you are, when you get where you're going, where will you be?

God, being both Creator and Savior, has an absolute claim on every human life. Every individual is an object of God's love, and every person is created a person of choice. Herein is the reason I differentiate between the journey *of* life and the journey *for* life.

Be All God Wants You to Be

In life, you are challenged to "be all you can be." I applaud the challenge and encourage the effort, but . . . there is a greater challenge:

Be all that *God* wants you to be.

It's your choice. It is up to you.

You may think you are self-made and that you do not need God, but you are *not* self-made. You are God-made, and you need God. You cannot achieve life's fullness on your own. You cannot pay your debt! A self-fulfilling life of accomplishment and the accolades that follow may satisfy the ego, but these will never satisfy the soul.

How tragic that the only gods many serve are the objects of their own hands. Yes, idols! Some refuse to begin the journey *for* life because of roadblocks and obstructions. Some obstructions are mental: "I just can't believe that." Others refuse to travel unless they are in charge. For them it becomes "my way or no way."

God is not unaware of this arrogance. Yet He is patient. Man's arrogance does not cause God to love less or care more. God is "not willing that any should perish" (2 Pet. 3:9 NKJV).

Decision Time

Transitioning from the journey *of* life to the journey *for* life is one decisive step, and from this giant step the journey *for* life begins, "little by little," one step at a time.

On the journey *for* life—as on any journey—you begin by making a choice. The first step is a step of faith. God's full purpose may not be known to you at the beginning; however, through obedience and faithfulness to God, "little by little" He will make it known to you. David prayed in Psalm 17:5—"My steps are on Your paths; my feet have not slipped."

I was an invited speaker for a Christian youth camp in Florida, sharing the platform with award-winning, Hall of Fame gospel composer Ira Stanphill. Ira knew about the commitment and cost required to travel on the journey *for* life, as captured in his song "Follow Me."

To follow, you must know *who* you are following, *where* He is, the *direction* He is leading, and you must understand that you don't move unless you are certain He is leading. In their search for Christ, the wise men from the East followed a special star. When the star stopped, they stopped, and ultimately the star led them to Jesus. That is a good strategy for today. On the journey *for* life, our Guide is God's Holy Spirit, and His purpose is to make Jesus known.

Why Begin the Journey *for* Life?

Everyone on the journey *of* life, even though created by God, is estranged from God. We are not manufactured robots. We are not creations of some cosmic, impersonal power void of personality. As God's creation, we are gifted by Him with purpose and ability for special assignments.

> You are a special person.
> There is no other *you*.
> Be the person God wants you to be.

As you develop your talents and gifts—dream. Visualize the future. Be dedicated to your call and purpose. You will find you are never alone.

We all live in the same world. There are no supermen, no superwomen. To suggest that those who travel on the journey *for* life have all of life's answers would be untruthful. In fact, it is such outlandish claims as this that make many who travel on the journey *for* life ineffective in their witness to those on the journey *of* life. The way to success on the journey *for* life requires total commitment that must be acknowledged and embraced by those who travel on it.

The journey *for* life is a journey beyond ourselves, a journey begun by those who believed before us—those who paved the way by sacrifice, perseverance, and hard work, inspiring their descendants and those who would hear to carry the torch, to build bridges of understanding where needed, and to manifest conviction and concern where the intolerance and indifference of others would compromise foundational values.

Follow the rules for holy living recorded in Colossians 3:1–2: "Since, then, you have been raised with Christ, set your hearts on things above, where Christ is seated at the right hand of God. Set your minds on things above, not on earthly things" (NIV).

On the journey *for* life, how are others aware of your journey? What are you doing to dispel darkness, to bring light?

The journey *for* life is not a destination. Each advance is just a continuation of the journey. The journey *for* life can be likened to space exploration. There will always be new horizons, more to explore.

As a boy, I looked forward to planting a garden. Inevitably my lack of patience would evidence itself as I would prematurely disturb the ground to observe the growth process, especially of the radishes.

As I learned from my gardening experience, there are no shortcuts on the journey *for* life. Growth is a process of seedtime and harvest. Keep in mind that we advance "little by little" as we are prepared for the conquest.

Where would Joseph's family have been without Joseph's journey? (God's total plan had not yet been revealed.) What would our world be like if, just for a moment, we would be patient and trust God's promises rather than doubt them?

Don't blame God for all of the problems of life. We are responsible for much of our trouble. Disobedience leads *away* from God; obedience leads *to* God.

The journey *for* life takes time. God has not provided an instant success manual, a "Journey *for* Life for Dummies." Life is a process. Preparation and conditioning are essential. You cannot shortcut the process to maturity. Proverbs 14:12 reads, "There is a way that seems right to a man, but its end is the way to death."

Success on the journey *for* life is often considered as arriving in heaven at the end of an earthly pilgrimage. Yes, heaven is promised to every traveler on the journey *for* life. However, heaven should be considered as a long-term goal. Many travelers are so "heavenly minded" that they are of no earthly good. Given the option, most travelers I know want to go to heaven, but not on the next bus.

I want you to be aware of and consider your options. You have observed others in the trenches on the journey *of* life as well as the journey *for* life. You have been challenged by some and disappointed by others. Every life includes periods of anguish, regrets, grief, loss, suffering, and lament. We each experience these, but not everyone has . . .

Hope.

On the journey *for* life, there is hope. God is the source of hope. His Word is our hope. You can have hope!

The Main Event

Jesus began His journey toward the cross in a wilderness encounter with the devil. For the devil, it was a "no-holds-barred" engagement. It was not a heavily promoted, sold-out event. It was not a twelve-round World Championship fight. It was not the

World's Strongest Man event with the trophy going to the last man standing.

It was a "No Spectators Allowed" event. This event would last for forty days. No attendants were available to support and encourage. It was a bare knuckles battle of the ages, void of physical blows yet as intense and as stressful as any man has ever known.

Why? What was at stake?

The redemption for this world was at stake. The rebellion that began in the heavens had found its way to earth. The weapons were truth vs. lies. The participants? The Author of truth vs. the father of lies.

For Jesus, the battle is already over. He later declared, "It is finished." But for you and me, the conflict continues—not because our victory is not assured but because each of us is a "free moral agent"—a being of choice—and our personal choices determine our destiny. As passive as some may be, the journey *of* life vs. the journey *for* life is spiritual warfare. The mind is the true battleground of our lives.

In Philippians 4:8–9, Paul wrote: "Finally brothers, whatever is true, whatever is honorable, whatever is just, whatever is pure, whatever is lovely, whatever is commendable—if there is any moral excellence and if there is any praise—dwell on these things. Do what you have learned and received and heard and seen in me, and the God of peace will be with you."

It must be made clear by all who would follow Christ on the journey *for* life that this message of sacrifice will not be popular with the masses. Speaking about commitment, Jesus also said in Luke 9:62: "No one who puts his hand to the plow and looks back is fit for the kingdom of God." The purpose here is not an attempt to discourage travel on the journey *for* life; rather, this is an attempt to encourage an honest assessment of the cost.

As mentioned before, Jesus told of a rich, young ruler who went away sorrowful after assessing the cost. But this is not the end of the story. Benefits do flow to those who consider the cost and follow Him. In Matthew 19:29, Jesus said, "Everyone who has left houses, brothers or sisters, father or mother, children, or fields because of My name will receive 100 times more and will inherit eternal life."

All who travel on the journey *for* life are on a mission. Jesus said to His Father, "As You sent Me into the world, I also have sent them into the world" (John 17:18). Travel on the journey *for* life is differentiated by the God we serve. As the Lord said through Moses to the children of Israel, "You must not make a covenant with them or their gods. They must not remain in your land" (Exod. 23:32–33). God's directive to them was to "possess the land," and He would enable them to do it.

Bad alliances have destroyed the hopes of many. The allurements, promises, and momentary contentment abruptly ended in helpless, hopeless despair. Moses made a choice that led him from Pharaoh's palace to the desert. He "chose to suffer with the people of God rather than to enjoy the short-lived pleasure of sin" (Heb. 11:25).

The journey *for* life is not a board game. There are no free passes or "Get Out of Jail Free" cards. The journey *for* life is the *essence* of life. It is not a game of chance. However, any way you consider the journey *for* life, it has its rewards.

Success on the journey *for* life is about making a difference in life—both in your life and the lives of those you influence. Many travelers on the journey *of* life aspire to more fulfillment, but they lack knowledge of anything that could satisfy their aspirations and desires.

Inside every person is a God-shaped vacuum. It is identified by many titles in the struggles of life, but the thirst is not quenched nor the hunger satisfied short of relationship with God.

The journey *for* life is a life of purpose and promise—promises from the Almighty for all who have counted the cost, believed on Him, and walked in obedience to God's Word.

God has obligated Himself to His Word. Jesus said, "If you remain in Me and My words remain in you, ask whatever you want and it will be done for you" (John 15:7). "No good thing will he withhold from them that walk uprightly" (Ps. 84:11 KJV).

The greatest achievement on the journey *for* life is to know God personally, love Him, and serve Him. Being an adventure, the journey is not mapped out or formulated ahead of time. The destination at times may appear illusive and seem an impossible quest. But lend your ear: there are countless testimonies of fellow travelers on the journey *for* life who bear witness of success in this pursuit.

In Hebrews 12:1–3, it is recorded, "Therefore since we also have such a large cloud of witnesses surrounding us, let us lay aside every weight and the sin that so easily ensnares us, and run with endurance the race that lies before us, keeping our eyes on Jesus, the source and perfecter of our faith, who for the joy that lay before Him endured a cross and despised the shame, and has sat down at the right had of God's throne. For consider Him who endured such hostility from sinners against Himself, so that you won't grow weary and lose heart."

People throughout the world nurture a mind-set of beliefs in the hereafter—the approval of God and promised rewards. Due to this illusion of lavish rewards in the afterlife, many—not fearing death—are willing to die as terrorists, taking many lives in the process via suicide bombs and other destructive means, seeking whatever defines success for them on the journey *of* life.

But the belief system for those who travel on the journey *for* life has a foundation. This foundation is not an illusion; it is the Word of God. Jesus said: "Heaven and earth will pass away, but My words will never pass away" (Matt. 24:35).

Motivated by love for everyone, God has commissioned all who travel on the journey *for* life to share His love and truth with a global perspective, inviting all to receive life. Wherever people are, God is God, and God is the same in His awesome love for everyone. Does God love those who are destitute less because of their circumstances? God has no elite class! The measure of our effectiveness on the journey *for* life is not how *different* we are but how *Christlike* we are.   •

Poverty, despair, wars, plagues, hurricanes, or other disasters never diminish God's love for man, and nothing can separate us from the love of God. Paul wrote:

> Who can separate us from the love of Christ? Can affliction or anguish or persecution or famine or nakedness or danger or sword? No, in all these things we are more than victorious through Him who loved us. For I am persuaded that neither death nor life, nor angels nor rulers, nor things present, nor things to come, nor powers, nor height, nor depth, nor any other created thing will have the power to separate us from the love of God that is in Christ Jesus our Lord!" (Rom. 8:35, 37–39)

God challenges us to test His love in the arena of life. As paradoxical as it may sound, the journey *of* life leads to the "ghetto" even though the primary goal is to escape the ghetto. Likewise, the journey *for* life does not always travel Main Street. It is not always the scenic route. The journey *for* life may lead to the ghetto. Many travelers, forsaking wealth and the conveniences of life, follow God's call to serve Him there, as did Mother Teresa. She said, "I knew where I belonged. I felt intensely that Jesus wanted me to serve Him among the poorest of the poor. Life is not worth living unless it is lived for others."

Follow the Plan, Make an Impact

Jesus said, "All authority has been given to Me in heaven and on earth. Go, therefore, and make disciples of all nations, baptizing them in the name of the Father and of the Son and of the Holy Spirit, teaching them to observe everything I have commanded you. And remember, I am with you always, to the end of the age" (Matt. 28:18–20). On the journey *for* life, God's call is for all who embrace the gospel to become proponents of truth. Travelers on the journey *for* life are not recruits; they are drafted and commissioned to the Great Commission. Jesus' command to His followers has always been two-fold: "Come, follow Me" and "Go ye."

Before you begin the journey, count the cost. Personal sacrifice in the face of conflict will be experienced; however, be encouraged— you have the promise of His presence and the assurance of success.

The mandate is to tell everyone. May we not be guilty of the Great *Omission* because of neglect. A challenging hymn I remember from my youth reflects my passion:

> Tell it again! Tell it again!
> Salvation's story repeat o'er and o'er.
> Till none can say of the children of men,
> "Nobody ever has told me before."

The mission message must be simple, clear, and, coherent. It must be complete, factual, and shared in love. It may be proclaimed in many ways—first and primarily by a lifestyle reflecting the essence of truth—never camouflaged or hidden but as a beacon light on a hill to shine brightly, encouraging others to boldly "shout it from the housetops." Christians must not go into the closet while others of competing agendas are coming out of their closets.

There are certain spiritual imperatives and mandates that must be adhered to on this mission. The psalmist wrote: "Let the redeemed of the Lord say so, whom he hath redeemed from the hand of the enemy" (Ps 107:2 KJV). In Mark 5:19, Jesus instructed one redeemed follower, "Go back home to your own people, and report to them how much the Lord has done for you and how He has had mercy on you."

On the journey *for* life, there are two elements: the *human* element and the *God* element—each dependent upon the other. God will not do the human part, and man cannot do the God part. Don't intervene—let God be God.

Stripped of all the related organizational and administrative functions of ministry, the overriding passion for those who *know* must be to *tell*.

There are times when this mission mandate can best be accomplished by the sharing of a personal testimony. Other activities are necessary and must take place; nevertheless, to tell is expedient. Too many travelers on the journey *for* life are more concerned about the process than the outcome. Successful witnessing depends more upon the message than upon the method. Paul declared, "I determined not to know any thing among you, save Jesus Christ, and him crucified" (1 Cor. 2:2 KJV).

Our best efforts should be in proclaiming the gospel, not defending it. God alone is the defender of His Word. Jesus said, "As for Me, if I am lifted up from the earth I will draw all people to Myself" (John 12:32).

The most potent force on earth will occur when Christians—in unity—put into practice what they preach.

Renew Your Purpose

In order to accomplish this mission, I propose a renewal of purpose whereby *who* we are, *where* we serve, and *what* we possess will be the primary means that enable us to share the truth, resulting in others joining us on the journey *for* life. Paul wrote to the Romans: "Now I am speaking to you Gentiles. In view of the fact that I am an apostle to the Gentiles, I magnify my ministry, if I can somehow make my own people jealous and save some of them" (Rom. 11:13–14).

Our mission is pure. To share the gospel is not to be a confrontational, flag waving, publicity seeking endeavor. We have the message that must be shared. Dr. Frank Page, pastor of Taylors First Baptist Church and former president of the Southern Baptist Convention, said, "By not sharing the gospel, we are saying to them (to those who do not know), 'Find your own road.'" Where would you be if you had been left to find your own way?

Paul wrote: "If our gospel be hid, it is hid to them that are lost: in whom the god of this world hath blinded the minds of them which believe not, lest the light of the glorious gospel of Christ, who is the image of God, should shine unto them" (2 Cor. 4:3–4 KJV).

Jesus is the answer for the world today. He is the Good News that those who don't know, need to know. Without this knowledge, they are lost!

On the journey *of* life, a person may have stature, wealth, and acclaim; nevertheless, to have everything except Jesus is to be lost. Jesus said to Nicodemus, "I assure you: Unless someone is born again, he cannot see the kingdom of God" (John 3:3). Our mission mandate is to make Him known. Other cultures may not accept our message or morality, but we must be diligent in keeping them from imposing their morality on us. Our morality is not a closet experience. "Let your light shine" (Matt. 5:16). A true witness will be motivated by a sincere desire to challenge those on the journey *of* life to an open, honest, sincere, intellectual consideration of the claims of Jesus.

Take a look for yourself.

Investigate for yourself.

Certain Greeks were looking for Jesus. Their desire was simply expressed to Phillip, a servant of Christ: "Sir, we want to see Jesus" (John 12:21).

After Hurricane Katrina, Dr. Richard Waters, president of Holmes Bible College, related the experience of a man—somewhat familiar with the Bible but not a Christian—who, observing Christians on mission in New Orleans said, "This is the first time I have seen it off the pages of the Bible."

Many refuse to open their eyes and see Jesus because to do so would be to question their own core beliefs and bring discomfort to them in their comfort zone. But in life and death matters, truth cannot be compromised. Reality must be faced.

Some young people in a Christian Sunday school class where the gospel was presented as a matter of life and death objected in these words: "We don't like this; it makes us uncomfortable." While they may fear such words and resist them, discomfort is a part of life, and everyone will experience it. Not everyone will believe, but some will. Always strive to leave the door open for further discussions.

What about your comfort zone? Has it been tested recently? Put it to the test.

Commit to What Challenges You

As noted earlier, Isaiah, in recording God's invitation, wrote: "'Come now, let us reason together,' says the Lord. 'Though your sins are like scarlet, they shall be as white as snow; though they are red as crimson, they shall be like wool'" (Isa. 1:18 NIV). Without the test of reason, how can you know? Without this step toward faith, how can you ever be certain concerning life?

Jesus said, "The thief comes only to steal and kill and destroy; I have come that they may have life, and have it to the full" (John 10:10 NIV). What a paradox!

> The journey *of* life—save it to lose it.
> The journey *for* life—lose it to save it.

Our effort on this mission must be singularly focused on communicating hope, assurance, and peace. Illusive *inner* peace and *world* peace are only attainable in Jesus Christ.

What is your evidence that what you embrace will not disappoint and fail you, that it can stand the test of God's Word? Do you still have lingering doubts? When all else fails, when hope is gone, when you don't know where God is and you don't have a clue that God knows or cares about you—what are you going to do? What did many of the victims of Hurricane Katrina do? This is real time. Real life. This is not church—this is *life!*

I heard Bobby Welch, former president of the Southern Baptist Convention, relate a post-Katrina episode that illustrates my point. A high-ranking officer in the Louisiana State Highway Patrol, after seeing so many Southern Baptists said, "I'm from (a church of another denomination). I don't know where they are. I'm thinking about changing religion."

"I wouldn't do that," Bobby Welch replied.

"Why not?" the officer inquired.

"You can change religion over and over, and nothing will change. That's not what you need."

"What *do* I need?"

"You need Jesus."

The officer, realizing his need—right there—allowed Bobby Welch to introduce him to Jesus. That's what being "commissioned to a mission" is all about. It means meeting people at the point of their need, giving a cup of water in Jesus' name.

When isolated by life's storms and floodwaters, when you are wondering, "Does anybody know where I am?"—God does know. And through servant hands, He is looking for you.

Expect Hostile Opponents

Travelers on the journey *for* life encounter adverse circumstances and hostile opponents. Jesus told us to expect them and prepare for them.

Paul wrote about just such times: "We don't want you to be unaware, brothers, of our affliction that took place in the province of Asia; we were completely overwhelmed—beyond our strength—so that we even despaired of life . . . so that we would not trust in ourselves, but in God who raises the dead" (2 Cor. 1:8–9).

This is an age of pluralism. On the journey *for* life, be considerate. Don't be offensive. While some among us caution, "Soften up on Jesus as the only way," how can we? God without Jesus Christ is idolatry. God is still in control. Don't believe the lie that society is too far gone.

In our world, Islamic fundamentalism is a real, present threat. Islamic fascists are endlessly scheming for new ways to destroy the "infidels." Christians are murdered, not because of what they do but because of who they are. How could America ever forget the fuel-laden airplanes that became weapons of mass destruction? The lethal gases? The suicide bombs? Even so, as Christians, it is not wise to ridicule what is sacred to others. Unfortunately, some Christians, at times, have resorted to this tactic.

> Don't demean.
> Show respect for the dignity of others.
> Build bridges.

There is no level playing field for the proclamation of the gospel. It appears that everything except the gospel receives an open hearing. To illustrate, I share the following news clip from Canada: a Christian missionary to Muslims was arrested for preaching the gospel. The charge? A hate crime!

Christians around the world find themselves victims of unprovoked persecution. Even so, as the "called" continue to share the gospel, many around the world, including Muslims, are coming to faith in Jesus Christ. Dr. Richard Land, president of the Southern Baptist Convention's Ethics and Religious Liberty Commission, has said, "If God's name uttered in a profanity is protected speech, even if it's offensive to believers, then God's name invoked in prayer is protected speech."

Disrespect for other religions is condemned while Christians are demeaned and defamed, all in the name of diversity. Disrespect for Christians and for Christian symbols should receive the same media coverage and condemnation as non-Christians. Regardless, travelers on the journey *for* life must continue to show respect even though it may not be reciprocated. Hostile witnessing should never be a tactic in the Christian arsenal. The whole armor of God is defensive. Witnessing is not a bold, military action. It should never be confrontational. There is already enough conflict in the world.

Force, coercion, ridicule—this was never the style or method of Jesus, and it must not be ours. Paul wrote: "We persuade men" (2 Cor. 5:11 KJV).

The Holy Spirit is a dove, not a screaming eagle. He is often "a still small voice." Develop the tact of being able to disagree without being disagreeable. When Paul wrote to the Ephesians, he was chained to a guard night and day. Even though he was an ambassador sent by the King of heaven and earth, he did not have diplomatic immunity. His chains were not his concern. His request was that he might be bold enough in Him to speak truth in faith, and to see the gospel of Christ change the lives of all who would believe.

The Bible identifies the devil as the adversary. As you face persecution on your mission, be encouraged by Jesus' words. Nothing—absolutely nothing—will keep Jesus Christ from fulfilling His purpose. He said, "I will build My church, and the forces of Hades will not overpower it" (Matt. 16:18).

This will happen as those on the journey *for* life fulfill their assigned mission. God will not surrender His sovereignty to any nation, people, or political system. The power to accomplish this mission resides in the called: "You will receive power when the Holy Spirit has come upon you, and you will be My witnesses in Jerusalem, in all Judea and Samaria, and to the ends of the earth" (Acts 1:8).

His commission to us is to take the message to the world—*all* people—every individual.

What does it mean to witness? Sharing, not proselytizing. Proclamation, not condemnation. Never engage in an in-your-face approach to dialogue. America is a land of growing diversity.

- The world's largest Buddhist temple is located in America.

- The world's largest Muslim training center is in America.
- The world's largest Jewish population resides in the United States of America.

It is not the "melting pot" we might remember; nevertheless, it is still the "land of the free and home of the brave."

The purpose of any witnessing opportunity is to promote honest consideration—an honest inquiry—to the claims of Jesus. A good witness presents the opportunity for others to believe or dis-believe. Those of other religious views are of no less value to God. Every person on planet Earth is a creation of God and an object of His love.

On the journey *for* life, witnessing is a command to follow, not an individual's option. Peter wrote: "Always be ready to give a defense to anyone who asks you for a reason for the hope that is in you" (1 Pet. 3:15).Many are not sure about God. How can they know He is able to make a difference in their life? The instructions for witnessing are specific:

Begin where you are. Follow the example of Andrew, who witnessed to his brother Peter. What a find!

Be faithful where you are. No one knows where God's jewels are. He does. Consider the witness of Stephen. Saul of Tarsus, who became Paul the apostle, could not withstand the powerful witness of Stephen as he was being stoned to death. Will others know by observing you?

Go! No area is to be isolated or abandoned. All the world is the mission arena. Wherever man is, God is. John wrote: "The Son of Man has come to seek and to save the lost" (Luke 19:10).

However, our going is not always to be foreign soil. Religious diversity has eroded much of America's heritage and weakened her as a Christian nation. America has become so diverse that she has become a fertile mission ground to Christian missionaries from around the world. Could our great mission of exporting the gospel now be overcome by missionaries from other parts of the world *importing* the gospel to America?

Where are America's absolutes? Has she lost her way? Has she lost her moorings? Sodom and Gomorrah did. Jesus wept over Jerusalem—would He weep over America today?

C. S. Lewis's words from *Mere Christianity* might be applicable here: "It is since Christians have largely ceased to think of the other world that they have become so ineffective in this one."[2]

Fear not, all you travelers on the journey *for* life. It is not what goes on in the USA that determines what God is doing in the world. God is global. He is involved in the affairs of the whole world. He is the God of the universe.

Where Are You in Your Search?

Do you have all the answers to the questions of life? If there is any degree of uncertainty, any shadow of doubt, don't close the door of *honest inquiry*. Don't chance eternity, thinking you are right, when it is possible to know for certain.

The Bible declares: "The entrance of thy words giveth light" (Ps. 119:130 KJV). Until you know, don't stop your quest—wherever it leads—until you have a sense of purpose, peace, and assurance.

Be sincere in your search. If there is something better—something that satisfies—ignore the others and commit to that which totally satisfies you. However, if the journey *for* life is what its proponents say it is, embrace it—whatever the cost.

There are many voices competing for a hearing. Why is the preponderance of the voices prejudiced against the Christian message? Are not Christians responsible for some of it? Is the proclamation always pure?

> Make it simple.
> Don't add to it.
> Don't take away from it.

At times, it appears that our differences are more essential than the core message. What is the purpose of our witness? It was prophesied by Isaiah and referenced by Jesus concerning Himself and His mission: "The Spirit of the Lord is on Me, because He has anointed Me to preach good news to the poor. He has sent Me to proclaim freedom to the captives and recovery of sight to the blind, to set free the oppressed, to proclaim the year of the Lord's favor" (Luke 4:18–19). Is there a more potent mission anywhere?

To the extent that I have believed truth, my life has been greatly blessed. As Christians, we are not promised that the arena will become more accommodating. Persecution against Christians is increasing and intensifying. In many parts of the world, Christians endure great hardship because of their Christian faith and witness. Even in America, Christians are under attack. Many are ridiculed and hauled into court because of their witness.

Could this be because there is no defense against love? Even so, we must show love and be conduits of love.

Regardless of the opposition encountered, Jesus is Lord, and He will build His kingdom.

The early followers were threatened. Some were beaten. Some were imprisoned, yet even in prison, they prayed. They did not pray for safety or deliverance but for boldness while on mission. Retreat is not an option on the journey *for* life. "Go ye" is the mission.

Where is our confidence? "Not by might, nor by power, but by my spirit" (Zech. 4:6 KJV). Wherever the gospel is given free expression—in love—it will overcome conflicting views held in place by force and fear.

Again, some have suggested that we engage the soft-sell approach in our personal witness. For me, I cannot help but be passionate and bold because of what I have experienced and the difference this journey for life has made in who I am. I know what it is to fail without Him. I also know what it is to overcome every obstacle *with* Him.

The desire to soft-pedal meaningful dialogue around sensitive differences of religion and culture, all in an effort not to offend someone while maintaining a semblance of peace, does not foster any position. Any engagement of sensitive issues should not be coerced, forced, or couched in language that demeans either position. Intellectual honesty considers the views of others respectfully, and this courtesy should be reciprocated. Truth does not stand or fall based upon the forum where it is presented or the experience of any individual, regardless of how convincing their argument. Truth rests upon that which is changeless—the living Word of God, which remains when all else has failed.

Knowing what I know—considering all that is accessible on the journey *for* life—all of my sales instincts motivate me to close the deal. Why would anyone resist such a compelling offer? As a salesman, I am programmed to "ask for the order."

4

"I WISH I'D KNOWN THAT SOONER"

Shared Jewels from Life Experiences

How often have I heard that? How often I have said that? And at my stage in life, I still find myself saying: "I wish I had known that sooner." I also have many younger friends who through the years have said to me, "I wish I had known that sooner."

After hearing this comment over and over, I began to think, "Why isn't someone speaking, teaching, and writing to satisfy this desire?" I will attempt to accomplish this by sharing observations and lessons from my school of experience—the school of hard knocks. Read carefully!

My motivation is for you to have the advantage of knowing now—sooner than I did—the useful lessons and principles I am able to share from my experiences. Some of the things "I wish I had known sooner" are:

- I wish I had learned *patience* sooner—not to act impulsively but to wait. Patience pays high dividends. Our society is cursed by the compulsive desire for instant gratification. We joke, "I want patience, and I want it *now!*"

- I wish I had learned sooner to be more *attentive* to those close to me.

- I wish I had never *embarrassed* another person in public—especially a child—*my* child!

- I wish I had known sooner how to express *thanks*, especially to those who have influenced my life. I wish I had practiced being thankful sooner.

- I wish I had known sooner that, when it comes to work, I can't do *everything*. My knowledge of what needs to be done already exceeds the hours in a day. It is easy to consider yourself invincible, which may be acceptable when your business is small. However, growth can quickly change that. Through experience, I have learned that you must plan and prioritize so that the most important functions don't get left behind.

- I wish I had known sooner how much *little things* count.

- I wish I had learned sooner how to say *"yes."*

- I wish I had learned sooner how to *forgive* my own mistakes and the mistakes of others, to realize that mistakes are often learning platforms.

- I wish I had learned sooner to ask questions, stop, and *wait* for the answers.

- I wish I had learned sooner to *invest in others*. A person is never bigger than when he bends down to help someone in need.

- I wish I had understood the term *due diligence* sooner. Due diligence is the process of investigation, research, and analysis needed in order to manage risk. Simply stated, it is thinking things through, doing your homework. Due diligence and planning is never wasted time.

- I wish I had learned sooner to *delegate*. When you delegate, you multiply yourself. The exponential effect that follows well-defined delegation of authority to act is amazing. Not only does this process develop leaders, it also makes the person who delegates appear even smarter. What if Jesus had not delegated? He was only here for a brief period and He knew that He could not change the world alone. His work would continue through those He commissioned and empowered when He said, "The one who believes in Me will also do the works that I do. And he will do even greater works than these, because I am going to the Father" (John 14:12).

- I wish I had learned sooner to *compliment* and express my *gratitude* for the contributions of others.

- I wish I had learned sooner to *believe in myself.* Paul wrote in Philippians 4:13, "I am able to do all things through Him who strengthens me." To be self-confident, I must believe that I am somebody because I am God's creation and I am here for a purpose.

- I wish I had learned sooner the value of *rest.*

- I wish I had known sooner how to *empathize.* This lesson is only learned in the trenches. After I was diagnosed with advanced stage prostate cancer, one of my early calls was from Dave Henschel, vice chairman of Oxydental Petroleum. Dave was an acquaintance of mine and a great friend of Chuck Ramsay, my close friend and associate. Dave is a prostate cancer survivor, and while I was wrestling with the process for treatment, his words were valuable. His research had been extensive. He could speak in layman's words to the pros and cons of various treatment strategies and make available to me his knowledge and guidance. Anyone can sympathize, but not everyone can empathize.

- I wish I had learned sooner how to *think*.
- I wish I had learned sooner how to *reason*.
- I wish I had learned sooner how to *listen*.
- I wish I had learned sooner to *write down* good thoughts and to take notes when listening and when reading.
- I wish I had learned sooner to *chase fewer deals* and spend more time with Jane, our children, and our grandchildren. I wish I had learned sooner to *stay in touch* with family, friends, and associates.
- I wish I had learned sooner to *build bridges* and never to burn them.
- I wish I had learned sooner the value of God's gift of *others*.
- I wish I had known sooner that I do not always have to be *right*.
- I wish I had learned sooner to be an *encourager*.
- I wish I had learned sooner to be a *Good Samaritan*. I wish I had learned sooner how to say, "Put that on my account."
- I wish I had learned sooner the *power of touch*.
- I wish I had learned sooner the value of *personal testing*.
- I wish I had learned sooner never to hold a *grudge*.
- I wish I had learned sooner to say "Why *not* me?" rather than "*Why* me?"

- I wish I had learned sooner how to say "*I love you.*"
  I grew up in a family that was not affectionate that way.
  Love was just assumed, but spoken love is bonding love.
- I wish I had known sooner the value of the book of
  Proverbs.
- I wish I had known sooner the value of *good nutrition.*
- I wish I had known sooner that you can *let go.* You can
  give up and move on. Never dig a hole deeper. Admit it
  when you are wrong. Apologize, mean it, and move on.
- I wish I had known sooner that you don't have to fear
  the *unknown.*
- I wish I had known sooner that *peace of mind* is far
  better than the attractions of life.
- I wish I had learned the lessons of *obedience* sooner. The
  standard for success on the journey *for* life is obedience.
  God's standard is: "To obey is better than sacrifice"
  (1 Sam. 15:22). King Saul's *disobedience* led to his
  being rejected by God as king. Charles Malik, former
  Secretary General of the United Nations, said, "Success
  is neither fame, wealth, nor power; rather it is seeking,
  knowing, loving, and *obeying* God."
- I wish I had learned sooner the effectual power
  of *prayer*—to take *time* to pray and to pray about
  everything. Especially in business, professional affairs,
  and relationships, prayer is powerful. There have been
  times when property deals appeared so promising,
  I thought taking time to pray might mean losing the
  deal. I felt it looked too good to be true. In retrospect,
  I wish I had prayed. I often found out later that it *was*
  too good to be true.

- I wish I had been an earnest *student of the Bible* sooner. Knowledge of the Guide Book is a hedge, a fortress, and a shield against sin. The psalmist wrote: "Thy word have I hid in mine heart, that I might not sin against thee" (Ps. 119:11 KJV).

- I wish that I had understood sooner the lessons of *"little by little"* as recorded in Exodus 23:20–30. Life is a process, not an event. Life cannot be accelerated. I want it now, but God knows best.

- I would have fought fewer of life's battles in my *own strength*, realizing that God would have fought them for me.

- I would have destroyed my *personal idols* sooner and realized God's blessing and provisions for the abundant life.

- I would have learned that *God's promises* are not diminished because of the time involved in the process. How many blessings have I lost doing things my way?

- I would have known sooner that the journey *of* life and, at times, the journey *for* life is filled with the tragedies of those who advanced beyond their ability to manage.

What a ready resource "little by little" is for all of life. Angel guidance and protection are readily available for all who travel on the journey *for* life (see Exod. 23:20, 23). I can testify from my personal experience that these are an infinitely more reliable and valuable resource than any global positioning system that can be purchased.

Where is your journey taking you? Are you prompted now to make a course correction? If so, let Matthew 6:33 be your guide: "Seek first the kingdom of God and His righteousness, and all these things will be provided for you" (Matt. 6:33). Stop thinking you can't make it, and start thinking that by the grace of God you *can* make it. We can never hear Philippians 4:13 enough: "I am able to do all things through Him who strengthens me."

Are you succeeding by this standard?

5

SUCCESS, BUT NOT BY EVERYONE'S MEASURE

*S*uccess. Everybody talks about it and desires to have it, but what *is* success? According to the dictionary, success is "attaining one's desired end, a favorable termination of a venture." Success is generally associated with the attainment of wealth, fame, or position.

On the journey *of* life, success (as defined above) is the usual measure of an influential life. On the journey *of* life, the accumulation of multiple assets and a growing balance sheet may open many doors as a person dreams and builds, but—is this a true measure of success?

Perceptions of Success

The measure of success on the journey *of* life is influenced by an individual's circumstances: the environment he lives in, his perceived social status, the professional degrees he's earned, the prestige of the university he attended, as well as his recognized accomplishments.

For some, success may mean "moving on up," as portrayed by the Jeffersons on the television series by that name. Many applauded accomplishments may follow high achievers on the journey *of* life, yet success is ever illusive. Someone else will always have more, and the craving—the insatiable desire to be on top—will remain unsatisfied. If "having all the toys" is the measure of success, circumstances will change. The economy is cyclical, markets are fickle, fortunes come and go.

For years I observed an enterprising real estate promoter work hard and create what at the time was a significant real estate portfolio. His balance sheet showed a net worth approaching $35 million. He had the accolades and recognition, the trappings of success, but within a few months, he was broke. It did not have to be that way. His focus was wrong. He did not manage his assets.

He did not follow through on the many opportunities to develop, manage, and sell his prime properties in the normal course of business. Therefore, his bubble burst. His positive attitude and many perceived friends were not enough to maintain his status and save his business.

Success is earned in the trenches where conflict, adversity, heartaches, and loss are experienced. Success is not bestowed. Success has its toll, its price.

> Success is a competitive journey.
> As you travel you will encounter enemies.
> Not everyone wants you to succeed.
> You must earn your way.
> Not everyone plays by the rules.

"Know the state of your flocks, and put your heart into caring for your herds, for riches don't last forever, and the crown might not be secure for the next generation" (Prov. 27:23–24 NLT).

What is commonly called "success" must be protected and cared for with the same diligence with which it is acquired; otherwise, it can be wasted away. Many travelers on the journey *of* life want you to fail and will assist in the process of making it happen. If the measure of success is the achievement of wealth, fame, or position, it can be as alluring as a rainbow and as distant as the proverbial pot of gold at its end.

Perceptions of success are very fluid. What one person perceives as success may only be a plateau to someone else in its pursuit. It is not my purpose to demean high achievers who attain the world's measure of success. All values on the journey *of* life are not in conflict with the values of the journey *for* life. Many of these achievements are needed on the journey *of* life; however, they are not essential to success on the journey *for* life.

Attitude of Success

A newly-hired traveling salesman wrote his first sales report to the home office. It stunned the top brass in the sales department because it was obvious the new "hope" was an illiterate, for here is what he wrote:

"I have seen this outfit which they ain't never bought a dime's worth of nothing from us, and I sole them a couple hundred thousand dollars of guds. I am now going to Chicawgo."

Before the illiterate could be given the heave-ho by the sales manager, along came this letter from Chicago: "I cum hear and sole them haff a million."

Fearful if he did, and fearful if he didn't fire the illiterate, the sales manager dumped the problem in the lap of the company president.

The following morning, the ivory tower members were amazed to see the two letters posted on the bulletin board—and this memo from the president tacked above:

"We ben spending two much time trying to spel instead of trying to sel. Let's wach those sails. I want everybody should read these letters from Mr. Gooch, who is on the rode doin a grate job for us, and you should go out and do like he done."

Failure is an attitude of doubt. To fail is to give up, to succumb to what is perceived as failure. The journey *of* life is lined with disappointments and failures. What is the preferred course of action when you face failure? Make a course correction.

> Resolve not to fail.
> Remember your dream.
> Recommit to your purpose.
> Regroup.

This is possible on the journey *for* life because God redeems and restores. Consider the work of the potter in reshaping the marred pot in Jeremiah, and the prodigal returning to the father in Luke 15. God is *for* you! Paul wrote: "If God is for us, who can be against us?" (Rom. 8:31 NIV). Don't quit! As this poem says:

> When things go wrong
> as they sometimes will,
> When the road you're trudging
> seems all uphill,
> When the funds are low,
> and the debts are high,

And you want to smile,
but you have to sigh,

When care is pressing
you down a bit,
Rest if you must,
but don't you quit.
Success is failure
turned inside out,
The silver tint
of the clouds of doubt,

And you never can tell
how close you are,
It may be near
when it seems afar.
So, stick to the fight
when you're hardest hit,
It's when things go wrong
that you mustn't quit.

Every basketball fan knows of the exploits of Michael Jordan on the court. He is acclaimed to be the best basketball player ever, but did you know that Michael was cut from his ninth-grade team?

On the journey *of* life, many travelers endeavor to keep the Ten Commandments and live moral lives according to the values set forth in the Bible. The truths of the Bible *are* good for life, even for those who don't acknowledge the Author.

The value system of travelers on the journey *of* life often exceeds those of many who travel on the journey *for* life. For them, purpose in life is found in good works contributing to the quality of life for others.

Some Things Success Is Not

- Success is not always what is perceived by others. I heard that behind every successful man is a surprised mother-in-law.
- Success is not without personal sacrifice, and is not guaranteed by following the crowds on the road most traveled.
- Success is not a snapshot at some isolated moment. It is neither in the valley nor on the peak. Success is the next mountain.
- Success is not achieved by selfish ambition. A successful person is not a self-made person.
- Success is not singular. Others influence every life: family, friends, teachers, church leaders, role models, heroes, business and professional associates.
- Success is not an individual sport.
- Success is not always measured by what appears to be positive outcomes.

Achieving any measure of success is a process; it is not an instant happening. Patience is required, and the patient person will be rewarded. Others may devise shortcut strategies in order to find success, but every shortcut has its price. Prisons are full because of failed strategies designed to circumvent the law. Any element of success that compromises core values is not success.

The journey *of* life is where you first discover yourself. It is where you find yourself innately, traveling with the masses on the road most traveled. For many travelers, this is a journey of selfish ambition, where taking care of "numero uno" is the primary purpose of existence. On the journey *of* life, the boundaries of a person's comfort zone are seldom exceeded. "Let others look out for themselves" is their motto. The journey *of* life can be an arena where life is lived selfishly, without moral convictions and ethical boundaries.

But what will you be left with when you have stored all of life's gains and you face the unknown?

In Luke 12, Jesus told about a rich man who had skillfully amassed a fortune and became concerned about what to do with his abundance. "He thought to himself, 'What should I do, since I don't have anywhere to store my crops? I will do this,' he said. 'I'll tear down my barns and build bigger ones, and store all my grain and my goods there. Then I'll say to myself, "You have many goods stored up for many years. Take it easy; eat, drink, and enjoy yourself."' But God said to him, 'You fool!'" (Luke 12:17–20).

In verse 15, Jesus' teaching had said, "One's life is not in the abundance of his possessions." Earlier He had said, "Do not store up for yourselves treasures on earth" (Matt. 6:19 NIV). Every person should be challenged to use his or her talents and energy wisely. What you invest in others lives on. What you do for self dies with you, without making a positive impact on others.

The greatest tragedy in life would be never to experience the journey *for* life.

You who are traveling on the journey *of* life: when you get where you are going, where will you be? Will life have meaning and purpose? Will you be fulfilled and satisfied?

Staring death in the face, Queen Elizabeth I cried, "Millions of money for an inch of time." She was empty and emotionally bankrupt and hopeless.

How does one change the course of his life from the journey *of* life to the journey *for* life? It is by personal choice. You begin the transition by realizing that change is possible, and by your choice the new life begins.

Now, you will not succeed on your own. Success on the journey *for* life is not based upon your performance, your achievements, or how others perceive you. The journey *for* life is a new way, a new life, with the Bible as your guide. On the journey *for* life, you begin a journey on which you can exceed your fondest dreams. By contrast, success on the journey *of* life begins where you are *now*, not where you are going.

Life is not a coincidence; nor are *you* a coincidence. What might be observed as coincidences are planned occurrences in the mind of God preparing us for travel on the journey *for* life and enabling us to be His hands extended to others.

Material possessions are never the measure of success on the journey *for* life; nevertheless, having possessions along with our gifts and talents—when these are dedicated to God—places us in position to be a success on the journey *for* life.

When I was a teenager, my dad introduced me to Napoleon Hill, author of *Think and Grow Rich*. I had a personal visit with him and I read his book, but *Little by Little* is not a book about the power of positive thinking.

The wise man wrote in the book of Proverbs 23:7—"As a man thinketh in his heart so is he" (KJV). I am a positive person, and I applaud those who radiate a positive mental attitude. But positive attitudes alone are not enough. Much good in life is accomplished by those focused on personal needs and the needs of society.

I invite you to join me on the journey *for* life—not a journey of getting or receiving but of *being!*

What Is Success on the Journey *for* Life?

Success is an inner knowing of what you should do, then being about the business of doing it. George W. Truett, longtime pastor of Dallas First Baptist Church, said, "Success in life is simply to know the will of God and to do it."

Success is a peaceful, inner knowing that you are doing what only you can do, being only who you can be.

Success is having a sense of God's purpose for your life and being fulfilled in its pursuit. Success apart from purpose is empty, meaningless, and never satisfies. "Set your minds on what is above, not on what is on the earth" (Col. 3:2).

> Success is always a team effort.
> Success is a documentary.
> Success is pouring yourself into others.

Success is an eternal measure that will be realized when, like Paul, you can say, "I have fought the good fight, I have finished the race, I have kept the faith. In the future, there is reserved for me the crown of righteousness, which the Lord, the righteous Judge, will give me on that day" (2 Tim. 4:7–8).

Success Is Faith

On the journey *for* life, success is the selfless giving of ourselves for others, where you move from your comfort zone into the risk arena. In this arena, the focus of life shifts from me to God, and faith becomes the driving force prompting action. How far will faith take us? Faith's horizons are infinite. God will provide the opportunities of service, and purpose will be realized. Ask yourself, "As I travel, what evidences am I leaving on the journey *for* life that prove I have been here? When I am gone, will I have made a difference? Will I be missed?"

Success Is Possessions under Christ's Control

Success on the journey *for* life is not without price, but it cannot be purchased. Your travel on this journey is not based upon something you can do to gain entrance. Your travel voucher has been purchased by another. However, your traveling requires commitment and personal sacrifice. Jesus gave the challenge to take up the gauntlet in these words: "If anyone wants to come with Me, he must deny himself, take up his cross, and follow Me" (Matt. 16:24). "Whoever does not bear his own cross and come after Me cannot be My disciple" (Luke 14:27).

> I'm for success.
> I strive for success in everything I do.
> I want *you* to be successful.

Now, hear me clearly. This is not a New Age motivational, self-help, get-rich-quick, solve-all-your-problems-in-minutes gimmick. Success will not be achieved by ignoring the facts in life, then saying the right words and mailing your check to some designated post office box this side of heaven.

Little by Little is a Bible-based approach to life-giving direction and guidance to those who dare to experience the all-encompassing meaning of life.

Success Is Service

On the journey *for* life, success embraces service, making a positive difference in the lives of others as we aspire to heaven. Jesus said, "I assure you: Whatever you did for one of the least of these brothers of Mine, you did for Me" (Matt. 25:40).

Success Is the Opportunity to Influence

Travelers on the journey *for* life are on exhibit. We are being watched. We must always keep in mind how we impress and influence others by our actions and our attitudes. Actions and attitudes can speak volumes when our words cannot be heard. On the journey *for* life, we belong to God. We are God's ambassadors—God's hands extended to others.

How can we best serve Him and influence others? It will be by who we are, not by what we possess. The Great Commission is not about how many properties we own or how many deals we make. On the journey *for* life, our best contributions will be made in the role of the Good Samaritan.

On the journey *of* life, the masses are battered, bruised, and bloodied. Most passersby are too self-focused to observe or to be inconvenienced by the hurts of others. What an opportunity exists then to manifest God's love and make an eternal difference in the lives of others. Remember, God's greatest gifts are not things but opportunities.

Success Is Costly

How many of the hurts of others have you put on your eternal credit card? Success is measured by selfless concern and compassion for others. This is a way of making investments in that which outlasts physical life.

Jesus said, "Whoever gives just a cup of cold water to one of these little ones because he is a disciple—I assure you: He will never lose his reward" (Matt. 10:42). Every deed of kindness in Jesus' name will not be without its reward—another step of success on the journey *for* life. Selflessly meeting the needs of others is sometimes costly. In order to meet the world's need of a Savior, it cost God His Son. It cost Jesus His life. And success on the journey *for* life will cost you *your* life.

Paul's testimony was: "I have been crucified with Christ; and I no longer live, but Christ lives in me" (Gal. 2:19–20). But remember, as Jim Elliott said, "The man is no fool who gives up that which he cannot keep to gain that which he cannot lose."

There is no success outside the will of God, and no failure within the will of God.

Success Is a Gradual Process

Success is a gradual process that is realized only as a person through the dedicated use of his gifts finds peace and fulfillment on the journey *for* life. Success comes from investing yourself in others as you travel, as others believe in you, encourage you, affirm you, and assist you—and as you believe in yourself. We should each thank God for family and friends whose support for us enables us to be successful on the journey *for* life.

Success is not a straight line. In fact, in investment terms, the chart line of our journey *for* life is often quite ugly. If you expect to see a gradually ascending upward line on this journey, you will be disappointed.

How would King David's life look projected on a chart graph? How would progress look on the journey to the Promised Land by the children of Israel? How would the apostle Peter's life look? These would not appeal to financial investors who buy and sell by the charts.

On the journey *for* life, there are ups and downs, highs and lows. As you travel, you will observe that the elevator of success is broken; you must take the stairs. Sometimes you miss the mark, you take hits, you stumble, you fall. Unfortunately, not everyone cares. But you keep going just the same, gradually climbing.

Success Includes Other Travelers

Quite often, those who seem to care least are fellow travelers on the journey *for* life. We are family on the journey *for* life and, like families, we have our stressful times, misunderstandings, quarrels, and conflicts. The journey *for* life is no place for jealousy, envy, bitterness, and selfishness. Characteristics consistent with travel on the journey *of* life often surface among those who travel on the journey *for* life.

"I have too many troubles of my own to be concerned with yours."

"I don't have time to listen to yours, but please lend me an ear, listen to mine."

On the journey *for* life, the concern is to be for *others*. On the journey *of* life, the golden rule may be "He who has the gold rules" or "Do unto others before they do unto you." However, the Golden Rule of the Bible is "In everything, do to others what you would have them do to you, for this sums up the Law and the Prophets" (Matt. 7:12 NIV). On the journey *for* life, success is measured by *this* Golden Rule.

Success Is a Challenge

The journey *for* life is not utopia. There are many enemies. Adversity is ever before us. Its challenges are numerous. Life does not always turn out the way we plan. September 11, 2001, has changed that forever. Terrorism has forced changes in the way we think, plan, and dream. The God of those on the journey *for* life is not everyone's God.

Perception as to the meaning and purpose of life and death is the motivation that propels most people to commitment and action. At times on the journey *for* life, the only comfort we have is a sense of purpose that compels and drives us on in our service to God and others.

How do I prepare for success on the journey *for* life? How do I get out of the doldrums, the mistakes, the failures, and the disappointments of the past?

Success for some people is satisfaction: "I never had it this good, and this is good enough for me." How limited we become by our negative thinking. We are the product of our thinking.

Success Is Now

It's time to live in the moment of the *now*.

Live one day at a time.

Enjoy life one day at a time.

Appreciate the moment.

The past is over. You can't relive the past. But you can profit from the past. The past is preparatory for the present and the future. Don't dwell on what you have missed. I know what it is to be disappointed, to hurt, and to stare failure in the face. I also know what it is to resolve a different outcome.

Sometimes, now is God's time. Tomorrow is God's time also. Sometimes His purpose is for us to wait—patiently, productively, expectantly. "Little by little," He is accomplishing His purpose as we are made ready by the experiences of life.

Success is not a look back. It is not a look forward. Success is what is happening now!

Doubt blinds. Faith sees. Inquire of God who He wants you to become. "You can't soar like an eagle while you are scratching around with chickens." All things are possible. Trust! Believe! Never allow doubt to obscure patient waiting. Trust is a part of faith.

Success Is Trust in God

Lessons of history teach us that those who received the promise often had to wait and trust. Abraham was promised to be the father of many heirs; however, according to Genesis 21:5, he was one hundred years old when Isaac was born.

Trust in God for your success. God can be trusted. He will keep His word.

When was Joseph successful? Was it when he received his coat of many colors from his father? When his brothers envied him? When he was sold as a slave by his brothers, and when Potiphar, one of Pharaoh's officials, purchased him? When Pharaoh put him in charge of Egypt? When he revealed himself to his brothers in Egypt?

Be patient. Success will happen in time—on time.

Don't try to fake success. Don't try to manipulate circumstances. God has promised, and God keeps His promises. Moses wrote: "God is not a man who lies, or a son of man who changes His mind" (Num. 23:19). God is not a man; therefore, He does not have the limitations of man. He can be trusted. He is worthy of your trust.

God does not hear you as a man, and God is not going to answer your prayers, requests, and petitions as a man. God is going to answer based upon who He is.

God's view of your situation is not distorted or biased. God speaks truth. Our adversary, Satan, speaks lies. God is not bound by the natural, explainable ways of doing things. He is not limited by our understanding, our strength, or our ability. God controls the outcome, which is only hindered by our lack of faith, our unbelief. If you believe God's Word, you will receive what God has promised.

Success Trumps Circumstances

Expect to be a part of the minority in the faith walk. Success is not determined by the majority.

Joshua served Moses as one of the twelve spies sent to scout the land of Canaan. He and Caleb resisted the majority report of unbelief and, according to Numbers 14:24, the Lord said, "Since My servant Caleb has a different spirit and has followed Me completely, I will bring him into the land where he has gone, and his descendents will inherit it." This occurred because they were men of faith, vision, courage, and loyalty. They lived in obedience to God and His Word.

On the faith walk, never look at circumstances; always look to God. As I heard Andy Stanley, best-selling author and founding pastor of North Point Community Church in Alpharetta, Georgia, say: "God's word always trumps circumstances."

What do want to do for God? What is the dream God has placed in your heart? Making a difference in the lives of others separates those motivated by faith in God's Word from all others. "May He give you what your heart desires and fulfill your whole purpose" (Ps. 20:4).

True success. Go for it!

6

SIGNIFICANT INFLUENCES
ON THE JOURNEY

*M*ost individuals can point to those who have significantly influenced their journey and achievements. A prominent influence is family. Family is God's idea!

God ordained marriage in the beginning, and the family unit became the first institution on earth. "Whoso findeth a wife findeth a good thing" (Prov. 18:22 KJV). Contemporary thought may differ as to the make up of the family unit, but with God this is a settled issue: "Male and female created he them" (Gen. 1:27 KJV). Adam and Eve became the first residents in the Garden of Eden. God blessed them and said to them, "Be fruitful, multiply, fill the earth" (Gen. 1:28), and they became the first parents.

Spiritual values within the family are foundational for success on the journey *for* life. Jesus said, "Everyone who hears these words of Mine and acts on them will be like a sensible man who built his house on the rock. The rain fell, the rivers rose, and the winds blew and pounded that house. Yet it didn't collapse, because its foundation was on the rock" (Matt. 7:24–25).

In this chapter, we'll look at the influence of family on your journey—both how you can benefit from it and how you can bless others through it.

Parents

Jane and I established our home on a strong value system—the values she brought from her family and the values I brought from mine. By God's grace, we are now an extended family of faith. This did not happen by chance; it was by choice. Family values must first be taught and then practiced in real-life situations and relationships. However, there is no family plan for travel on the journey *for* life. Each traveler must have his own ticket.

Today more than ever, the traditional family is under attack. There is no norm. Diversity is the New Age cry. Scoffers scorn biblical absolutes.

Personally, I am not concerned about what is politically correct as it regards family. I am concerned about what is *right*. Popular opinions do not square with truth. Success on the journey *for* life is not based upon what is politically correct. Knowing and doing what is right determines destiny.

Satan attacked the first family by questioning God's purposes. This is the same argument Satan has used from the beginning, and Jesus said it would continue: "Just as it was in the days of Noah, so it will be in the days of the Son of Man" (Luke 17:26). Even so, God has a standard, and He has said, "When the enemy shall come in like a flood, the spirit of the Lord shall lift up a standard against him" (Isa. 59:19 KJV).

The role of parents (and grandparents) is a demanding one. There is no greater responsibility on earth! Ralph Waldo Emerson wrote: "The creation of a thousand forests is in one acorn."

Knowledge of the Bible is essential in establishing faith principles for parenting. Successful parenting is a joint venture between a father and a mother. These parenting roles should never be in conflict. Each is important.

From the moment of birth, the teaching role of parents begins. Neglect this role and the family will be the loser. Many teaching opportunities will be missed if parents don't begin early. Never relinquish the teaching role to the school and church. Too much is at risk! The best and most productive way for parents to teach is by example. "Be there" for your child.

Parents earn or forfeit the respect and confidence of their children by the example they set before them. Advice abounds on successful parenting and is often shared without request. However, most of these counselors give up on the advice after they become parents.

The best and most practical way to learn how to be parents is in the school of experience. How many times have I had to acknowledge to Jane and our children, "I blew it," as we were growing and developing as a family! On occasion I would follow that confession by reminding them, "I've never been the parent of a teenager before."

I've never been too swift as a gardener either. Parenting is much like being a gardener:

> First, understand the crop desired.
> Set specific goals.
> Pay the price.
> Be patient.

Whether the desired harvest is gathered or a crop of weeds is produced depends upon the gardener.

A visitor from Great Britain was asked what impressed him most about America. His immediate reply was, "The perfect way the parents obey the children." I recall reading somewhere: "One of the first things noticed in a backward country is that children are still obeying their parents."

As a parent, I have always wanted to be worthy of my children's respect. I strive to make my life model what I speak. I don't always meet the measure. Most of the times as husband, father, associate, and employer, I have felt remorse and pain when I have lost my cool. I know me! I understand my disposition. Sometimes I am just *too human*. My guilt threshold is high and my personal discipline will not allow me to leave misunderstandings unresolved. I must sincerely make amends—quickly—learn from my mistakes for my own well-being, and become a better example for others to observe and follow.

Paul wrote: "In your anger do not sin: Do not let the sun go down while you are still angry" (Eph. 4:26 NIV). On occasions when I am speaking or teaching I will say, "Jane and I have never gone to sleep on an argument." With the audience gazing in disbelief, I conclude my point by saying, "There have been a few nights when we did not sleep very much."

When the time came for our children to leave home for college, we could only trust that our efforts at parenting during their dependent years had adequately prepared them for a new world out there, a world with all kinds of influences over which parents will then have no control. When that moment arrives, we must continue to commit them to the Lord and trust that the values we have planted as seeds in their lives will produce the desired outcome. Even at this point, *don't leave the results to chance*. Though they are no longer at home, we continue to pray for them daily at the family altar. Remember, prayer is a powerful force available to those who travel on the journey *for* life.

Grandparents

What would family be without grandparents? Not everyone is dealt the same grandparent hand. A perfect hand is when you have two loving and caring grandfathers and two loving and caring grandmothers. If it were measurable, the excitement and interaction between grandparents and grandchildren would go off the charts.

Jane and I had immeasurable joy in observing our children grow up interacting with four healthy grandparents. I grew up with only one grandparent, and she greatly influenced my life. That was my Grannie. I share her with you throughout this book. My maternal grandmother died when I was very young, and I have no active memory of her. My grandfathers each died at a young age. I only wish I had known them. I know I missed much by their premature deaths. I do remember my Grannie!

A class of eight-year-olds answered the questions, "What Is a Grandmother?" as follows:

- "A grandmother is a lady who has no little children of her own. She likes other peoples."
- "Grandmothers don't have to do anything except be there when we come to see them. They are so old they shouldn't play hard or run. It is good if they drive us to the store and have lots of quarters for us."
- "They don't say, 'Hurry up.'"
- "Usually grandmothers are fat, but not too fat to tie your shoes."

- "They wear glasses and funny underwear."
- "They can take their teeth and gums out."
- "When they read to us, they don't skip. They don't mind if we ask for the same story over again."
- "Everybody should try to have a grandmother, especially if you don't have television, because they are the only grown-ups who like to spend time with us."
- "They know we should have snack time before bedtime, and they say prayers with us every time, and kiss us . . . even when we've acted bad."

Of all earthly mortals, can anyone be so immortal as a grandparent? Grandparents have:

Extraordinary vision.
Time for you.
Confidence in you.
Encouragement for you.

Jane and I share the immense joy and excitement of being grandparents. We have seven "perfect" grandchildren. I just happen to have a picture—would you like to see it?

In birth order they are: Meagan, Lindsay, Mitch, Baleigh, Anna, Abbey, and Carson. Each of them makes me vibrate with pride. Jane is the picture-perfect, Norman Rockwell *Grammie*. She does it with love and style. Being Granddaddy is awesome!

Jane and I had good mentors for being grandparents. My parents, with thirteen grandchildren, are "pros" at grandparenting. When our twins were born, Jane's parents became "rookie" grandparents, and the lessons I learned from them I have tried to emulate as a grandparent.

The Family Altar

On our wedding day, Jane and I began our married life by establishing our family altar. For us, this began a time of daily devotion, a time of togetherness to acknowledge God for who He is and to invite Him to be our guide on our journey *for* life. Our family altar is not some stationary place but a time and place wherever, whenever we choose to meet God.

Nothing is more important in our daily lives than this sacred time realizing that when we come together in His name, He has promised to be present with us. In our home, I assumed the lead role in our family devotions; however, in practice, Jane is a strong coleader.

For us, it is a family altar but not a private altar. Daily, family and friends who happen to be with us gather for family devotion at a convenient time.

After we were blessed with children and as they grew, they became active participants in this family time. We were amazed and challenged by their uniqueness and by what they caught in the process. Sometimes the children would plan our devotion. When Donnie and Ronnie were quite young, on one occasion—without us knowing it in advance—they brought saltine crackers and a large glass of grape juice as elements for a "communion time" at our family altar. This was a precious moment. Psalm 127:3 says, "Children are an heritage of the Lord" (KJV).

On another occasion when it was family altar time, what a surprise Donnie and Ronnie had concocted to get my attention! This had been a day they spent cleaning one of our vacant rental houses for the next tenant. What they had found was a treasure for their mischievous minds. They had stowed this treasure under my bed, and was I surprised at devotion time when they produced a collection of *Playboy*-type magazines as though they had found a secret of mine, mischievously asking, "Dad, what are these doing under your bed?"

The magazines didn't remain there long. That's my story and I'm sticking with it! How thankful I am that I had not set that kind of an example for them and we all could enjoy the joke.

Our family altar is open to share each of our needs and desires. We have learned that there are no insignificant happenings in our lives. We bring them all to our family altar. "Christ is all and in all" (Col. 3:11).

Our family altar continues to be our daily gathering place, a solace for life's surprises and a refuge from life's storms. Every family should have a family altar. "The family that prays together stays together."

Our Family Story

Now, let me back up and catch up. Jane and I wanted a family. But before we knew Jane was pregnant, she diagnosed herself as having "food poisoning."

It wasn't food poisoning.

We were excited when we knew we were going to become parents, and at our family altar we prayed often for a healthy child who would grow up, acknowledge God, and live for Him.

As the days and months slowly passed, Jane and I were not ready for the events as they began to unfold. Around seven months into the pregnancy, unusual things (at least for us) began to happen. During the night, I suspected labor, but Jane said, "No way!" Even so, enough happened through the night that we were at the doctor's office the first thing in the morning. When the staff contacted Dr. Dacus at the hospital, he gave instructions for Jane to wait in his office for him. She waited and I drove the short distance to my office to wait for her call.

Dr. Dacus arrived in his office and was explaining to Jane that she was experiencing false labor, when suddenly her water broke. This time, both Jane's and Dr. Dacus's diagnoses were wrong. Remember, all of this was happening just seven months into the pregnancy.

Two telephone calls were quickly made—one to me, and one to Greenville General Hospital.

I made two other calls quickly to the expectant grandparents. There was significantly more excitement expressed by Jane's parents than mine. Mom and Dad are parents of five children and grandparents to thirteen. They were old hands at this.

Arriving at the hospital, Jane was quickly separated from me (they did things differently then), and Jane's parents, the Leslies, soon joined me in the waiting area. After a little wait, Mr. Leslie, expecting a drawn-out process, went back to his office and before he arrived there, Jane delivered.

Our son Donnie was born but, Dr. Dacus's comment in the delivery room was, "He's too small for her to be as big as she is.

Let's see if there is another one." Looking again, our son Ronnie was discovered.

Dr. Dacus came to the waiting room to give me the report: "You have twin boys, but they are way in the woods." It did not take long for me to understand what he was saying.

In such a brief period of time, I experienced excitement, despair, and then the faith I lived by surfaced as I prayed, "Lord, Jane and I prayed for a healthy child, and You chose to give us two boys. What we prayed for one, I now pray for two."

Word of this urgent need quickly spread, and many others joined us in prayer. After a long day, time came for Jane to rest. Before I left the hospital, we embraced—our heavy hearts beating as one—united in our faith and trust in God.

On my way home, I stopped by to see our longtime friends Bill and Sybil Thomas. I shared the events of the day with them, and they thought I was joking. After a brief visit there, I went home to a lonely house.

Again, at our family altar—alone this time—I prayed. And it seemed as though I was enveloped by a holy, comforting presence. Sensing that God was near and had heard my prayer, I experienced a confidence that everything would be all right. In this confidence I was able to sleep restfully through the night.

In order of importance, an individual's love for God followed by love for one's spouse, there is no greater challenge given than to provide wholesome nourishment and balanced Bible-based development for their children.

Our family would not be complete until God blessed us with Deborah. Again, Jane didn't get the timing right. Deborah was born three weeks early, and unlike the birth of Donnie and Ronnie, we were ready this time.

What a charmer Deborah would be. A ball of energy from the beginning. As she was growing up, others would say that her presence "lightened up the room." She is so much like her Mother and namesake, and unlike her Mother she calls me a "pussycat."

Upon her arrival, even though she could not yet participate, Deborah would be present with us at our family altar. As Jane and I had done with Donnie and Ronnie, Deborah was presented to the Lord and dedicated to Him.

Our children have always been full of energy.

But our family altar also enabled us to face the urgent issues of life. Years later when the doctor said to us, "We are sitting on a keg of dynamite if it's what I think it is, and it can blow at any time," he got our attention.

Deborah was just starting the second grade. She had fallen off the monkey bars at the school but at the time did not seem to be hurt. In fact, she had walked home after school with some friends. We would learn later that she had lain down on the grass several times during that walk. She told us she was okay, but she was not acting normal. Something was not right. She lay on her bed and when some friends came to see if she wanted to play she said, "No."

Bedtime came, and after everyone was in bed, we heard a horrible scream. I got to her first. She was sitting up in bed and told me that her shoulder hurt. It soon felt better and she went back to sleep.

The next morning she felt fine, dressed for school, ate breakfast, and was about ready to leave when she screamed again. The morning pain was from her left side, and again it quickly went away. She had no fever and she wanted to go to school. Jane and I decided to take her to the doctor instead. Jane spoke with him privately, telling him about her screams and her shoulder pain. He checked her and found nothing abnormal. However, upon observing her more closely he saw she wasn't as vivacious as normal. They did a couple of tests and found nothing dramatic. The doctor then advised us not to hesitate to call if there was any problem, that he would tell the doctor who would be on call that night what tests he had done.

Just before we left the doctor's office, he decided maybe a pediatric surgeon should look at her. When he called, the surgeon was just going into surgery at the hospital and told us to come by there. As Jane and Deborah were checking into the hospital, they were asked if that was Deborah's normal color. Jane looked and realized her coloring had changed. They performed some more tests at the hospital and determined she had a serious problem. That's when we were advised: "We are sitting on a keg of dynamite if it's what I think it is, and it can blow anytime. We won't know for sure until we operate, but we need to wait as long as we can since she ate breakfast because having eaten recently makes surgery dangerous."

An intern stayed with her from that time until she was taken into surgery. The discovery of a ruptured spleen confirmed their suspicion. Jane thought the intern was just being friendly, but I later learned he was watching for any sign that they would need to operate immediately.

Jane went to the office to admit her and then called to update me on what was happening. I quickly called Jane's parents and arranged for them to take care of Donnie and Ronnie, and then I rushed to the hospital.

Jane observed when the intern was trying to show me what they suspected and what they were going to do that I kept stepping back. Later I would tell her that I just couldn't watch, knowing it was Deborah they were talking about.

Surgery went well, but it was long into the night before anyone could see her. I had gone to be with the boys. Jane stayed at the hospital and finally called and said she could go in the intensive care area to see Deborah. However, they warned Jane concerning what to expect since they were giving her blood. As it turned out, they allowed Jane to sit with her all night until they took her back to her room the next day.

Deborah was very weak and could not speak above a whisper. It seemed like it was several days before she could sit up.

Donnie, Ronnie, and I stopped to buy Deborah a big bear on our way to visit her. A doctor friend told me, "You don't know how lucky you are that she didn't die." *Lucky* was not the correct word. We were *blessed.* Throughout the entire process, family and friends had fervently prayed for a good outcome.

As the doctor was leaving her room, Jane followed him to the elevator and began to ask if what he told me was true. The doctor said, "Don't ask; you don't want to know." Again when he was about to dismiss her from his care weeks later, Jane said, "Can I ask that question now?" He said, "Now I can tell you that she may have lived a few more hours but certainly not days if we had not operated when we did."

For the future, the pediatricians advised us to contact them immediately anytime she had a fever or felt bad because treatment would need to be started immediately. Without a spleen, you can't wait to see if you'll get better because your immune system is not there.

On the journey *for* life, limitless promises and guidelines abound in the Scriptures as examples for those who will accept the challenge to "train up a child in the way he should go; and when he is old, he will not depart from it" (Prov. 22:6 KJV).

Life's greatest resolve was expressed by Joshua: "If it doesn't please you to worship the Lord, choose for yourselves today the one you will worship. . . . As for me and my family, we will worship the Lord" (Josh. 24:15).

In life, this one measure of success transcends all others. God's plan, expressed by Jesus is to "let the little children come to me, and do not hinder them, for the kingdom of heaven belongs to such as these" (Matt. 19:14 NIV).

For many parents, inside the hedge of prayer, love, shelter, and security that they sacrificially provide for their child, they often approach an impenetrable wall of resistance from a child that reads: "Private Area. No Trespassing." The best efforts of caring parents appear only to exasperate the separation. Have you found yourself there?

There are so many voices, real and imagined, unrelentingly tossing potent grenades of criticism your way. Don't listen to them! You don't have to accept the condemning, pious, hypocritical platitudes of those who are master players of "The Blame Game."

> Resist perceived failure.
>
> Don't give up.
>
> When you've given your best, you are not a failure.

Nothing on earth is more important than family! A village may be important, but family is essential. Don't neglect your family. Unfortunately, some families—even clergy, missionaries, or earnest Christians on the journey *for* life—are neglected because a parent excuses his absence saying: "I must not neglect God's work." Family is important, and God has never called anyone to neglect his own family in order to care for someone else's family. Your family *is* God's work, and your family must be your priority.

For as long as I can remember in our family, the Bible has been the guidebook for family living. According to God's plan as recorded in the Bible, each individual is to be part of a monogamous family unit.

The Truth about Family

The traditional family is foundational for those who travel on the journey *for* life, and if the family is to survive and influence our culture, it must be modeled beyond the home and church, wherever struggling dysfunctional families may be—on your street, on Main Street, in the inner city ghettos, or to those of the upper classes, wherever they reside. There is no adequate substitute or replacement for the family. No better plan or idea improving God's original plan has evolved.

God's blueprint for functional family living is in the Bible. Our homes must provide a nurturing atmosphere where parents, with the resources God provides, inoculate those in our homes from the godless influences so prevalent in our society and, too often, influences that are allowed to invade our God-fearing homes.

Family is where I first learned about God. My parents were obedient to biblical instructions given by Moses to remember and teach God's Word. I learned at an early age that God loves me.

When I was a child, our family was a singing family (ahead of our time). Mother was a singing lady. As she would do her work around the house, she would be singing the songs of the church and the songs of the village culture. On Saturday nights family and friends would often gather around the radio to enjoy the music of "The Grand Ole Opry."

Dad would accompany us with his guitar when our family would sing songs of the church like:

> Jesus loves me this I know,
> For the Bible tells me so;
> Little ones to Him belong,
> They are weak but He is strong.
>
> Yes, Jesus loves me,
> Yes, Jesus loves me,
> Yes, Jesus loves me,
> The Bible tells me so.

Learning that "Jesus loves me" through song has continued in our home with our children and grandchildren. We would often gather around the piano to sing as I played. Occasionally Jane and I are reminded of these sessions when we come across recordings of past sessions. The precious memories and moments they revive are priceless.

As a functioning family unit interacting together, we learn from each other and from God's instructions—"little by little"—how to live and work together on the journey *for* life. God through Moses instructed family leaders to be faithful in passing His Word on. "Only be on your guard and diligently watch yourselves, so that you don't forget the things your eyes have seen and so that they don't slip from your mind as long as you live. Teach them to your children and your grandchildren" (Deut. 4:9).

God's word is clear and instructive concerning marriage and the family. Paul wrote: "Do not be mismatched with unbelievers. For what partnership is there between righteousness and lawlessness? Or what fellowship does light have with darkness?" (2 Cor. 6:14). The choice of a compatible, believing marriage partner is essential for a wholesome marriage. There is reason for a period of courtship prior to marriage. Call it "due diligence." It takes time to know each other. Don't rush into marriage. Christian marriage is to be entered into as a lifetime commitment. I know of no better definition of marriage than that of the *Baptist Faith and Message*: "The uniting of one man and one woman in covenant and commitment for a lifetime."[3]

On the journey *of* life and the journey *for* life, marriage can be as different as addition is to multiplication. Addition is applicable to the journey *of* life:

$$1 + 1 = 2$$

Multiplication is applicable to the journey *for* life:

1 x 1 = 1

It is recorded in Genesis 2:24—"Therefore shall a man leave his father and his mother, and shall cleave unto his wife: and they shall be one flesh" (KJV).

One in life. One with God.

As paradoxical as it may sound, it is true. Even so, evidence mounts that traditional marriage is in trouble. Marriage is under attack, and without God's intervention it will only get worse. However, "with God all things are possible" (Matt. 19:26). In a functional family the members learn how to:

Appreciate and respect differences.

Manage conflicts.

Support each other.

Encourage each other.

Honor each other.

Love each other.

And through the process, they learn the most important lesson of all. They learn how to be obedient to God, which is the key to receiving all God has promised, enabling success on the journey *for* life.

From listening to and observing many critics of Bible truth, this is the message repeatedly heard: "This is a new day. Get your nose out of the Bible and stop using an archaic book of stories as your crutch for existence. The Bible has served its purpose. Study the Declaration of Independence. It says 'All men are created equal.'"

True! All men are created "by God," and all men "are equal" in God's eye. There is no higher authority. There is no *other* authority!

Paul wrote, "Everyone must submit to the governing authorities, for there is no authority except from God, and those that exist are instituted by God" (Rom. 13:1). We cannot acquiesce what we believe to be truth just because we are accosted by those of other views—especially as they relate to marriage.

Reduced to its simplest equation, what does God say? Paul wrote:

> For God's wrath is revealed from heaven against all godlessness and unrighteousness of people who by their unrighteousness suppress the truth, since what can be known about God is evident among them, because God has shown it to them. From the creation of the world His invisible attributes, that is, His eternal power and divine nature, have been clearly seen, being understood through what He has made. As a result, people are without excuse. (Rom. 1:18–20)

Because of man's continuing rebellion and disregard for God's authority, God ordained and established the governing authority of the state. Unfortunately, the state has assumed authority beyond what God ordained, and chaos reigns.

As a free moral person, man's choice—not God's anger—is the reason for the depravity and perversion that is depicted by Paul in the first chapter of Romans and even now is so devastatingly prevalent throughout the world. Could the inquiry of the king recorded in 2 Chronicles 34:21 also be applicable to our nation? "Go. Inquire of the Lord for me and for those remaining in Israel and Judah, concerning the words of the book that was found. For great is the Lord's wrath that is poured out on us because our fathers have not kept the word of the Lord in order to do everything written in this book."

There are many trophies of God's grace, bearing witness to renewal of purpose and changed lives. Simon Peter is a good example, not in his swearing and gross denials but in what he became when he was restored. Wherever you are on your journey—however hopeless your life may seem—there is hope.

Restoration Is Possible

What is restoration? A place where even God will no longer remember our sins, missteps, and wrongdoings. According to Jeremiah 31:33–34:

> "This is the covenant I will make with the house of Israel after those days"—the Lord's declaration. "I will place My law within them and write it on their hearts. I will be their God, and they will be My people. No longer will one teach his neighbor or his brother, saying: 'Know the Lord,' for they will all know Me, from the least to the greatest of them"—the Lord's declaration. "For I will forgive their wrongdoing and never again remember their sin."

Why? Not because of who we are. Not because of what we do, but through repentance, submission, and obedience.

Something is terribly wrong when Christian marriage mirrors secular marriage and the rest of society does not recognize any difference.

Restoration Is God's Answer

Restoration is what redemption is all about. Don't allow the mistakes and failures of your past to undermine your future with God. It is possible to start over—in many instances with the same partner—and united in faith you may begin to experience a wholesome, fulfilling marriage, "until death do us part."

If your marriage is not what you had hoped for, don't give up. Divorce is not God's answer.

Every marriage, whether begun on the journey *of* life or the journey *for* life, has periods of stress and conflicts. Couples who work through these times often find their marriages refocused and stronger. An unwholesome marriage can be redeemed!

How can this be?

On the journey *of* life, self is so important. But on the journey *for* life, self is lost in God and in selfless service to others in His name. It's true that purpose may be diverted and distorted, but with desire and resolve, purpose can be restored.

Unfortunately not every family unit will survive. Sometimes family conflicts cannot be resolved amicably. It may be too late in the process at this juncture. Precipitous acts by one or both partners involving many other lives are so complex that any solution other than divorce would be too disruptive, resulting in further chaos for family members.

Even then, there remains hope.

The word "dysfunctional," with all of its connotations, does not mean that an individual from a dysfunctional family cannot find success on the journey *for* life. There are many testimonies of success by individuals rising from the ash heap of personal trauma, motivated only by personal desire and faith to a better life. Dysfunctional family relationships are not new to God. The dysfunctional family began with Adam and Eve. If you find yourself in a dysfunctional family, life is not hopeless.

First, remember, "God is love." He loves you, and God does not love by degrees. The apostle Peter said, "In truth, I understand that God doesn't show favoritism, but in every nation the person who fears Him and does righteousness is acceptable to Him" (Acts 10:34–35). God does not love a member of a functional family more than an individual in a dysfunctional family. Jesus' death on the cross settled this issue forever. His love is *to all* and *for all*. "For God so loved the world that he gave his one and only Son, that whoever believes in him shall not perish but have eternal life" (John 3:16 NIV).

The Bible teaches individual responsibility. God's promises are to individuals, not families. Nevertheless, a godly parent's resolve and dedication can do much to point the way. Again, as Solomon wrote: "Train up a child in the way he should go; and when he is old, he will not depart from it" (Prov. 22:6 KJV).

That is such a comforting word! God's "whosoever" includes everyone, but the choice is personal and individual. It depends upon you.

In today's stressful times, conflict and strife based upon "what an individual wants" continues to devastate families. Personal sensitivities cause tempers to flare and fits of anger are expressed both verbally and physically. But family harmony is more important than family possessions.

Abraham had it right. Because of his faith in God's promises he gave Lot his choice of direction and they parted as family. Faith in God was Abraham's confidence while Lot's choice was motivated by avarice and greed. His was not a walk of faith; it was a walk of sight focused on the moment.

What is true for individuals and families is also true of nations. The children of Israel's disobedience to the commands of God caused them to become a dysfunctional people. Seldom have God's chosen people been in total surrender and complete obedience to God. Even though they were and continue to be a dysfunctional people, God did not nor will He destroy them. God loves them, and His heart yearns for them to return to Him.

Sadly, the United States of America has strayed from her spiritual foundation. The Judeo-Christian principles upon which America was founded are not descriptive of America today. God's universal call as recorded in Jeremiah 3:14 says, "Return, faithless people . . . for I am your husband" (NIV). In Jeremiah 3:18, the Lord says, "In those days the house of Judah will join with the house of Israel, and they will come together from the land of the north to the land I have given your ancestors to inherit."

What is the problem? Sin. In Proverbs 14:34 it is recorded, "Sin is a disgrace to any people."

What is the solution? In Proverbs 28:13, it is recorded, "The one who conceals his sins will not prosper, but whoever confesses and renounces them will find mercy."

God is a loving God. God is a forgiving God. "If we confess our sins, He is faithful and righteous to forgive us our sins and to cleanse us from all unrighteousness" (1 John 1:9).

Family is not to be isolated from today's diverse culture. Those from strong families must *change* the culture. Families may be disintegrating, but God's Word provides answers that really work.

Societal pressure continues to redefine marriage and family, forcing acceptance of some court-ordained substitute for the family institution God ordained. The majority may not accept Bible-based, Judeo-Christian morality; nevertheless, we must be diligent in keeping others from imposing their morality on us. God-sanctioned morality must not be relegated to a closet experience. It must be visible and evidenced in society. Heterosexual marriage is still God's model.

While we are building our strong families, our commitment must also be to help restore the dysfunctional family and to assist struggling families. When the family is threatened, the foundation of society is threatened. Constant pressure with no outward evidence of success can cause one to despair; however, surrender is no option. God's miracles are still available to redeem and restore failing marriages.

In some families, the dysfunctional misfortune begins at the marriage altar. Many marriages should never have happened. Unfortunately this problem only continues to accelerate. The USA has the highest divorce rate in the world. It appears that in marriage, America models Hollywood rather than the plan God instituted.

Other contributing causes to dysfunctional families are:

- The role and control of money.
- Alcoholism and drug addiction.
- Health problems. We did say in our vows "in sickness and in health," but now—"this is more than I can bear."
- Suicide. Never, never a right way out.
- Divorce. Something is terribly wrong when divorces exceed marriages.

As travelers on the journey *for* life, what is our commitment to the dysfunctional families around us? If we respond in a positive way, we may be God's means of healing to a family, a community, and a nation—for God and for good.

Generational Family Markers

In other families, there are distinguishing generational family markers. Notable is the high profile of the Joseph P. Kennedy family.

Senator Edward Kennedy, losing his presidential hopes after the incident at Chappaquiddick, inquired whether there was a curse on his family. During the past several generations of the high profile Kennedy family, many have asked if there *was* a curse on this family. Whatever the cause, there has been a sequence of tragedies over several decades. Consider the following short list, which does not reference issues like divorce, adultery, or alcoholism:

- Joseph P. Kennedy, Jr., Joe's eldest son, the great hope of his father for the American presidency, is killed in a plane crash in 1944, age twenty-nine.
- Kathleen Kennedy, Joe's second daughter, dies in a plane crash in 1948, age twenty-eight.
- John F. Kennedy, the thirty-fifth president of the United States, is assassinated in Dallas in November 1963, age forty-six.
- John F. Kennedy's son, Patrick Bouvier Kennedy, born prematurely to the president and his wife in 1963, dies three months before his father's assassination.
- Robert F. (Bobby) Kennedy, Joe's third son, is assassinated in June 1968, age forty-two.
- Senator Edward M. (Ted) Kennedy, Joe's youngest son, drives a car off a bridge on Chappaquiddick Island in July 1969, after a party. His aide, Mary Jo Kopechne, is found dead in the submerged car. Ted's political career may have survived the questions and speculation surrounding this event; however, it cost him whatever chance he may have had to become president of the United States of America.
- Bobby Kennedy's son Joseph is involved in a car accident in 1973 that leaves a female passenger paralyzed for life.

- Ted Kennedy's son, Edward, Jr., has his right leg amputated in 1973 because of cancer.
- Bobby Kennedy's son David dies in 1984 of a drug overdose.
- Ted Kennedy's son Patrick is treated for cocaine addiction in 1986.
- Ted Kennedy's nephew, William Kennedy Smith, is acquitted of rape in 1991.
- Bobby Kennedy's son Michael is killed in a skiing accident in December 1997, age thirty-nine.
- John F. Kennedy's only surviving son, JFK Jr., dies in a plane crash in July 1999 (exactly thirty years after Chappaquiddick), age thirty-eight.

The opinion of others may conclude that the events that have been enumerated are not a curse but rather a dysfunctional family driven by a patriarch of obsessive ambition unwilling to settle for less than his selfish goals.

What is a curse? Some would say it is something inflicted on the descendents of an individual who has offended God. Throughout time people have been puzzled by tragic events and circumstances called a "curse" that seem to follow or shadow certain individual families. Could this be what the ancient Greeks called a family curse, or are we just observers of coincidence?

In most biological families, there are recognizable traits and characteristics—markers—that make it easy to identify its members. Why is it that in many families there does not appear to be a legacy of faith? Whatever the reason, the pattern did not begin with recent generations.

In Exodus 34:7, Moses wrote: "He will not leave the guilty unpunished, bringing the consequences of the fathers' wrongdoing

on the children and grandchildren to the third and fourth generation." From these words we learn that sin and disregard for God
and His laws may bring havoc on families for generations.

Not all families who suffer multiple misfortunes are on the
scale of the Kennedys; however, the impact may be very real and
devastating just the same. Regardless of the slant historians and
others may place upon such tragic markers, the source of it all is
sin and *total disregard* to the commands of God. Life does not need
to happen that way.

Sin began in the Garden of Eden. And evidences of sin's curse
continue to abound. Family curses, generational family markers,
and dysfunctional families are very real and observable. Being a
victim of these may seem unfair if you struggle helplessly and hopelessly in their grasp, groaning and crying for a way out. But if this
describes your plight, don't let anyone relegate you to the defeat
and agony of your past. Regardless of the extent of your misfortune,
don't despair. God also said in Deuteronomy 5:10 that He shows
"faithful love to a thousand generations of those who love Me and
keep My commands." There *is* a way out.

Generational Blessings

Many families have clearly repetitive patterns of good fortune. "Where sin abounded, grace did much more abound"
(Rom. 5:20 KJV).

God is just. The Bible's message is clear and understandable.
Grace is available for all. Be encouraged. Sin's curse can be broken.
The desired change is not in the genes; it is in the heart.

A family curse, an adverse generational marker, or being locked
in a dysfunctional family—perceived or real—is not the end of the
story. You can experience release. You can be free!

And what sparks the desire to be free? Knowledge.

Jesus' parable of the prodigal son, recorded in Luke 15:11–32, illustrates this poignantly. The prodigal had squandered his wealth in wild living. Needy and desperate, with nowhere to turn, he took a job foreign to his culture and began to feed pigs. He became so hungry that he considered eating the pig's food, yet no one gave him anything.

Then by a sovereign act of God, "he came to his senses" (Luke 15:17). He remembered his father's house. Remembering was followed by resolve. No longer willing to remain where he was, he began his journey home thinking of what he would say to his father: "Father, I have sinned against heaven and in your sight. I'm no longer worthy to be called your son. Make me like one of your hired hands" (Luke 15:18–19).

Still, a long way from home, his father saw him, ran to him, embraced him, and kissed him. The prodigal began the speech he had rehearsed, but the father, ordering a celebration, would have none of that. The prodigal was alive and restored.

There are many prodigals on the journey *of* life. I have a friend of many years whose family was marked by alcoholism for generations. Would alcoholism engulf him? Indeed, its ravages had begun to take hold. A lifestyle was developing that could go nowhere but down. Much like the prodigal—in a somber moment that can only be birthed by God's Holy Spirit—he "came to his senses." In a cataclysmic moment, he determined, "No more!" On his knees, he retraced his steps and was embraced by the Heavenly Father—delivered from the clutches of alcoholism and the personal ambition and drive toward success on the journey *of* life. By a work of God's grace, he is now positioned on the journey *for* life.

I don't have a better friend on earth than Dr. James M. Ford. We now travel the journey *for* life together—supporting each other, encouraging each other, and influencing others to travel it with us. In life, whether the journey *of* life or the journey *for* life—no matter how far you may have wandered—God is not so remote that He is unaware of you, your circumstances, and your need.

> Realize who you are.
> Realize who your Father is.
> Resolve to break out of the mold.

Many wayfaring travelers on the journey *of* life today ask: "Where is this elusive peace in the midst of such turmoil?" It will not be found in scripted spoken words, magic formulas, or the works of man's hands. There is nothing you can do to achieve it, deserve it, or earn it. It is only obtainable by grace—unmerited favor. God is a God of grace, and grace is a work of God.

Sin does impact generations; however, grace exceeds sin and also impacts generations. In Acts 2:39, the apostle Peter proclaimed, "The promise is for you and for your children, and for all who are far off, as many as the Lord our God will call.

As parents, Jane and I experience the joy that children can bring to a functional family. What a legacy! What a heritage we have! How proud our children make us as parents. Observing them achieve on their own—while instilling meaningful values in the lives of our grandchildren—is the best reward we can experience on the journey *for* life. The successful harvest of the seed planted in the lives of our children and grandchildren will be our greatest lifetime achievement.

Where Generational Markers Begin and End

Without realizing it, parents have destroyed the dreams of a child by showing favoritism or partiality for one child over another.

When did the prodigal brother's problem begin? Diligently guard against such an occurrence. When this is allowed to happen, it often repeats itself in the succeeding generation. Consider how this was manifest in Isaac and repeated in Jacob. Should this occur today, grace is still the answer.

Sometimes, in families, the best efforts of a child to show honor, respect, and care for parents fail. Parents sometimes are jealous of each other. One parent may want the love and respect of the child while resenting any love and devotion expressed by a child to the other parent. In other instances, a parent may be envious or jealous of a child due to no fault of the child. Often, a child's expressions of love and concern are refused by one or both parents. Even so, we must obey God and continue to honor our parents.

For better or worse, children mirror their parents. As a parent, have you seen yourself in the actions of your children? As a child, have you seen yourself in your parents? Do you like what you see?

Like the prodigal when he "came to himself," you can break free from the controlling, seductive grip of your environment and circumstances. You don't have to remain bound by the village culture, the sins of past generations, or generational markers

The controlling culture I remember as a young person has blended into the past. I have moved on, and I am free. Nevertheless, those memories remain indelibly etched in my mind. Peter said, "In truth, I understand that God doesn't show favoritism, but in every nation the person who fears Him and does righteousness is acceptable to Him" (Acts 10:34–35).

Be encouraged: The better life can be yours.

I have known families where identical markers of disease, affliction, and death in one generation followed like clockwork in succeeding generations. A father dies of a heart attack at age fifty-two, and his son dies of a heart attack within months of being the same age. A Christian father in his forties forsook his family in a moment of passion, embracing a life contrary to all he had believed and practiced. Subsequently, his son, who followed a call to Christian ministry, had a similar adulterous affair in his forties that destroyed his home.

Is this just coincidence? Does it result from the sin of a previous generation? Is it a family curse? Is it caused by something in the gene pool? Is it psychosomatic?

None of the above? All of the above?

Once repeated, some even came to expect it as though the inevitable must happen. Job said, "The thing I feared has overtaken me, and what I dreaded has happened to me. I cannot relax or be still; I have no rest, for trouble comes" (Job 3:25–26).

Multitudes inquire: Is there a way out? Is there hope? Can this cycle be broken? Is retribution possible? What is the way out? How can I be set free?

Sin has been a part of the human predicament ever since Adam and Eve sinned in the Garden of Eden. Even so, God had a better plan, and He would not give up on them. God in love told Adam and Eve of a better day to come. Redemption is a plan conceived in the heart of God before creation. In Genesis 3:15, God said to Satan: "I will put hostility between you and the woman, and between your seed and her seed. He will strike your head, and you will strike his heel."

God continued to implement His plan by calling a man named Abraham. Through him, God intended to have a man of faith who would know Him and serve Him. From Abraham would come a chosen nation from which Jesus Christ the Savior of the world would come.

This drama would continue to unfold. But Satan would not give up, and he has continued to attack and distort God's plan and promise through the generations.

God's promise to Abraham and Sarah was to be through Isaac and his seed. However, Abraham and Sarah could not wait for God to fulfill His promise. (Ouch! I have been there.) Consider the impact of their impatience when Sarah gave Abraham her servant to "lie" with Abraham, resulting in the birth of Ishmael. This was not according to God's plan. The resultant cultural clashes created the conflict and havoc that have continued for generations in the extended family of Abraham.

Yes, sin is generational. Indeed, sin extracts an awful toll, but never beyond the reach of grace. Grace, too, is generational!

Paul wrote: "Where sin multiplied, grace multiplied even more, so that, just as sin reigned in death, so also grace will reign through righteousness, resulting in eternal life through Jesus Christ our Lord" (Rom. 5:20–21).

God's plan continued through Joseph. Joseph's journey *for* life began as a youth. His mother, Rachel, had died—leaving him to learn about life and godly living from his father, Jacob. Joseph would also learn deep spiritual truths and exploits of faith from his grandfather Isaac. You can almost sense the trauma and the drama as Isaac recalled the events of the day he lay on the altar as his father Abraham raised the knife that would complete Abraham's sacrifice of obedience.

Jacob, now called Israel, loved Joseph more because he had been born to him in his old age. He ordered a multi-colored robe tailored for his special son. Was this wise? This obvious expression gave Satan an opening for attack.

The Lord was with Joseph, and he learned to listen to God. God gave Joseph dreams and the ability to interpret the meaning of the dreams. At the same time, Joseph's brothers were listening to another voice.

Yet everything that happened in this unfolding drama was under God's direction to ultimately preserve Israel's family according to God's promise given to Abraham. In Joseph's life, we see the unfolding of a much greater plan. It takes place "little by little" over a period of more than one hundred years, beginning with God's call to Abraham and Abraham's obedience to God. Through Joseph we learn that though the righteous may suffer in a corrupt world, God's plan will ultimately triumph. God had promised Abraham descendents as numberless as the stars in the heavens and the grains of sand on the seashore.

We observe Joseph's life and wonder, "Where is God? Has He forsaken His promise?" Joseph's journey *for* life was off the beaten path. God has promised to always be with us, just not at the Ritz-Carlton. There would be many similarities between Joseph's life and Jesus' life. Remember, Jesus had no place to lay His head.

You cannot always gauge God's plan for your life by a casual observance of the circumstances of the moment. The trends of the moment are not necessarily permanent directions. You may feel confident and adequate in your own strength, but when adversity comes, you will quickly realize your limitations, begin to lose hope, and become desperate and dependent. When this happens, recall Proverbs 3:5–6: "Trust in the Lord with all your heart, and do not rely on your own understanding; think about Him in all your ways, and He will guide you on the right paths."

Some seven hundred years after Joseph's death, David was anointed king of Israel. At an early age David had developed a heart and desire for God, and as a youth he accomplished great exploits in the name of God. David was an unknown to man, but

David was known by God. In people's eyes, David was the least likely of Jesse's sons to be king over Israel. Yet as unlikely as he was, David was God's choice, and God instructed His prophet Samuel to anoint him king.

Why?

It would be twenty-five years before he would become king. God's timing is not always according to our calendars. Many who are called by God, like Moses and Paul, spend much time in "Desert University" before they matriculate. In time, God would acknowledge David to be "a man after my own heart" (Acts 13:22 NIV).

Nevertheless, Satan observed the weakness of another of God's called servants, and he went into attack mode. David, then the king, stumbled off the journey *for* life in the episode with Bathsheba, causing irreparable havoc in the kingdom. The "man after God's own heart" became guilty of adultery and murder.

Nevertheless, at a God appointed moment, David had a reality check during an encounter with Nathan, God's prophet. Even so, there followed in David's family: rape, murder, incest, rebellion. True, David repented and he was restored, but at the cost of what might have been. How many of us wrestle with a nightmare of what might have been?

Another generation followed David, led by his son Solomon. Even though Solomon was the product of a dysfunctional family, Solomon had "all the toys." He was born into position, wealth, and fame. He was gifted and blessed with great wisdom. It is recorded: "The queen of Sheba heard about Solomon's fame connected with the name of the Lord and came to test him with difficult questions. But I didn't believe the reports until I came and saw with my own eyes. Indeed, I was not even told half. Your wisdom and prosperity far exceed the report I heard" (1 Kings 10:1, 7).

But from Solomon's perspective it all became vanity.

What did it take to restore and establish dysfunctional Simon Peter, enabling him to become the powerful witness Jesus had foretold when He said, "Simon son of Jonah, you are blessed because flesh and blood did not reveal this to you, but My Father in heaven. And I also say to you that you are Peter, and on this rock I will build My church, and the forces of Hades will not overpower it" (Matt. 16:17–18).

In a short period of time he was elevated from the pit to the pulpit. From cowardice and denials to the fearless proclamation of the gospel, often in a hostile environment, Peter had received the infilling of the Holy Spirit, never turning back to the old life.

On the journey *of* life, Paul had studied with the masters. But his learning was not wasted. All his training and study had equipped him for his journey *for* life, which would be realized in his defense of "The Way" before kings and rulers and to the Gentile world.

In his defense before Festus and Agrippa, Paul spoke with such power and passion that Festus interrupted him:

> "You're out of your mind, Paul! Too much study is driving you mad!" But Paul replied, "I'm not out of my mind, most excellent Festus. On the contrary, I'm speaking words of truth and good judgment. For the king knows about these matters. It is to him I am actually speaking boldly. For I'm not convinced that any of these things escapes his notice, since this was not done in a corner!
>
> "King Agrippa, do you believe the prophets? I know you believe." Then Agrippa said to Paul, "Are you going to persuade me to become a Christian so easily?"
>
> "I wish before God," replied Paul, "that whether easily or with difficulty, not only you but all who

listen to me today might become as I am—except for
these chains." (Acts 26:24–29)

In summary Paul would say, "I have fought the good fight,
I have finished the race, I have kept the faith" (2 Tim. 4:7). Paul
had realized success on the journey *for* life.

The Impact of Family Influences

Consider the following lesson in contrasts from the early
1700s.

Around forty years ago, Yale University conducted an extensive seven-year study on how a person's actions in life affect the
lives of his or her children. This study was focused around the lives
of two men: Max Jukes and Jonathan Edwards. Max Jukes was an
atheist who believed in the abolition of laws and rules. He formed
an organization called the Freedom Movement that preached free
sex, no laws, no formal education, and no responsibilities. Jonathan
Edwards, on the other hand, was known by all as the "disciplinar-
ian," not because he disciplined his children harshly but because
he was a self-disciplined man. He became a preacher who believed
in leading by example. He authored two books on the subjects of
physical fitness and kindness. Mr. Edwards later became involved
in teaching people to be responsible for their daily actions. Both of
these men were chosen for their diverse beliefs, but also because
they both fathered thirteen children. Here are the legacies they
left behind:

Max Jukes	Jonathan Edwards
1026 descendants	929 descendants
300 convicts	430 ministers/314 war veterans

27 murderers	75 authors
190 prostitutes	86 college professors
509 alcoholics and	13 university presidents
drug addicts	7 congressmen/3 governors

The outcomes were all predicated on personal choices early in life. Jukes and the woman he married traveled a road of wrong choices. Follow his descendants, and you will observe no significant contribution to society but a trail of crimes and tragedies which cost millions to the state of New York.

Next, consider Jonathan Edwards, minister and theologian. Edwards married a woman who shared his values and commitment to live a life of positive influence with amazing results.

The place where you are in life now is the result of choices you have made in your past years. Whom have you influenced? Where are they headed?

God does not mete out his vengeance as a curse. However, God does punish those who sin. Sin separates man and God. "And be sure your sin will find you out" (Num. 32:23 KJV).

Clarence McCartney, who pastored First Presbyterian Church of Pittsburgh, Pennsylvania, wrote that your sin would find you out "in time, in conscience, and in eternity." Most of us don't count on our sin being exposed in this life. Our view of sin is different from God's. We count on time being our ally until a "more convenient season" comes. Then we will deal with the sin question.

Amid today's high-tech advances, we no longer have the cover of time. Even if we *could* have the cover of time when others don't know and don't care, we live with ourselves and we know.

Peter denied his Lord with an oath and was overwhelmed with the rush of guilt when he looked into the eyes of Jesus.

Judas betrayed Jesus, and under the guilt of conscience hanged himself.

Having escaped in time and having drugged your conscience, you cannot escape God's judgment. You will face God. Satan's attacks on God's servants are focused attacks. John wrote of him in John 10:10—"A thief comes only to steal and to kill and to destroy." Satan has a "playbook" designed for your destruction. As the author of Hebrews wrote, Satan is aware of "the sin that so easily ensnares" you, and this point is where he will attack. (Heb. 12:1)

> He is not timid.
> He has no sympathy.
> His mission is to destroy.

But as Paul wrote, "If God be for us, who can be against us?" (Rom. 8:31 KJV).

As with the prodigal son, not all Christian parents are blessed with each child following their example. Years ago in the city of Philadelphia, there was a family of good reputation. The family consisted of: a father, who died of a broken heart because of the shame that came to him through a son who was a disgrace to the family; a mother, who was a beautiful person; and another son, who was very respectful and obedient and became a physician. After the father's death, the prodigal boy started away from home and aimlessly drifted farther and farther away.

One day on his journey *of* life, the young man had a great yearning to see his mother. You can drift on and on, but there is something about a mother's love that you can never get away from. The mother–and–son bond will never leave, no matter what the mother does to you or what you do to your mother. Thank God for family and godly mothers.

Starting toward home, he felt greatly ashamed to enter the old house, but still he knew if he could just see her, she would welcome him.

Arriving at the door, it flew open—and he became wrapped in his mother's arms as she welcomed him home with a forgiving kiss. Exhausted, he soon retired for rest.

During the night his brother came to the door: "Mother's dying." Rushing into his mother's room, dropping to his knees, embracing his mother, he cried, "Mother, you must forgive me."

Looking into his face with a smile, she said, "My son, I forgave you long years ago. All this time I have been waiting for you to accept my forgiveness."

How like the forgiveness of Jesus Christ! Ever since Jesus died on the cross, God has been waiting for you to accept His forgiveness and begin your journey *for* life—to experience God's promised blessings.

As mentioned before, "The Lord is slow to anger and rich in faithful love, forgiving wrongdoing and rebellion. But He will not leave the guilty unpunished, bringing the consequences of the fathers' wrongdoing on the children to the third and fourth generation" (Num. 14:18). Yet God does not leave us here. He completes the expression of His heart in Deuteronomy 5:10—"showing faithful love to a thousand generations of those who love Me and keep My commands"

Knowing about God created an earnest desire in my heart to know God. Prior to knowing God in a personal way, my life—like many others—was self-centered, directionless, without significance and purpose. And without Jesus Christ, yours will be also.

Don't close these pages yet! Remember the challenge of "honest inquiry," and read on! There is no more compelling example of "honest inquiry" available for consideration than that of Saul of Tarsus, who became Paul the apostle as recorded in the Acts of the Apostles, chapter 9. Saul was the leader of the opposition who sought to discredit the seven men chosen by the apostles to assist in the daily service ministry activities so that the apostles might not neglect the ministry of the Word of God. Stephen, full of the Holy Spirit, proved to be too much for them. "They were unable to stand up against the wisdom and the Spirit by whom he spoke" (Acts 6:10).

Trumped-up charges were brought against Stephen, a mockery of a trial was held, and Stephen was stoned to death. What a powerful revelation Stephen was to the grace of a loving, caring God even while being stoned to death! Luke recorded the event like this: "They were stoning Stephen as he called out: 'Lord Jesus, receive my spirit!' Then he knelt down and cried out with a loud voice, 'Lord, do not charge them with this sin!' And saying this, he fell asleep" (Acts 7:59–60).

While this was taking place, Saul was standing there, giving approval to Stephen's death. The Holy Spirit was also there, observing Saul and making indelible impressions of these happenings in his mind and spirit. Apparently unmoved, Saul continued breathing out murderous threats against the Lord's disciples.

Then, on his way to Damascus with authority to destroy any who belonged to the Way, a sudden light flashed around him. "Falling to the ground, he heard a voice saying to him, 'Saul, Saul, why are you persecuting Me?'" (Acts 9:4).

What a transforming moment! Saul's journey *of* life was over. He was changed. As Luke recorded the moment, Saul's name was changed to Paul, and his name change was followed by a more drastic change as Paul would later detail: "Therefore if anyone is in Christ, there is a new creation; old things have passed away, and look, new things have come" (2 Cor. 5:17).

Thus Paul began the journey *for* life.

What a compelling, convincing, powerful staffing Person is God's Holy Spirit. He looks beyond the veneer of man's exterior and observes the heart. Who else but God could have known the potential in the life of Saul?

Corporate America spends billions engaging "headhunters" to search out competent key executive and administrative personnel. Oh, for the gift of outcomes like Paul in our search for leadership today on the journey *for* life.

We can have such outcomes today! Jesus left us with a promise and a plan for such results. He said: "Seek first the kingdom of God and His righteousness, and all these things will be provided for you" (Matt. 6:33). What an illustrative example Paul became of the grace of God.

Be encouraged by the example of Paul and don't ever become discouraged in your search for truth. God knows you. He knows where you are, and He is in control of the events of life. In your search—

Be patient.
Don't fret.
You can trust God's timing.
He may not be early, but He won't be late!

God is no respecter of persons, and as followers of Jesus Christ, we must respect everyone. The message and mission for those on the journey *for* life is to proclaim the message of hope and freedom offered to all through Jesus Christ.

Not everyone has hope; however, there is hope for everyone. This hope has motivated me to share the powerful truth of *Little by Little*. The future for traditional marriage and the family on the journey *for* life is unlimited in potential. Family values, family unity, family support—this is God's way for traveling on the journey *for* life. As Jesus said, "If you continue in My word, you really are My disciples. You will know the truth, and the truth will set you free" (John 8:31–32).

And that truth can be generational for your family also.

The Village Culture: "That's Just the Way We Do It Here"

What do I mean by the *village culture?* It is the generally accepted beliefs, customs, and practices imposed by those who assume leadership roles upon those subservient to them.

A *mill village* is a community where the houses are owned by the company and rented to the mill workers. The rent on the three-room house on Cox Street was ninety cents per week, including utilities, and this was deducted before pay was distributed. In the village, there is usually a general company store where the workers can purchase merchandise on *credit.*

The culture of the cotton mill village era was very distinct. A retrospective look is often quite informative, revealing, and therapeutic. Let's talk about it.

In the small village town, there were basically two types of people: the town people and the cotton mill village people. The town people were more educated. They were the merchants, doctors, bankers, supervisors, and the mortician. These groups were differentiated by lifestyle, and there was very little if any social interaction between the groups.

The village was generally inhabited by medium to large families. As a rule, the parents were poorly educated. In these depression times, most of the children left school to work in the cotton mill to help support their families. The average age of these youthful employees was eleven to fourteen, and they worked under the supervision of an experienced adult.

There was no apparent end to this cycle as each generation repeated the pattern. My Dad told me that many public schools held graduation exercises at the end of the sixth grade. It still bothers him that he did not make it to this level.

The social activities of the village were usually associated with the village churches, and the limited sports activities of the village were subsidized by the mill. Cultural activities, including fine music, dancing, and the arts were considered sissy and soft, and those who participated were scorned.

On Saturday nights, the Grand Ole Opry, broadcast from the Ryman Auditorium in Nashville, Tennessee, captured the village's attention. Those who owned a radio would move it to the porch, and the neighbors would gather for the hoedown.

The village culture was predominant even in the churches. The churches were a culture within a culture that mirrored the dogma of the larger culture. Church doctrine and rules were dogmatic and dictatorial—and enforced. Adults who had grown up in the church were independent, opinionated, and overly sensitive to any indication of a critical attitude as to their judgment and leadership.

Children were not strangers to harsh treatment by adults. Spankings ruled the day with little or no explanation as to why, and this cycle seemed to be generational also. At this time, life was generally more difficult for girls than for boys.

Church has always been a part of my life. Outside our home, the first place my parents carried me was to church. If the church doors were open, the Shaw family was in church. Church was the focus of family life. In retrospect, it was a very narrow and limited focus.

The village church met often in Honea Path:

- Saturday night
- Sunday morning Sunday school
- Sunday morning worship service
- Sunday evening services
- Mid-week prayer meeting on Thursdays

(Dad told me that Thursday was the night for our mid-week service because other churches had their mid-week prayer meetings on Wednesday night. With that logic, I wondered why we met on Sunday at traditional hours like the others.)

In addition to all these services, several "revivals" were scheduled throughout the year. Often these meetings would be protracted, lasting two weeks or more.

In that period the church leadership would discipline those who challenged the culture. Our family value system and lifestyle were influenced by what the local church leaders approved.

There was a very clear distinction and separation between what composed the *sacred* and *secular* issues. It was a class distinction. In the environment in which I grew up, it was ingrained in me that the highest, most spiritual service an individual could give to God was in full-time occupational ministry. So as I approached high school, my mind was fixed upon serving God vocationally. Did I have a passion and desire in that direction? Yes! Did I have a divine call to vocational ministry? That was a question I would wrestle with for a long time.

The church culture had a very devastating effect on me. As a young schoolboy, I did have an inferiority complex. I saw myself as I thought others saw me. In my mind, I was different. The village culture had taken its toll and remained with me.

I did not attend the First Church. In my mind, the church I attended made me different. The church often reminded the members that *they* were not "our crowd." Our church was a "separated" church. These were Satan's thoughts working on my young mind.

During an after-Christmas show-and-tell at school, I listened to others talk about their toys, bicycles, and balls. My time came, and I timidly told of the Bible I had received. Others were not responsible for this. It was my mind-set.

Growing up is painful; nevertheless, I did. I now know who I am. I realize that God has a plan and purpose for my life. Even though I have not always known God, I cannot remember a time when I did not believe in God. Learning about God as a child from those in relationship with Him created a desire in me to know God myself.

I cannot recall when I first realized God loved me. In my youth, in fact, love was not a common word at our house: I don't remember Dad telling Mother he loved her or hearing Mother tell Dad she loved him. I guess I just knew I was loved. I just did not hear the words "I love you."

Recently I began to ask my Dad, "Has anyone told you they love you today?" At first he would hesitate and not answer. Then I would say, "Well, *I* love you." What a blessing I receive now when he replies, "I love you too, son."

When you feel love, communicate it.

One author I've read captured the essence of my memory. "We didn't hear much about a loving God. We were told God is good and that was supposed to be enough. Otherwise the God of my memory is one the tribe of Israel would have recognized, an angry God, a vengeful God, a God who will let you have it upside your head if you strayed, transgressed, or coveted. Our God had a stern face and a message of damnation from the pulpit, scaring us to death. If we didn't understand and asked questions, we were brushed aside and told it was a matter of faith so [eat your dinner] and be quiet."

When answers were given to probing questions, the answers were usually very simplistic. (Remember, these leaders were generally uneducated.) Serving God was based upon simple assumptions. Others did your thinking for you. Those who disagreed with the opinions of the church leaders were *wrong!* Church loyalties were established not by church doctrine but by what someone in church leadership did for you. Yes, church politics, though masked, were evident.

Often, church leaders were so opinionated that they considered those of other denominations "lost." It was easy to assume that the little village church had a corner on truth. Their creed was: "We're right; others are wrong."

These were good people, the "salt of the earth." Nevertheless, they were bound by tradition as much as the Pharisees of Jesus' time.

Not long ago, I drove my Dad for his appointment with a neurosurgeon. While we were waiting for his appointment, Dad finished scanning a newspaper. Putting the paper down he told me, "When I was a boy, reading a newspaper was a sin." He explained the church position like this: "Time should be spent reading the Bible."

Sins were very obvious in that kind of culture. The litmus test for church membership was whether or not you used tobacco products or drank alcoholic beverages. Money was evil, so it was a virtue to be poor. If a person attained a degree of material success or accumulated significant material possessions, others questioned, "What had they done wrong?"

I remember attending a very conservative religious gathering at a resort hotel where those attending were described by the bartenders and others like this: "These folks came here with a ten-dollar bill and the Ten Commandments, and so far they haven't broken either."

Most residents of our village owed their existence to Chiquola Mill, Honea Path's primary employer. Pay was pennies an hour, and employees resided in mill-owned village houses that they never expected to leave. Material possessions were few, usually purchased on credit and subject to weekly debt payments to local merchants. Tennessee Ernie Ford must have had Honea Path in mind when he sang, "I owe my soul to the company store." Neighbors borrowed essentials from neighbors when possible, striving to put food on the table and to eke out a meager existence.

Most of the citizens assumed things would ultimately get better. Olin D. Johnson had been elected United States senator, and he was from Anderson County. Senator Johnson was already a legend, entrenched in Old South "one-party" politics. There were no Republicans in that part of the world. In that culture, the word "Republican" was almost a swear word. No, God is not a Republican, but neither is He a Democrat.

This culture was okay for me as a child, but as my mind developed and expanded beyond those horizons, there were far too many questions and too few rational answers. Early in my life, I was in fear of God. I perceived God as some austere being who was ready to *zap* me for anything I did wrong. I heard more about God's judgment than I did about His love. This cultural image of a demanding God took years for me to overcome.

Almost everything done outside church activities was wrong. The list of what a person could not do was long. And I'm not sure I ever saw the "can do" list.

Try as I did, I could not fit the world of my dreams into this programmed, restrictive, controlling culture and environment.

With all the answers, how could so many people struggle with issues of life and be without hope?

In my search for truth, I'm glad I did not become satisfied with the surface knowledge of the culture around me. I am thankful for my exposure to God's unadulterated truth. I shudder to think that I might have been satisfied too soon, that I might have sold out too cheaply and missed the promptings of God's Holy Spirit as well as the mental challenge in my search for truth.

Paul expressed it like this in his letter to the Romans: "Oh, the depth of the riches both of the wisdom and the knowledge of God! How unsearchable His judgments and untraceable His ways!" (Rom. 11:33). "Now to Him who is able to do above and beyond all that we ask or think—according to the power that works in you—to Him be glory in the church and in Christ Jesus to all generations, forever and ever" (Eph. 3:20–21).

An unknown poet expressed it like this:

> You can only see a little of the ocean,
> Just a few miles from the rocky shore.
> But out there beyond our eyes horizon
> There is more, so much more.
> You can only see a little of God's goodness,
> Just a few golden nuggets from His boundless store.
> But out there beyond our minds horizons
> There is more, immeasurably more."

In many cultures, there is such a limited vision as to the greatness of God. Biases, lack of knowledge, lack of faith, and just simple lack of trust limit what God desires to do for everyone today.

My faith in God's promises began early in my life. One of my favorite Sunday school songs expresses it like this:

Every promise in the Book is mine
Every chapter, every verse, every line
It is written in the Book divine
Every promise in the Book is mine.

Claim God's promises to you. Believe—and receive: "No good thing does he withhold from those whose walk is blameless" (Ps. 84:11 NIV).

Grannie: The Widow Matriarch

Magnolia Bray, who would become my Dad's mother, was married at the age of fourteen to Elmer Shaw, who was nineteen years old. My grandfather, who is also my namesake, was a farmer near Donalds, South Carolina. The money crop at the time was cotton.

I know very little about Granddaddy Shaw. I recall hearing that he was a religious person, but he was no saint. Dad said he had a relationship with God, but he was a "backslider," not unlike many believers today.

Elmer died in 1919 at just twenty-nine years old. Dad would be four years old in August of the year Granddaddy Elmer died. There was an epidemic of Spanish influenza in the early 1900s, around the time of World War I. Approximately five hundred thousand people died in the USA, and Honea Path was not exempt. My Dad recalled hearing about it like this: "A person would be sick today and dead tomorrow. Bodies in the mortuary were stacked like cord wood."

Unlike my siblings and me, Dad's family did not begin with a strong religious heritage. Grannie was a proud widow recognized by many as "the prettiest woman in Honea Path." Nevertheless, she was not too proud to do whatever task was necessary to provide for her children. She would provide for them by doing washing and ironing for others. She also became a sharecropper with help from Dad.

Grannie was a very gifted and enterprising person. She was an artisan with needle and thread and with her sewing machine. She made clothes for herself and her children and supplemented her income by sewing and making clothes for others.

At this time in Grannie's life, she was not a religious person. Religion and church were for others. However, that would soon change drastically. The village gossip became: "Did you hear about Magnolia? She got religion."

That may be the way others saw it, but for Grannie, it was a life-changing encounter with Jesus Christ. A revival was sweeping the little town of Honea Path, and in the words of my Dad, "Our mother heeded the call."

My! How things changed when my widowed grandmother got saved. Grannie became the matriarch of the Shaw family. Through her, the spiritual foundation that continues to support our family was established. She expressed it like this: "As I was sweeping the floor, a sweet little voice whispered to me, 'Believe that you are saved.' I believed, and that settled it for me."

Grannie was about twenty-six or twenty-seven years old at this time, and when she got saved, she was a different woman. This was her exodus from the journey *of* life to the journey *for* life. For Grannie, it was a new beginning. Instead of carrying a heavy widow's load of responsibility, it now became a shared load. Her sin load of guilt was gone. She heard Jesus say, "Take up My yoke and learn from Me, because I am gentle and humble in heart, and you will find rest for yourselves" (Matt. 11:29).

Being a widow with three children, Grannie knew her human limitations. She told me that when she realized she could not provide an education for her three children, she began to pray that they would be able to send her "grands" to school.

I know the significance of Grannie's prayers because I became the first member of the Shaw family to earn a college degree. I earned a bachelor of arts degree from Elon College (now Elon University), having first graduated from Emmanuel Junior College and studied at Bob Jones University.

Growing in her new faith, she would learn that she served One who was limitless. She would sing:

> Leave it there, leave it there,
> Take your burden to the Lord
> And leave it there.
> If you trust and never doubt,
> He will surely bring you out.
> Take your burden to the Lord
> And leave it there.

What a legacy I have!

Grannie used to tell me, "Son, I want to go home." I knew what she meant, and I didn't want her to leave. She was such a treasure for me.

More recently, Dad has been echoing those same sentiments about home. Grannie would often say to me, "Son, the only reason I want to stay here is for you grands." I'm not at that point yet. I want to go, just not on the next load.

Dad: My Mentor and Example

My dad, William Erby Shaw, was the middle child of three, the only boy between two sisters. After his dad died, he quickly became "the man of the house" and at ten years old, Dad and Grannie did the sharecropping together. Dad told me that he worked like a man at only ten years old. Because of the extreme circumstances, he was unable to complete the fourth grade.

Dad told me that even then he had some talent for music. At school in Donalds, South Carolina, he had been selected to perform in the Christmas program; however, because of family circumstances he left school before the Christmas play.

Dad has continued to exhibit musical talent through the years. As a boy, his love was the banjo and the guitar. Grannie helped him get a guitar from "Roebuck" (Sears and Roebuck). Dad shared with me how some people questioned his musical talent. One instructor said, "You can't even pat your foot and keep time." Dad proved him wrong. At ninety-three years old, he still plays the guitar and sings.

In those struggling years, music was a pastime for him. For years he was a member of a gospel quartet that he says was "pretty good."

Enjoying a good story must be in the Shaw genes. Like my Dad, I always try to have a good story available. This trait was also characteristic of his granddad. Recently he shared with me a favorite story of his granddad. "He would say to someone, 'You always put your left shoe on last.' After some ensuing discussion or argument, he would say, 'Why not? The one remaining is left!'"

Even though Dad did not finish the fourth grade, he became a well-educated man because of his inquisitive mind and love of knowledge. Dad received very little formal education; however, he was elected a founding member of the Oral Roberts University Board of Regents. Through his years of service, he was recognized and awarded an Honorary Doctorate of Laws degree because of his input and insight.

As the man of the house, Dad began work at the village cotton mill when he became fourteen years old. Prior to that, Dad had kept his younger sister while Grannie and his older sister Irene worked in the cotton mill. On the job, Dad worked long hours for less than ten cents an hour. Also, after his regular job at the mill, he would clean machinery for other workers for extra pennies. On these days, he could earn an extra thirty to forty cents a day.

Around this time, Grannie began telling Dad about the religious meeting at the Hall. This created a dilemma for him; he had to choose between a movie and the revival meetings.

Later, Dad decided that "if someone would go with him, he would attend a tent revival meeting." While there, he went forward at the invitation.

When Dad and I were discussing this event, he told me that he went to the altar under conviction. This conviction stayed with him about two weeks, and then he just accepted by *faith* that he was saved (born again). When Dad testified before the church to being saved, Grannie did an old-fashioned Methodist shout! That even *sounds* old-fashioned, but that is what happened.

Jobs were too scarce to complain, so Dad worked long, laborious hours for little pay while at the same time searching for an opportunity to do more for his family's financial security. Like Mom, Dad's workday did not end when he left the mill. Dad was ambitious and dreamed of a better life. He sought advice and opportunities about how he might find additional work to help pay the bills.

About this time, a brother-in-law started selling Watkins Products door-to-door in another town. On the occasion of a visit to Uncle Olin Saxon's home, Dad observed that Uncle Olin was a Watkins Product dealer. Traveling with him as he made some house calls, Dad thought, "I can do that." He was able to borrow twenty dollars from the paymaster at the mill. He obtained a ride to Greenville where the Watkins Product Distribution was, and with this he acquired products to demonstrate and then write orders for future delivery. The loan would be paid back at a dollar per week without interest. Grannie was really concerned about this loan. She thought she would have to pay it back. This was Dad's first business venture.

There are some needs that only money can satisfy. Dad believed that a few extra dollars invested wisely along with his time and effort would make the difference in enabling him to provide for his family. But, where would this money come from?

Dad's older sister Irene was a caring, giving person. Her only tangible asset was the cash value that had accumulated on her meager life insurance policy. This she had accumulated by making weekly premium payments. Aunt Irene shared Dad's ambition and dream and lovingly loaned him this cash value amounting to sixty dollars. From such a little seed, through the years—"little by little"—God provided amply for both the need of brother and sister.

Not having a family car presented a challenge to Dad for delivering the products. He solved this problem by engaging my brother Larry and me, accompanied by our "Little Red Wagon" to be the delivery team.

By the way, let me share with you the history of the Little Red Wagon. One of my first memorable Christmas gifts was this wagon that Larry and I received. Recently, Dad told me how they were able to purchase it. Chiquola Mill, where Dad and Mother both worked, had a Christmas Savings Plan. Dad committed fifty cents a week for a total savings of twenty-six dollars. I remarked, "Dad, the wagon didn't cost $26.00."

"No" he said, "that $26.00 was for all our family Christmas."

"Little by little," Dad's work on dual jobs—plus other odd jobs—began to pay off. Dad purchased the family's first car! It was a used 1932 Chevrolet purchased in 1939. The Little Red Wagon had served well and was retired. Soon, Dad was able to purchase a brand new 1941 Chevrolet!

About this time, gasoline began to be rationed because of the energy demands of World War II. What good is a new car—*any* car—without gasoline? This presented a real dilemma for Dad. How could he service his expanding territory without fuel for the car? Gasoline was available and less restrictive for "commercial vehicles." Again, Dad innovated!

The 1941 Chevrolet "morphed" into a truck and qualified for the more liberal "T" rationing sticker. How did this happen? The back seat was removed from the car, and the barrier separating the rear seat from the trunk removed. Then the two backside windows were painted black and—*eureka!*—the family car was now a "commercial vehicle."

Let me describe for you the "convenience" of travel for a family of six in a "truck" with no backseat. Fortunately, this was prior to seat belts being required for passenger travel. Quilts were spread on the car's floor, and this padded floor and makeshift pallet became the children's place to sit, play, and sleep.

Product sales continued to pick up, and Dad's talents were soon recognized. He was offered the opportunity to establish a dealership in another town.

The Shaw family's exodus from Honea Path, South Carolina, finally brought us to Greenville, South Carolina, where our family living really changed. From living in a company house in the cotton mill village in Honea Path, to subdivision living in Greenwood, South Carolina, with numerous inconveniences along the way, the family moved to downtown Greenville. We lived, worked, dined, shopped, and played "Downtown." At this time, it was not "cool" to live in downtown Greenville. This was over sixty years ago, and very few families lived there.

But the Shaw family lived downtown out of necessity, challenged by the opportunity for Dad's expanding role with Watkins Products. He was now a distributor.

Our first Greenville "home" was on East Coffee Street, one-half block off North Main Street. We moved into a place that served as an office/distributing center for Dad's business and living quarters for a family of six. This was upstairs over what was then "The Sanitary Barbershop," directly across the street from Charlie's Steak House, a Greenville landmark that continues to thrive today.

Regardless of the negative culture of the church and village, Dad had a desire for a better life. He would have a lot to overcome before faith would lead him to believe he could be successful and prosper as a Christian businessman. When his ambition to succeed would surface, he would often be reminded of how people lost their assets during the Depression. Dad did not know anyone financially blessed in the local church. No one in his church talked about how to make money and put it to work for God. Dad wanted to prosper in order to support his family and advance God's work.

Dad told me that on one occasion he was meditating, desiring to know how to get close to God. At that moment, I walked by where he was. Instantly his answer came by inspired impression: "Just like that boy gets close to you."

Today Dad spends many hours reading and studying the Bible. And occasionally as we visit, he ponders: "I wonder what I might have accomplished had I received the benefits of an education."

My Dad was always ambitious. He wanted to do more, accomplish more. He dreamed. He desired. And he did.

On one occasion, sharing his plight and concern with Dr. G. H. Montgomery, who was a minister friend and mentor to my Dad, Dr. Montgomery, observing me, replied, "You see that boy there?

You can be everything you ever wanted to be in him." He can be justly proud. Dad didn't have anything but desire and drive, a praying widow mother, and a growing faith in God.

When I was inducted into the Greenville Entrepreneurial Forum, I was asked the question: "Who is or was a mentor for you?" Quickly I answered, "My dad was and is a mentor for me. Dad taught me the work ethic by example. In order to support a

My dad at the empty tomb.

growing family, he became an innovative entrepreneur. Dad was one of the early developer/builder entrepreneurs after World War II in Greenville. I am a second generation real estate developer/builder and investor. The third generation is in place with my twin sons Ron and Donnie at the helm, following the same tradition. Thousands of developed residential lots and hundreds of homes continue to grace the Greenville landscape because of his continuing entrepreneurial spirit."

Mother: Age Slowed Her Down, But She Still Retained Her Mettle

My mother did not have an easy life as a child. She was the sixth of eleven children—six girls and five boys. Difficult family circumstances would only allow her to finish the sixth grade in school. Even then, she had to take her younger brother to school with her.

At times she would be responsible for babysitting her younger sister. Once on Mother's babysitting watch, her sister's clothing caught fire, and before Mother could get help from the neighbors, her sister who was following her died.

Mother did not have the legacy of growing up in a Christian family. Her father died when she was about ten years old. When I inquired as to the circumstances of his death, she told me that her dad's brother-in-law "shot him over a woman."

As a young girl, fourteen years old, Mother was afflicted with typhoid fever. She was near death, thinking she was going to die. After her recovery, her mother (who was not a Christian) asked her, "What would have happened had you died?"

This was not Mother's first consideration about her soul and spiritual matters. She remembers being "under conviction," going forward in a Baptist church without finding the peace and assurance she was searching for. She would continue to have questions about heaven and hell, and while attending a revival service in the old community hall in Honea Path, she was saved.

Mother and Dad's courtship centered around going to church together and participating in church socials and activities. This relationship led them to the courthouse where they were married at eighteen years old.

Resources were scarce at our house. Our family existed from pay period to pay period. Depression times necessitated that both Mother and Dad work in the local cotton mill. Mother was always an example of hard work. Though often pregnant, she worked a full shift at Chiquola Mill as well as doing all the necessary things at home to meet the needs of a growing family. She was a great cook and kept the house immaculately clean. Dad often said, "There's not a lazy bone in her body."

Mother and Dad's combined efforts continued to be necessary in order to provide food, shelter, and clothing for a family of six. Mother was a good manager of the limited household funds available. She could stretch a dollar while saving some for a rainy day. I still marvel at how she could save a little money out of the weekly budget.

When I started work, Mother began to share her art of saving with me. According to her gospel, "You save by not spending." This was not altogether to my liking. Money was made for spending—at least, I thought so at the time. Nevertheless, Mother was the bank, and I made my initial savings deposit with her. When I would come home from selling newspapers, Mother would shake me down (not really) to find the money I had made and put it in savings for me. Dad may have taught me how to work, but Mother taught me how to save. Winston Churchill said, "Savings is a fine thing, especially when your parents have done it for you." I agree. However, I don't think Mother's plan is what he was referring to.

Mother always prided herself in how she cared for her children. We were always neat and clean, but combing a boy's hair just before he goes to bed was a little too much care. I was an active boy and I could get dirty. However, I was never dirty for long. One time I asked her, "MaMa Shaw, didn't you know a dirty boy is a happy boy?"

Mother was a persistent person and at times could be very convincing. During World War II, most Americans were on edge. Millions of their sons were in the military on foreign soil. At home, air raid drills were common. During a drill, the warden would make sure that the regulations were followed. All lights in a house had to be completely subdued. During some drills, Mother would give subduing the lights her best effort while at the same time continue wrestling to finish giving four children their baths. At times a little light would be visible around the blackout shades, and the warden would appear at our door. In Mother's convincing way, she would inform him, "The children are getting their baths." She would prevail with his admonition to "Hurry!"

It was common knowledge in the church and the village that Mother was a good cook. But this came to an end much too soon as arthritis and age took their toll. Before this, however, she was unequaled in preparing the best steak dinners. They were served hot and juicy from the broiler to the plate. If heaven has a steakhouse, it will be called Mittie Lou's Choice Steaks.

Sundays often found ministers and others around our table. As a child, this created a problem for me. You see, at Mother and Dad's, the custom was for the adults to eat first. This custom would not be generational for Jane and me. When our home was established, our children and now our grandchildren eat first.

Mother and Dad would often come to our house for family meals, and I could not bypass the opportunity to point out to them that at our house the children eat first. Of course, there's room for exceptions with most rules, and we would usually usher Mother and Dad to the front of the line.

Mom's journey *for* life ended Christmas Day 2007. She is at home with Jesus, but still very much in my heart. She is one of my greatest influences.

Jane: Everything I Ever Wanted, More Than I Dreamed Possible

One person who influenced me greatly—and in the process stole my heart—was Norma Jane Leslie. Jane is all I could have hoped for as my wife.

First on my mental list for a soulmate and partner on the journey *for* life was that God would put someone into my life who would be a committed Christian and have a vibrant, personal relationship with Jesus Christ. Jane is such a person.

Let me tell you about Jane.

Being raised in a Christian home and regularly attending Sunday school and church were important foundational components on her journey *of* life. When God's Holy Spirit caused Jane to contemplate the journey *for* life, here's what happened—in Jane's words:

> Christmas mornings at our house were amazing when I was growing up. The living room was so full of toys and gifts that they often spilled over into our dining room. They were all for me because I was an only child. When I think of those years, it is not the *things* but the *love* that I remember most. There was never a

doubt that my parents loved God, each other, and me! We took two big trips a year and many small ones. I had lots of friends who were always welcomed and felt comfortable in our home.

As a teenager I was very busy and involved. I had everything the world says is important: love, security, things, friends, etc. On a few occasions when I was quiet and alone, I remember thinking, "I need something to think about" because there was a hollow feeling inside.

One night I heard a man say he had taken his friend to talk with the minister because he wanted him to become a Christian. While the minister was explaining the plan of salvation to his friend, this man realized he had never accepted Christ as his personal Savior. I realized I was in the same situation. I had grown up in the church, been involved in all areas of church life, but never asked Jesus to forgive my sins and come into my heart. At that moment I did, and what a difference He has made in my life! On the outside there was probably no change, but on the inside I was new and alive. The hollow feeling was gone, and in its place I received the peace that Jesus gives.

I remember the first time I really—really—looked at Jane. She was my sister's friend and I knew her from church and her occasional visits to our home.

Wow!

This time I saw her differently. I filed this "look" and emotion away in my mind, pondering over it and never getting away from it. At the same time, my heart was affirming my interest. How could one person grow up to be so beautiful, so complete? Where had I been not to notice this sooner? No cocoon ever produced such a lovely butterfly.

Even though there were other girlfriends along the way, the seed of that "wow" moment continued to develop in me. The more I observed her, the more I knew I wanted to explore interesting possibilities that could meaningfully impact my journey *for* life.

The moment came! Our dads were business partners, and as fate would have it, Jane was in the office having a little difficulty with a Spanish translation for a Sunday school lesson she was to teach. Finally, I knew why I had studied Spanish! Jane got help with her Spanish, and I got a date!

Time swiftly passed. Jane was off to Columbia College and I was off to Elon College. I would see Jane as often as I could. It just did not seem right for her to be at Columbia College and me to be elsewhere. Perhaps, and in retrospect, the benefit accrued to both of us because it gave us the opportunity to meet and date other people. But "little by little," the possibilities of the relationship began to tug at my heart as we continued to see each other.

Steady was not the word, but *often*, at least for a while. Columbia College being a girl's school in the same town with the University of South Carolina didn't help a lot. Jane was having a good time dating other boys while we were separated by miles. I did not like that development, but not to be outdone, I discovered Greensboro College—at that time a women's college in North Carolina not too far from Elon—and visited there frequently.

As in most relationships, things are not always smooth. Periodically there are bumps in the road. In our relationship, I just remember one, but the bump really hurt.

Was it my fault? Perhaps I had not effectively communicated my love to her. Perhaps I was crowding her.

As some people express it, perhaps she "needed space." I knew I loved Jane and could not cope with the thought of someone else having her. Jane had some steady, long-term dating relationships in high school. I had dated other girls; however, no long-term relationships. I had experienced hurt in past relationships; I didn't want to hurt again.

What was the bump?

Jane told me that on the following weekend, a USC guy (now you know why I support Clemson) was riding to Greenville with her to visit some family. That was true, but I discerned more. I was right! I strongly objected to this arrangement and told her that if it happened, I was out of the picture.

It happened!

I was gone, and out of touch.

Professionally I was becoming a good negotiator, but in this relationship, I had played the only hand I had. Had I lost? I don't know the game of poker, but I wondered, "What hand was she playing? Was she bluffing? Was she just "cool"? If it was a game, who would blink first?

As I hurt, I asked myself, "Was it happening again? Did I have a fragile heart when it came to love and romance? Surely, I had not just become another guy to Jane. I had never known Jane to deliberately hurt anyone."

I don't believe Jane knew how hurt I was. I probably masked it well, but she had played the card I did not want to see. Did she really care for me? Did she want me—just later?

Going back to Elon College that night was lonely, and I hurt! Why does disappointment in love hurt so?

How had that evening impacted Jane?

I would later learn that she had not taken me seriously when I told her I would be out of the picture if she brought this "friend" with her to Greenville to "see his family." Jane told me that after not hearing from me for a few weeks, she began to think I meant it. Did my absence, discontinued frequent letters, and no phone calls from me concern her?

During the period, when mail time came, Mrs. Leslie or Kate (the maid) would ask, "Did she get a letter today?" Like the country song, the answer was "No letter today."

Let me tell you about Kate Williams. She continued to work for Jane and me until retirement, and we were family to her for the rest of her life. When health issues would not allow her to care for herself, we cared for her as we had for Jane's parents. Kate died recently at ninety-six years old.

We may have been out of touch, but Jane was not out of my heart and mind. Later Jane told me, "When you were away, I realized how special you were."

We were out of touch for a short while (it seemed long), then came graduation time at Elon College. I think Jane's mother suggested she remember my graduation with a gift. (Thanks, Mom!)

Jack and Jane. Who wouldn't love her?

She did, breaking the ice that led to what has been a wonderful happening on my journey *for* life. God knew what was to be. I knew what I wanted to be.

In retrospect, November 1958 was a very eventful month. Jane had a severe bladder infection at school, and the doctor suggested a recuperative week at home for her. College is no place to be when you are really sick. Jane knew Mom's care at home was just what she needed. I just happened to be in Greenville at this time, and I wanted to be with her as much as possible. I had a bug also that needed attention: the "love bug."

The past was now behind us, and I was anticipating the future. I guess I saw Jane as a captive audience and, as she remembers it, "He surprised me by asking if he could give me an engagement ring." Jane remembers telling her mother about me "popping the question." When I became aware that Jane had told her mother, I knew my odds were improving. I think I won Mom before I won Jane.

By the way, Jane did say yes!

Now, for the real task. I had to generate the courage to do the manly thing and ask Mr. Leslie for Jane. Yes, I was anxious. Yes, I was nervous.

The moment came when I told him that we needed to talk. His first comment was, "I've been hearing about this foolishness." At least it was not a surprise to him. Mom had done her job again. We had a good conversation, and I received his blessing.

Jane was soon over the bladder infection and it was back to college for her—recovered, and now engaged.

The lull in our relationship that had lasted for several months was over. The letters began again, and I kept the phone lines hot—and the road hot also—between wherever I happened to be and Columbia.

Exciting events began to happen.

We really knew it was meant to be, and while Jane finished the school year, I began construction of the house plan we had decided was for us. How could it be possible—the opportunity to begin our lives together in our own home? Jane's parents influenced the process, but Jane and I were fully involved. I was the contractor/builder.

Jane also was prepared to make a financial contribution to our marriage. Her parents had taught her good lessons of life and thrift. Jane shared some of these treasures with me. Here she shares some of their wisdom:

> Each year, Mother, Daddy, and I would discuss my allowance amount and how much I should expect to save from it. At the end of the year, they would match dollar for dollar everything I had saved over that amount. Even though I was young, I had some financial acumen and recognized the challenge and opportunity this plan afforded me.
>
> Daddy was thinking ahead, and when I had saved enough for a down payment, he suggested that I invest in a small village house to rent. Of course, financing would be required and the mortgage payment would be paid from the rent. The amount that was left over would be added to my savings.
>
> When I had saved enough to repeat the process, Daddy would recommend that we buy a second house. He found one that he thought was a good deal. Each time Daddy suggested we go look at it, I had something I thought was more important to do. (I was in high school by that time). When he said the owners needed an answer, I talked Daddy into buying it without my seeing it.

Later, when I found time to see my new purchase, we rode around for some time. I teased Daddy
about not being able to find the house he had bought.
Finally he stopped in front of a house and simply
asked, "Well, what do you think?"

"It looks terrible," was my reply. We discussed how
a new roof, new paint, and yard work would improve
it. Discouraged, I reminded him that we had spent all
my money on the down payment. After a few minutes, I looked at him and asked, "Did you really spend
my money on this house?" He laughed and replied,
"No, but I could have. You always need to check out
an investment for yourself because you may not think
it is as good of a deal as the other person does."

How many parents take the time to teach their children such
valuable lessons?

Through friends, Jane and I were introduced to the Furniture
Market in High Point, North Carolina. We were privileged to be
able to select custom-made furniture at wholesale prices and have
it manufactured and in place, ready for us when we returned from
our honeymoon.

Marriage is ordained of God. Marry right! Marriage is not an
experiment; marriage is for life! I could have missed Jane on the
journey *of* life, but on the journey *for* life, this marriage union was
meant to be.

Shared life is a wonderful life. The measure of success I have
known in my life has been exponentially impacted by Jane, and
it continues to this day. Jane brings sunshine to our family. She is
thoughtful, considerate, sharing, and loving. Jane is an only child;
I am one of five. I mention this because the stereotype of the
typical only child has never been applicable to the girl I have been
married to for forty-plus years.

Jane is my best friend, my soul mate, my confidant, my compass, and my adviser in relationships personal, spiritual, and professional. We do most things together. We enjoy being together. I rarely schedule business luncheons because Jane and I have a daily lunch date. Being with Jane is like a Bible study! I'm always learning something new.

We are not without disagreements or misunderstandings, but with the Mediator in our hearts, disagreements and misunderstandings are short-circuited and peace prevails.

7

FINDING MY PURPOSE

Fulfilling It with Significance

*T*he journey *for* life is about everyday life. And one of the necessary components of everyday life is work. Since we live in a free enterprise, career-oriented society, it is important that we have the right understanding and attitude about work.

I read a great story of a dynamic young man just out of college who applied for a position at a bank. The personnel officer asked him what he was capable of doing, and the young man replied he wanted to be a vice president. The personnel manager, quite shocked, said, "Why, we already have twelve vice presidents." The aggressive young man replied, "That's all right, I'm not superstitious."[4]

My friend Nido Qubein says, "If you're willing to work hard enough and smart enough, you can make something valuable come of your life."

Senator Jesse Helms said, "We have no limits if we partner our dreams with our willingness to work for them."

The dictionary defines work as "physical or mental effort to do or make something." Work is purposeful activity. Work is equally applicable to the journey *of* life as well as the journey *for* life. However, we don't all share the same attitude about or appreciation for work.

Some avoid work. The gospel of some is that they are exempt from work, and their lifestyle exemplifies it. One observation is certain: those who do not value work tend to migrate to the unemployed and welfare roles.

Some despise work. There are those who will do almost anything for money. A few of them will do an honest day's work for it. We have all heard the old adage, "I'm not afraid of work, I can lie down beside it and go to sleep."

Some worship at the altar of work. During a "Larry King Live" interview, Martha Stewart said, "My life is my business, and my business is my life." A total commitment exclusively to a job or position extracts a heavy price.

Some feel too important to work. For some unknown reasons, millions assume that the world is indebted to them. They approach life with their hand out, always receiving and never giving. A job, an occupation, any work is demeaning to them—an indignity they should not have to bear.

Wise King Solomon himself became confused about life and work. He wrote in Ecclesiastes 2:20, "I began giving myself over to despair concerning all my work I had labored at under the sun." What was Solomon saying?

Solomon was speaking of work from the perspective of carnal man. This is the only conclusion for anyone without the eternal perspective of the journey *for* life. Observing many travelers on the journey *of* life could lead to the same conclusion, thinking the rewards of work are meaningless.

The Necessity of Work

Work is a lost art in much of society; however, even in this age of technology, there is still no substitute for it. Machines and computers have not replaced it, and if they could, those who bypass work would be the losers.

Many people are content to live off the resources and accomplishments of others, and often they do so in style and substance. But success on the journey *for* life is a personal achievement that is not measurable by the criterion of what satisfies those on the journey *of* life.

Work requires commitment—the expenditure of a person's time and energy. An average person consumes more than one third of adult life devoted to work. So every young person should be taught the value of work early in life. Each child should be expected to participate in the work responsibilities of the home. A proper understanding and appreciation for work cannot be taught by indulgence. Responsible work habits must be taught by doing.

In a large family, home responsibilities must be shared. Growing up, each of the Shaw children had special chores to perform. However, work is something many children never experience in their formative years. Parents, remembering their own childhood, sacrifice to shelter their children. They pamper and indulge them, wanting them to have a better life than they knew.

I don't know of any worthwhile formula for success in life that bypasses work. God's formula for work expressed in the first book of the Bible is: "You will eat bread by the sweat of your brow" (Gen. 3:19).

Because of the failure of many to understand and apply the principles of the Bible to work, life is fraught with problems, disappointments, hurts, and needs. Paul's instruction to Timothy mirrors my desire: "Be diligent to present yourself approved to God, a worker who doesn't need to be ashamed, correctly teaching the word of truth" (2 Tim. 2:15).

As we train and teach our children and grandchildren, they should be given an adequate allowance based upon some work they are assigned to do. Any job, vocation, profession, trade, or craft is important and not inferior to any other. In terms connoting success, society may categorize work, but any honorable work is important and not second class. Regardless of the perceived status by others of work, *everyone should work!*

The Goals of Work

The goals of work vary. Most people must work for economic reasons. However, some are more fortunate than others. They have no economic problems; therefore, they have no economic pressure to work. Even those so blessed still need to practice the work responsibility of stewardship.

Work is more than a paycheck. Nevertheless, a paycheck is necessary—and a paycheck is one reward for work.

Work—productive effort—is necessary to sustain a vibrant quality of life. The goal of work is not just to make money and provide for your family; however, those are primary goals. The broad-brush stroke for meaningful work on the journey *for* life must extend to embrace the needs of others less fortunate.

The significance of work is in what it does for a person's self-worth and the benefits it brings to those under our roof and to others for whom we are responsible. However, our most significant work on the journey *for* life may not relate to our vocation, and it does not end at our front door. It may require a knock on a neighbor's door to offer a kind word and a helping hand. Even then, it is not enough just to help our neighbor. Jesus commands: "Love your neighbor as yourself" (Matt. 19:19).

Those who do not value work often perceive work to be a curse resulting from the fall of man. *Not so!* Work is not a curse, nor was man cursed. The "ground" was cursed because of man's sin. God's Word says, "The ground is cursed because of you. You will eat from it by means of painful labor all the days of your life" (Gen. 3:17).

Work is *God's* idea!

God worked and God's work continues. God's six-day work log in creation is recorded in the first chapter of Genesis:

- On the first day God created light.
- On the second day God created an expanse and called it "sky."
- On the third day He created land, sea and plant life appeared.
- On the fourth day He created the sun, moon and stars became visible.
- On the fifth day God created animal life.
- On the sixth day God created living creatures, and then God created man in His own image; male and female He created them.

Then, "God saw all that He had made, and it was very good" (Gen. 1:31).

Adam's work was to take care of the land (see Gen. 2:15). Contrary to what many think, this command to work was given to Adam while he still resided in the Garden of Eden, prior to his sin of disobedience. After Adam sinned, work then became toilsome.

Jesus Worked

John wrote about Jesus' work in creation: "All things were created through Him, and apart from Him not one thing was created that has been created" (John 1:3). Jesus—Creator God—came to earth, born of a virgin to complete God's redemptive plan. His time on earth would be limited to just thirty-three years, the last three encompassing His public ministry. When speaking of the work He came to do, Jesus recalled the words recorded about Him by Isaiah some seven hundred years before: "The Spirit of the Lord GOD is on Me, because the LORD has anointed Me to bring good news to the poor. He has sent Me to heal the brokenhearted, to proclaim liberty to the captives, and freedom to the prisoners; to proclaim the year of the Lord's favor" (Isa. 61:1–2).

With awesome obedience, Jesus accomplished the work for which He came to earth. And on the cross, in that excruciating moment just before He died, He shouted, "It is finished." I'm not writing about some kind of special effects animation. The cross is the true account of God at work on earth through the sacrifice of Jesus.

What love!

John recorded Jesus' words as to His purpose: "I was born for this, and I have come into the world for this: to testify to the truth" (John 18:37).

But now, to those who know Him, He is not a man, He is the Son of God, the King of kings, the Lord of lords. And at God's right hand, He is interceding for you and me.

Man's Work Goes On

After Jesus' resurrection, He delegated man to continue His work on earth. In Joshua 13:1, these words are recorded: "A great deal of the land remains to be possessed." Our work is to continue "all that Jesus began to do and teach" (Acts 1:1).

We can do it!

My friend, Dr. Hugh Morgan, says: "When God gives the *vision*, He provides the *provision*." Our unpossessed possessions can be possessed. The psalmist wrote: "Ask of Me, and I will make the nations Your inheritance and the ends of the earth Your possession" (Ps. 2:8). Our "land" to be possessed is to continue His Spirit-anointed work—no more, no less.

- Preach the good news.
- Proclaim freedom.
- Open the eyes of the blind.
- Release the oppressed.
- Proclaim the Lord's favor

Consider Jesus' plan for the future of His kingdom. He did not recruit the elite of His day. In fact, those He called to be His disciples were perceived by onlookers to be "unlearned and ignorant men" (Acts 4:13 KJV). Jesus did not focus on what these men had been. He focused on what they could become.

Was it a risky plan? Yes! But what an awesome responsibility. At times it was more than they could comprehend. At times they failed—and so will we! Jesus knew this and made provision for it; nevertheless, in spite of illiteracy, questionable backgrounds, factions, and momentary cowardice, they went on to accomplish the work He trusted them to do—the same work He trusts you to do. Look what they became!

To effectively delegate, a person must have a vision—a goal and a plan to achieve that goal. When you begin to delegate, you must give authority with responsibility, then take a step back. Initially it will not be easy; things may not happen your way; nevertheless, let go. Give others the opportunity to succeed. When you delegate, you challenge the best in yourself and the best in your associates, and in doing so, you receive their best and are freed to be your best.

My Work—God's Call

From my earliest recollection, my desire has been to serve God on my journey *for* life. I prayed to know God's purpose and will for my life.

When I sought counsel from others about how I could make my life count for God, a career in business was never mentioned. At that time, this was an expression of the mentality of the culture into which I was born. I was taught that all work was honorable, but the only way to render acceptable service to God was as a called vocational minister or missionary.

As a young man I was busy with secular endeavors. In my desire to render acceptable service to God, I performed *secular* work to have personal resources to finance my *sacred* activities. Being available and affordable (I don't know which was first), there was a demand for my services in Christian youth camps, camp meetings, revivals, and as a member of several gospel quartets. I was a captive of the culture and vision of that period.

What a release to my entrepreneurial spirit when I heard, "There is no difference between the sacred and the secular. To the Christian, everything is sacred." I did not become more sacred or secular. I was set free to serve God full time—right where I was.

Does secularism have a greater influence in society than religion? The secular view is that God is not in the system. A person's destiny is self-driven. Success depends on you. You set your goals and you make the rules. The secular view leaves God out of the equation. You are your own master.

But those who travel on the journey *for* life are not defined by sacred or secular. On the journey *for* life, the entire scope of life is sacred.

During this period, I was still wrestling with cultural moves as well as a heart desiring and searching to know how I could best serve God. Usually a call for service to God does not run contrary to a person's gifts and talents. Our challenge is to develop these to the maximum and be the best we can be.

Fortunately for me, I was motivated by the rewards of work, and many opportunities opened up for me. As Paul wrote to the Corinthians, "Working together with Him, we also appeal to you: 'Don't receive God's grace in vain'" (2 Cor. 6:1).

Man's work is a function of time and eternity. His work is accomplished on earth; however, honest and honorable work has both temporal and eternal value. Jesus said, "Don't collect for yourselves treasures on earth, where moth and rust destroy and where thieves break in and steal. But collect for yourselves treasures in heaven, where neither moth nor rust destroys, and where thieves don't break in and steal. For where your treasure is, there your heart will be also" (Matt. 6:19–21).

On the journey *for* life, the true meaning of work comes when we realize our work benefits others without being prompted by personal, selfish motives. Not all purposeful work will be compensated monetarily. On the journey *for* life, many contribute greatly to benefit others and never work outside the home. For example, what could be more valuable, more personally fulfilling, more rewarding to society than to "train up a child in the way he should go," having the promise that "when he is old, he will not depart from it" (Prov. 22:6 KJV).

Never yield to the temptation to compare your worth with the talents and accomplishments of others, becoming in awe of them, seeing your own talents and gifts as insignificant and meaningless. That may be the measure of some on the journey *of* life but not on the journey *for* life.

In our work, it is good to be reminded that God has no giants, just shepherd boys. Paul wrote: "God has given each of us the ability to do certain things well" (Rom. 12:6 NLT).

Your work, gifts, and calling are significant. They encompass your purpose. To emphasize this significance, Paul used a metaphor of the body: the foot, the hand, the ear, the eye—each in its function—is as necessary and important as the other.

On the journey *for* life, work is the primary means of our subsistence. Paul wrote, "If anyone isn't willing to work, he should not eat" (2 Thess. 3:10). He himself set a high example for all travelers on the journey *for* life to follow. He was learned, talented, and spiritually gifted for ministry, yet he often supported himself by making tents during his missionary travels.

Whatever our work and calling on the journey *for* life—be it tent making or tunneling (a term used to define various types of work as a cover to ferret out opportunities to live out our faith)— may we be found faithful and diligent in the pursuit of our work. Many in remote places of the world today, places where doors are closed to Christian missionary activity, follow this example of Paul. They work alongside natives in places where they are called, and their lives are a living witness in these places, opening doors to serve and teach.

Work on the journey *for* life has its demands and challenges. Those who commit to travel on it—whatever their vocation or call—are often very visible and are under microscopic scrutiny by those on the journey *of* life.

Honorable work is hard work—be it physical or mental—and it can be most intense. Nevertheless, there is no substitute for honest work and the satisfaction it brings to an individual. Even when you are in a responsible position with authority to delegate work responsibilities to others, your work is important, and you should always lead by example. Leadership has its role and it involves work.

The view of work for travelers on the journey *for* life must be Bible-based, and our work ethic must be evidenced in the work arena. Regardless of an individual's personal resources—be they small or great, earned or inherited—acquired resources will not satisfy a person's need to work. On the journey *for* life, we are recipients of so much that we should just roll up our sleeves and do the work at hand, always keeping in focus that our work is a means of our service to God.

- Work is mentioned more than 150 times in the Bible.
- Work is not demeaning.
- Work does not define who you are or what you are worth as a person.
- Work is an expression of who you are.
- A person's worth is not determined by a job title or the type of work done. Title and compensation may be the measure of self-worth on the journey *of* life. But on the journey *for* life—though important—they are never primary considerations. "Work hard and cheerfully at whatever you do, as though you were working for the Lord rather than for people. Remember that the Lord will give you an inheritance as your reward, and the Master you are serving is Christ. But if you do what is wrong, you will be paid back for the wrong you have

done. For God has no favorites who can get away with evil" (Col. 3:23–25 NLT).

- Work elevates a person's self image.
- Work allows a person to cultivate his God-given talents effectively in partnership with God, continuing God's creative process on earth.
- All meaningful work is not physical.
- Work takes on many forms, some of which are productive and stressful without being intensely physical.

At the end of the day, work well done should leave us with a true sense of accomplishment, fulfillment, and satisfaction. The greatest investment of your life is to spend it so that its accomplishments will outlive your life in the lives of others.

The transition from the journey *of* life to the journey *for* life is no make-believe comic happening. I grew up enamored of the Superman comics and movies. Clark Kent, the bespectacled news reporter for the *Daily Planet* on the trail of a story, would sense danger, step into a phone booth, and reappear as Superman. In real life, the change is a metamorphosis. The Holy Spirit now dwells in you, empowering you, living through you, transforming you "little by little."

Greek philosophy taught that menial (physical) work was beneath the gods, and that those of privilege could choose their pursuits of the higher way of religion or philosophy. If we cannot pray God's blessings upon our daily vocational activities, our vocation is wrong. Our best work is achieved when it is ordained and blessed of God. Below are questions and other matters to consider on being a Christian worker.

How Is the Journey for Life to Be Funded?

A laborer is worthy of his hire, whether in vocational church-related functions or whatever support roles we are called to perform, be it clergy or laity—sacred or secular. There is no difference except as to the office and work. Faithfulness in our work and our giving will adequately provide the necessary resources. Martin Luther said, "We are salt and light among those who don't believe."

Am I to live my life differently from eight to five because these hours relate to my "secular" job? On the journey *for* life, there are no segregated areas of your day.

Those Who Travel the Journey for Life Are on Exhibit

Christians are observed because there is a noticeable difference—a difference brought about by an inward change, reflected in an outward change in direction. On the journey *for* life, there is a change in loyalties and perspective. It was said of the early Christians, "They took knowledge of them, that they had been with Jesus" (Acts 4:13 KJV).

Are Religion and Work Compatible in the Work Arena?

The Christian faith is especially relevant in the workplace. However, a Christian must have sensitivity as to what is appropriate conduct in the workplace.

- The workplace is not a forum for witnessing, whatever the religion.
- The workplace is a display case. Christians in the workplace should be evidenced by their lifestyle.
- The workplace is a place where faith is to be lived out in pursuit of our responsibilities on the job.

- A work ethic is best taught by example.
- Diligence in the workplace has earned the opportunity for many to give witness to the difference between the journey *of* life and the journey *for* life.

On the job, the first obligation for those on the journey *of* life or the journey *for* life is to meet the requirements for which you are being compensated. Just being a Christian in the workplace is not enough. Those on the journey *for* life should distinguish themselves by giving more than is expected. The rote, mechanical, lackadaisical attitude toward work won't cut it. Passion in the pursuit of excellence on the job is required, even though it may not distinguish you from those on the journey *of* life. The door of opportunity to share the journey *for* life is best earned by a distinctive lifestyle. When it matters—

- Courage will be there
- Work related stress will be overcome
- Patience will be there
- Peace will be evident
- The distinctives will evidence themselves.

With these distinctives in view, they will be like seed planted that in due season will prompt others to wonder and perhaps inquire:

> "How can you face life the way you do?"
> "Why is your life different?"
> "What do you have that I don't have?"

Then you will have earned the right to share at the appropriate time and place the distinctives between the journey *of* life and the journey *for* life. That's the main part of the equation and you will have done it well.

What about Retirement?

Now, for the God part. Do you have the confidence in God to wait for His time? For the young who are beginning their travel on the journey *for* life, your career goals for work and retirement must be reassessed because of who you are in Christ. For the more mature, work does not end at retirement. Retirement is not a phase of life on the journey *for* life. Retirement is a release to "reFIRE." Retirement is not the last chapter in your life. Don't believe it!

"Re-Tire"—put new tires on your vehicle and "get going" for God! Retirement can be the freedom and release that allow you to be more fully engaged in the continuing work God has for you on the journey *for* life. There are more exciting, revealing, rewarding, enlightening chapters ahead.

Many who have had extremely rewarding vocations and professional careers have sensed the call and the release for service in a second career. This career becomes more focused because it is entered without the stress of the necessary, the routine. In this career they are liberated to serve God and others, expecting nothing in return.

Retired, volunteer workers often spend more hours and energy in their new careers, and because of their passion they appear to be as though they are the most highly compensated members of the team. Some even become so engaged in retirement that the thought crosses their mind that they need to go back to work so they can rest!

What Is Acceptable Work?

How do you represent God in your world and work arena? Your work ethic, your attitude toward work, and your attitude *at* work speak volumes about you and your character.

Today many are content to sponge off family and friends and abuse the welfare systems. Many of the employed who would never steal anything tangible are not troubled by giving less than their best on the job. If work matters to God—and it does—how we use our talents and gifts at work is an expression of who we are and a witness of our commitment to God, to His purpose and plan as we travel on the journey *for* life.

Many of our non-Christian coworkers are also people of integrity who display character and values consistent with the Christian view of work. A Christian in the workplace should be distinguishable by an uncompromising consistency of life and values.

Temptation is always lurking to cause us to compromise core values, such as honesty, integrity, and fairness. We should always resist such temptations by calling upon an available source of inner strength given by God that enables a person to manifest a Christlike character and work ethic. If you are going to *talk the talk*, you must *walk the walk*.

How Should We Balance Work and Rest?

Work is never absent on the journey *for* life; however, God never intended for us to work seven days a week. He expects us to balance the responsibilities of life. God Himself rested. Jesus took periods of rest and found the resolve to continue the work He came to do. Likewise, a set time for our rest and relaxation should not send a person on a guilt trip. Work and rest are necessary functions of a wholesome, fulfilled life. It's okay to "smell the roses."

- Rest is a God-sanctioned expression of the importance of work.
- Rest is really recuperative, enabling us to refresh and renew our focus.

- Our best work follows on the heels of regular times of rest.
- Rest is not a means of grace; however, rest enables one to grow in grace.

A person can be too demanding on himself in the workplace and become dysfunctional. It is easy to drift away from God by crowding Him out of your work, family, worship, and social life. In the process of leaving Him out, your priceless families and other things of value are sacrificed as you are in pursuit of wealth, status, and acclaim.

The consequences of selfish neglect in an effort to feed the ego are significant according to the writer to the Hebrews: "We must listen very carefully to the truth we have heard, or we may drift away from it. The message God delivered through angels has always proved true, and the people were punished for every violation of the law and every act of disobedience. What makes us think that we can escape if we are indifferent to this great salvation that was announced by the Lord Jesus himself?" (Heb. 2:1–3 NLT).

For all of this, what does a person gain? What a loss!

Are you working too long and too hard because you won't trust God to supply your needs? Again, as a friend often reminds me, "It's okay to smell the roses."

A workaholic may become worldly successful, but at what cost? The term *workaholic* is not a generic word applicable to all people who work long hours or hold more than one job. Providing life's basics for those we are responsible for is essential, whatever the sacrifice. Faithfulness has its reward. But remember, God is faithful! And balance in life's responsibilities is essential.

Paul wrote to Timothy: "Those who won't care for their own relatives, especially those living in the same household, have denied what we believe. Such people are worse than unbelievers" (1 Tim. 5:8 NLT). Yet it is a great injustice to yourself, to those you love, and to those who love you to link the provision of daily physical needs as your sole responsibility to others.

Let me share with you about a friend I miss dearly. He was brilliant in his chosen profession, and as his career developed he chose to be a private practitioner. In the process, the seasonal demands of his time would compel him to work around the clock. One of his sons observed this commitment and not in a demeaning way said, "I won't work like him."

His dad's earthly journey ended at fifty-six years of age. Consider what his dedication to his work cost him and his family. It was an inestimable expense, an unnecessary sacrifice. Even so, driven by his work ethic as he was, he accomplished many things on his journey *for* life. A litany of service to others follows him. He shared his plans and dreams for the future he anticipated, but many of his plans and dreams for the future on the journey *for* life died with him.

Work is a component of life. Work is *not* life. What is it you want to accomplish? Begin to do it now—in balance.

My Career Path and Calling

Since any statute of limitations that might have been applicable has expired, I can now disclose that my work history began under duress and could have been rightfully described as forced labor. At the Shaw house the children worked. I became the designated professional dishwasher as soon as I could stand in a chair and reach the dishes in the kitchen sink. I did not like washing dishes—it was not a boy thing. Nevertheless, Mama overruled and washing the dishes continued to be my job.

Often on Sunday evenings after attending compulsory church services—even though I wanted to eat—I would bypass eating and slip into my bed in an attempt to avoid dishwashing time. Even Mother would not wake me to wash dishes.

Dishwashing was just the beginning of my chores at home. Ironing was added to my responsibilities. As I became proficient at ironing simple pieces, the onerous job of ironing Dad's shirts was also assigned to me. Mother was demanding—these shirts had to be perfect—a constant challenge to my best efforts as week after week I continued helping her with the ironing. Washing dishes and ironing clothes was not the vote of confidence I wanted from her.

I was active and inquisitive and, according to Mother, impatient. I had dreams to fulfill; however, my dreams would be on hold until later.

In time, I became my Dad's helper and found satisfaction in this role. Dad was becoming more and more successful in developing his Watkins Products route, and he needed help with the deliveries. Dad did not own a car—he walked his route carrying a heavy handheld product display case. My brother Larry and I owned the Little Red Wagon, and we became Dad's helpers. At delivery time, the delivery vehicle would be loaded with products, and we would pull it from house to house while Dad made the deliveries and collected for the products.

I also assisted Dad when the products arrived at the Honea Path railroad depot. With the Little Red Wagon in tow, we would walk to the railroad station and transport the sold products to our house, awaiting delivery time. Dad's sales were increasing and these trips became more frequent. As they say in Jamaica, "No problem!" You see, the Little Red Wagon was not a cheap import. It was made for heavy-duty work.

An exhilarating experience was mine when Dad would allow me to be with him as he went from house to house selling Watkins Products. Observing him develop and exhibit his salesmanship made me so proud of him. Perhaps Dad was not aware of it at the time, but he was planting seeds that would impact my life forever.

I learned how to work observing my Dad work. When Larry and I were helping Dad deliver products, I observed that the payment was not always in cash. A lot of product was delivered on credit until payday. The term "Pay you Saturday" must have been coined in Honea Path.

I learned as a boy helping Dad that you get ahead using what you have. Don't make excuses. Innovate! Dad did!

Dad was a trader. I did not know what to call it at the time, but Dad often engaged in barter. Bartering was not something Dad had been taught. It was a natural progression of his creativity, born out of necessity. Many times we would return home with live chickens, butter, eggs, etc., which Dad had accepted in exchange for merchandise. Dad being a trader influenced my identification when CB radios came along and my handle became "The Trader." I fully believe my handle dated back to those early observations of Dad's trading skills.

When our family moved to Greenville, I had to adjust to the cultural shock of the thirty-five mile move from village to city. What a great place it would be to grow up. I soon began selling *The Greenville News—Piedmont* newspaper at the corner of East Coffee Street and North Main Street. My newspaper business was good. This was during World War II. Everyone was eager for the latest news. Donaldson Air Force Base, located in Greenville, was very active at this time. Many soldier boys frequented Walgreens at

Main and Coffee Streets. They came to eat, relax, and fellowship. The regulars became my buddies.

The officers greatly assisted my business. They would suggest to the enlisted men that they purchase a newspaper—then allow them to read the headlines—and repeat the process with the same newspaper many times.

Profits were great!

At this early age, I was learning to save most of the money I earned (Mother helped in this process) and in time, I began to invest it. On several occasions, *The Greenville News* featured the "young paper carrier" who was investing his savings in interest accruing War Bonds. My patriotism began early! Greenville was good to me!

In addition to selling the afternoon newspaper, I began selling Watkins Products—on my own. I was beginning to practice the art of selling I had learned by observing my Dad.

In the mornings when school was out, I would peddle products to the nearby store owners, restaurant owners, as well as employees and laborers at other downtown businesses. Living downtown at the time, I was a recognizable, enterprising young man.

Charlie Efstration, owner of Charlie's Steak House, recognized my ambition and became my friend and encourager. Not only did he allow me to walk among the restaurant tables selling newspapers, but he also became one of my best Watkins Products customers.

Growing up, I had very little playtime—and really, at that time, downtown was no place to play. Occasionally I was allowed to visit the YMCA just a half-block away from home. In retrospect, I remember more about work as a child than I do about participating in recreational activities. I was not pushed by my parents to work outside the home. I pushed my parents to allow me to work. That's not either a bad thing or a good thing; for me, it was a necessary thing. That doesn't mean I didn't play at all; I just didn't have the liberty to play all the time. While others were playing, I was making friends in the business community, and I enjoyed making friends—and making money.

Whether at work or play, I've always wanted to win. My Dad describes it like this: "If Jack wasn't winning, he would change the game." When I did play, I played to win. I still do! It was also at this time I was beginning to learn the value of giving a portion of what I earned to benefit others, a value that would become foundational to who I am. I will share how this developed in a later chapter.

Driven by ambition and living *downtown*, I worked:

- at home
- for *The Greenville News-Piedmont*
- at the Sandwich and Soda Shop in the Insurance Building on Main Street
- for Peterson's Manufacturing Jewelers
- for Dad selling Watkins Products
- for myself on various odd jobs on a regular basis.

As Dad's business continued to grow, he purchased a home for us away from the downtown business district. Without realizing it at the time, this initial real estate purchase planted the seed that has made the Shaw name significant in Greenville real estate.

Dad negotiated good buys and was able to realize a profit when he would sell one home and purchase another more accommodating home for his family. In retrospect, I guess we sold our several houses in the Augusta Road area too soon, but always at a profit. I will not second-guess Dad now.

Away from downtown Greenville, I was no longer selling newspapers on the street corner; I soon had a residential paper route of my own. I was able to increase the number of customers and at one point I was recognized for my achievements by being named a representative for *The Greenville News-Piedmont* at the Washington Monument Bicentennial celebration in Washington, D.C.

On this paper route, before completing my deliveries, I often took time to play. C. Dan Joyner's family lived on East Tallulah Drive, and it seems there was always an afternoon football game in Dan's front yard that I found difficult to resist. Yes, some customers did complain because this game delayed their paper delivery, and I also got home later than expected. Even today, Dan and I continue to enjoy reliving these priceless memories. Dan says, "Jack's the best paper boy I ever had." Dan has done pretty well for himself. He has built one of South Carolina's great real estate companies.

In addition to the newspaper route, I was able to provide a lawn mowing service for our neighbors and for my customers on the newspaper route in what became a prestigious and desirable community in Greenville.

By the way, the retired Little Red Wagon was then a relic, and I became the proud owner of a brand new heavy-duty bicycle that enabled me to develop my business.

Observing the opportunity to diversify further by selling Watkins Products to my customers on the newspaper route, Dad allowed me to become a dealer and establish a route of my own. My efforts were successful, and as Dad observed my selling skills develop, he eventually drafted me to train other agents in the art of door-to-door selling. Most of the time I would be training men considerably older than me, and at times I felt awkward doing it; nevertheless, I got the job done.

However, in direct sales, there is a lot of personnel turnover. In my role I would often be challenged to deliver orders other agents had written. Only a door-to-door salesperson would know how to appreciate such a dilemma. This aspect of my role was especially difficult. Personality is so important in selling. A good personality and a pleasant attitude often remove barriers and help break down sales resistance. Pressure sales tactics of other dealers who had moved on to something less demanding than door-to-door selling essentially became a resell if the delivery was accomplished.

I could deliver the orders I sold and often make additional sales to my customers at delivery time, but reselling the orders others had written was always a challenge.

The Watkins Products line was so complete that persistence in displaying the variety of products I carried in my sample case would usually uncover a need resulting in an order. Even when I was not invited inside a house, I gave my best efforts to suggest a product that might meet a need while standing at the front door. When all else seemed to fail, I would ask, "Are you bothered with roaches, ants, or other crawling insects?" The universal answer was "yes."

While asking, I was removing the trusty Roach and Ant Spray with the atomizer sprayer already conveniently installed. This allowed me to demonstrate the simple application, always followed by my offering a money-back guarantee. This approach was a winner, and I wrote many orders for this product. In my mind, I was a world-class seller of roach and ant spray.

Regardless of my sales ability, direct selling was not emotionally easy. There were many highs and lows. I would experience ups and downs—almost simultaneously. It takes courage and fortitude to knock on the doors of strangers. Many times I would knock on a door hoping no one would answer, but when they did open the door I quickly rallied emotionally, responding to the challenge before me.

In direct sales, confidence is essential. Don't fear! Ask for the order! Whatever your chosen vocation or profession, this approach is applicable whether on the journey *of* life or the journey *for* life. My advice to any young person, whatever your chosen career or calling, is to learn and develop the art of salesmanship. Observe those who are good at it. Study and practice and adapt their skills to your personality. If you can sell, you can face any challenge in life.

I continued to earn Dad's confidence, and he assigned more of his distributorship responsibilities to me. This would enable him to continue pursuing his interest in real estate opportunities, ultimately leading to a career in residential homebuilding, subdivision developing, and investments in various other real estate ventures.

The opportunity to observe Dad at work and to work with him was a priceless experience. I count it preparatory for all I have been able to achieve.

During high school and college, I continued to diversify my sales career:

- In college I became an agent for a local dry cleaning and laundry service working on a commission basis.
- I participated in demonstrating and selling washing machines from farm to farm in northeast Georgia.
- I sold L. B. Price mercantile products house-to-house.
- I sold *American Peoples Encyclopedias* for a division of Sears Roebuck & Company.
- I demonstrated and sold Wearever Aluminum Cookware, emphasizing it as a hope chest item for aspiring brides.

Upon graduating from Emmanuel Junior College (now Emmanuel College), I purchased my first car. This was not my ultimate dream car. However, that did not lessen the excitement of the moment. It was a new 1953 Chevrolet "150" two-door sedan purchased off the showroom floor of Thackston Chevrolet in downtown Greenville. What a proud moment!

However, it would not last. My friend and fellow Emmanuel College quartet member Stan Oliver, who later would be the father of Joe Oliver, the outstanding catcher for the Cincinnati Reds, described my new car this way: "No chrome, no radio, the cheapest thing on the road."

Nevertheless, it was mine! I could not prove ownership by the certificate of title because I was not of legal age. It was purchased

| DIAL 2-4451 | | Bill of Sale | | TERMS: NET CASH | |

THACKSTON CHEVROLET CO.
DEALERS
Chevrolet Cars and Trucks

104 COLLEGE STREET
GREENVILLE, SOUTH CAROLINA

SOLD TO Mrs. W. E. Cothran   DATE July 29,   195 3

ADDRESS 609 E. North St, Greenville, S.C.

COUNTY   SLSM Mr. Field

This will certify that I/we have this day purchased from THACKSTON CHEVROLET CO., the automobile or truck hereinafter described, upon the terms and conditions hereinafter set forth.

MAKE AND TYPE	MODEL	SERIAL NO.	MOTOR NO.	AMOUNT
1 1953 Chevrolet "150" 2-Door Sdn	A53A	060047	LAA852992	1732.00
Directional Signals				16.75
				1748.75
S. C. Sales Tax				40.00
S.C. License Tag Applied For				5.00
				1793.75

KEYS 8490   LICENSE

TRADE IN AND/OR OTHER PAYMENTS LISTED BELOW

| Special allowance for straight sale no trade in | 75.00 |

I/we hereby certify this is a true Bill of Sale.
THACKSTON CHEVROLET CO.   BY PREVIOUS DEPOSIT

By _____   THACKSTON CHEVROLET CO.   DOWN PAYMENT   1718.75

Sworn to and subscribed before me this   NO. PAYMENTS   EACH   1793.75

____ day of ____ 195__   7-29-53   (Balance Due Shaw)

My commission expires at   N. P. for S. C.   PAID   7-29-53   LICENSE
the pleasure of the governor.

in my Grannie's name. Even so, I could drive it, and I was responsible for making the payments on the note—which I did. By the way, Stan would often ride *with* me in "the cheapest thing on the road."

This chrome-less Chevrolet would not always be my ride. My dream car was still in the future. Since that first plain car, I have been blessed with some really neat automobiles.

While attending Elon College (now Elon University), I was a second-shift employee at Western Electric Company in Burlington, North Carolina. Being ent repreneurial, I "retired" from Western Electric. I took my modest savings and with two partners organized a used car business near Elon College. We rented a lot near the college to advertise and display the cars. On weekends and on the allotted class absences, my partners and I would travel to New York City and shop for vehicles on Jerome Avenue. This was an area of warehouse type buildings filled with used cars for exclusive sale to used car dealers. It did not take long for us to accumulate the number of cars our limited budget could handle. Then we would connect the cars, two by two, and begin our trip back to North Carolina. We were motivated by budget constraints; we traveled at night to eliminate hotel expenses. Upon returning to North Carolina, we would detail the cars for display. When these were sold, we would again travel to Jerome Avenue to repeat the process.

As Dad progressed in his real estate and construction business, I observed the opportunity to further diversify my activities by providing services on a subcontract basis, to him and other residential builders and developers. I began by cleaning windows, acid-cleaning brick, and performing final cleaning details for marketing or move-ins.

The next level for me was in real estate sales. I became a real estate agent for Leslie-Shaw, Inc. I was now "asking for the order" and being compensated on a commission basis, selling many lots and homes. All this would lead to my first real estate venture as an entrepreneur—building a house for sale. This embryo business would later become incorporated as "Jack E. Shaw Builders, Inc."

Again, I would innovate.

For a number of years our advertising agency promoted the activities of Jack E. Shaw Builders, Inc., using the nursery rhyme theme, "The House That Jack Built." This was a theme that caught fire in the Greenville market as it was showcased on television and promoted on radio by the "old lazy man." It was displayed on strategically located billboards. The billboards proved to be a very captivating advertisement, especially to the kids.

"The House That Jack Built" was one of the first animated billboards in Greenville, and parents would often share with me that their children would re-route them so they could see the caricature of Jack, the builder with hammer in motion. A more sophisticated billboard would follow, featuring Jack out of his overalls, now dressed in a suit and tie with briefcase in hand.

A successful business had begun that would be the umbrella for my diversification into other business opportunities. But not so fast—my work and career have not been without challenges and difficulties.

I learned early and often in the "school of hard knocks" about the cyclical nature of the housing industry and financial markets. Business is not without risk. There is no professional pain like that experienced when these cycles happen simultaneously.

Being a speculative home builder, you don't want to get caught in a down cycle with a large inventory of unsold homes.

I did!

What a lesson I was to learn.

This particular cycle caught me with thirty-five homes under construction. These homes were presently financed by construction loans or anticipated to be financed by construction loans from the local savings and loan associations. However, the financial markets changed like a bolt of lightning. The money faucet slowed to a trickle. Sales dried up and the homes I had under sales contracts pending loan approvals by the banks could not be closed. There were no mortgage funds available.

I had progressed a long way from that first speculative house I built. My competence and confidence swelled. The challenge was real. I could not build houses fast enough. I would sell one house and begin construction on two more. Then suddenly, without mortgage funds, I had no adequate source of revenue to service the construction loans that were in place.

Would the banks foreclose? Would I be out of business? That's the dilemma I was facing. What would I do?

I had looked everywhere—to everyone—finding empathy and nothing more. I quickly was at the end of myself with no help or hope in view. It was then I would discover that on the journey *for* life, God is my source.

As I began to understand this powerful truth, I changed the way I did business. I responded to the challenge of James 1:5: "If any of you lack wisdom, let him ask of God, that giveth to all men liberally, and upbraideth not; and it shall be given him" (KJV).

I was attending the annual convention of the National Association of Home Builders in Houston, Texas, when this truth overwhelmed me. In an instant, I had this inner knowing that I should immediately return to Greenville. Jane and our friends Marshall and Rebecca Nash did not understand this sudden, urgent compulsion of mine.

What had changed? The markets had not suddenly changed. I still had the inventory of unsold homes. Nevertheless, I had found my Source. God was becoming my source of wisdom and guidance. In times like these, you have to "think outside the box." There were people wanting to purchase my houses. How could I help them?

I began to innovate!

I discovered how to close sales through creative financing techniques: a bond for title, a balloon contract, and when sales were nearly extinct, I learned how to trade houses—a win-win strategy.

These strategies would enable me to create a monthly revenue stream to service the interest accruals on my construction loans until the cycle changed. When the markets did change, I would be ready! I would continue creating "The House That Jack Built" in multiple subdivisions.

Soon, I would further diversify by creating "The Apartments That Jack Built." The townhouse apartment market was in its early stages in Greenville, and I became an early apartment developer.

I was now ready (I thought) to develop "The Shopping Center That Jack Built." I had discussed building a small retail shopping center with my banker at C&S National Bank, and he assured me that when I was ready for financing, "the funds would be available." When the center was approximately 60 percent complete, I went to the bank to request funding. I was not prepared for the news. To my dismay, the banker who had assured me that funds would be available (not unlike what many developers experience in cyclical economic downturns) gave me these dismal words: "Upstairs (the ultimate decision makers) has said, 'No more real estate loans.'"

It had happened again!

This time I would learn a potent faith lesson. I had depended on the banker only to experience an empty promise. The banker was not my source. Banks may be an instrument used to supply my need, but *God* is my Source! Going to my source in prayer, I would realize adequate funds from unexpected sources.

I had acquired a good, hands-on knowledge of the construction business. I often say that I learned from the ground up, again with pick and shovel in hand. Building was the fulfillment of a dream for me. What I did not adequately understand at the time was how financial markets impacted my business and investments.

I have learned, sometimes too late, that God was not in every business or investment I ventured into. On my own, I've gotten ahead of God and suffered in the process. I have learned that God doesn't clean up the mess; nevertheless, when I call upon Him, I do receive wisdom and guidance to work through it. God has a way of filtering the fragment created by my haste and enabling me to right my course. I cannot be and should not be in every deal presented to me—not even the sure thing. That's a difficult lesson to learn. On my own I have settled for the good, only to find that by waiting, God had the best for me. First, take the test: What does God say? He has my best at heart, and He is never wrong.

I know what it is to be disappointed, to hurt, and to stare failure in the face. I also know what it is to resolve a different outcome.

What vs. Who

People often begin a conversation by asking, "What do you do?" rather than "Who are you?" My work is not my worth. Worth in life is determined by who you are.

Today, you may be compensated for the value your occupation brings to enterprise but that in no way establishes your worth. Your worth has been established by God as expressed in John 3:16: "For God so loved the world that he gave his one and only Son, that whoever believes in him shall not perish but have eternal life" (NIV).

Employers may have a pecking order in how they value work, but there is nothing demeaning about any work, be it manual labor defined by "the sweat of your brow" or the work of those who occupy the executive suite. All work is essential to complete the product or project. Speaking of work, Jesus said, "Look! I am coming quickly, and My reward is with Me to repay each person according to what he has done" (Rev. 22:12).

Make a Difference

When conditions are not ideal at work, what is your response? Do you follow the herd who complain and criticize, or do you become engaged in order to solve the problem? What contribution can you make to create an ideal workplace?

Don't become a part of the problem.

Help a coworker who has a work-related problem.

Smile.

Speak a kind word.

Your work ethic is a witness to who you are. On the journey *for* life, secular work is full-time Christian service. Our greatest witness for Him at work is to give 110 percent. The basic integrity of many on the journey *of* life challenges the work ethic of those who are lazy and uncommitted on the journey *for* life—those who talk the talk, but don't walk the walk.

Put yourself in your employer's shoes: would you hire a person to work for you with less commitment than you have for your job?

Personal activities should not invade work time. Lengthy visits at the water cooler and copier should be avoided. Personal telephone calls should only occur at break time.

Performance standards for work are universal and are equally applicable to the journey *of* life and the journey *for* life. On the job it will be your knowledge and work skills that will be observed and qualify you for advancement.

What would you do if you saw a coworker about to make a wrong move, knowing that this just might create the opportunity to advance? You already know what you *should* do. Can you honestly approach another person in your work experience and be as concerned for that person's welfare as your own?

A young homebuilder had a prospect who was also considering a more seasoned builder's house. The transaction would involve a trade-in house. The young builder asked the older builder, "How much are you going to allow for the trade-in?" Not only did he tell the younger builder the trade-in allowance, he disclosed to him how he had determined the value. What an example of character and integrity this was for the younger builder!

Was this necessary? No, not by the journey *of* life standards. With this information in hand, the younger builder immediately offered the prospect more. Did the higher offer make a difference? No! He purchased the other house.

Travelers on the journey *for* life are not to be confrontational. There is already enough controversy in the world. Bigotry comes in many shades and is spoken in vicious, vindictive words in many languages. We are called to be "salt and light." A Spirit-enabled life manifesting the grace of God is a powerful message. Follow that message and you will have done your part.

Leave the outcome to God. It is the work of the Holy Spirit to convict, convince, and convert—and He has promised to do it!

Today, Shaw Resources, Inc., is the corporate umbrella under which all the real estate developing, construction, marketing, leasing, managing, and consulting activities take place. Jane and I are blessed that our twin sons, Donnie and Ronnie, decided to associate with us in business. Shaw Resources is a third generation company—soon to be the fourth.

Donnie and Ronnie probably *caught* more quality work habits than they were *taught*. In their early years, they were on the construction sites with me. Recently, Ronnie was jokingly (I hope!) relating Donnie's and his work experience during those early years to our granddaughter Meagan with this story:

> When we were about Abby and Anna's age (our nine-year-old twin granddaughters) we would leave home early, and Dad would drop us out at a construction site with a broom in hand to clean the debris in and around the house or building. Around lunchtime, Dad would show up with sandwiches and eat with us. When one job was finished, we would be transported to another site following the same routine. Finally,

around 8:30–9:00, just before dark, Dad would show
up to take us home.

Ronnie is capable of fabricating a pretty good yarn, and when
he was pressed for more details, he hesitated saying, "I don't want
to say too much. I'm not sure whether the statute of limitations
has expired."

Today, in all our various enterprises, Donnie and Ronnie are
integral to everything we do. Shaw Resources continues to grow
and is in better hands for the future.

Purpose-Driven Work

Are you ready for a work assessment. Ask yourself:

- Why am I in the profession I am in?
- How does my work serve God?
- Is my work personally fulfilling?

Some people bound by the wrong vocation and work environment experience freedom and release when they realize they are
capable of doing something else.

- Is the work I am doing the work God wants me to do?
  Some have changed careers abruptly when challenged by
  this question.
- Do I desire change?
- If I change my work, could I better serve God and be
  more fulfilled?

The goal of work is not evangelism; the purpose and goal of *life*
is evangelism. On the journey *for* life, do God's work, God's way.

It's never too late to draft a work plan for a life God desires
to use. Coaches have a game plan. Generals have battle plans.

Builders have blueprints. Teachers have a teaching plan. Ministers have detailed outlines.

If you consult with those who are advancing in their work on the journey *for* life, you will sense that they are purpose driven. The guiding Holy Spirit gives them confidence, wisdom for life, direction in life, and meaning for life in their work, before their calling.

In life we encounter competing messages and agendas proclaiming to be the right way, the only way. Most of the religions of the world have a basic concept of salvation obtained through good deeds. This concept teaches that if you are a good person and do good deeds, you earn the right to enter heaven. Being good, being sincere, and having the best intentions are to be admired, but can each be misleading—and destructive. The rich young ruler answered Jesus concerning the commandments: "All these have I observed from my youth." But Jesus said: "Not enough!"

Works are important and necessary, but more is required, and this cannot be accomplished in isolation. Man may devise and scheme, but there is no other way. Paul explained it this way to the Corinthians: "According to God's grace that was given to me, as a skilled master builder I have laid a foundation, and another builds on it. But each one must be careful how he builds on it, because no one can lay any other foundation than what has been laid—that is, Jesus Christ" (1 Cor. 3:10–11).

Can you honestly approach your vocation and be as concerned for the business owners' welfare as your own? On the journey *for* life, we are called to show a caring, loving spirit. The concern of most people is, "How is it going to benefit me?"

How do you approach the interest of others?

Men are gifted by God with certain crafts and skills. In my career I have always wanted my compensation to be performance driven based on negotiated contracts, commissions, and incentives or on profits as an entrepreneur. For brief periods I would work for hourly wages or salary. Even then I would subsidize my earnings by performing contract work after hours.

I know what it is to labor. When I say, "I learned the construction business from the ground up," I speak of hard labor. Most of my early construction work was before the specialized machines that are now available.

Very often I observe individuals holding signs at an intersection that read: "Will Work for Food." In construction, you can always use more laborers. On one occasion my son Ronnie, attracted by the sign, stopped to offer assistance. The response was, "What type work is it?" When Ronnie explained the job was washing windows and doing yard work, the man holding the sign replied, "I don't do that kind of work."

Moonlighting is not a new term to me. I have done it. My dad might have even coined the term. In his door-to-door sales, his work ethic was: "As long as I could observe the inside lights edging around the window shades, I would knock on the door."

Banking from a Different Perspective: My Avocation

My fascination with banking began early in my career. I cannot recall when or where this desire was planted; nevertheless, a dream and goal of mine was to own or control a bank. Why did I have this fascination?

Bankers and merchants were the pillars of the communities where I lived as a young boy. I began negotiating with bankers before I was of legal age. My first car was purchased in my grandmother's name, but I was the one who received the banker's lecture as to my responsibility for timely performance of the obligation.

It seemed that everyone owed the bank money and wanted the banker's advice. Bankers controlled the flow of money, and most people are fascinated by the flow of money—theirs and others.

How would I begin my quest to own or control a bank? Naturally, it would happen "little by little."

Every growing business needs a bank, and I developed a banking relationship with the Bank of Greer. My business was growing. I was performing on my obligations to the bank, and the bank was enabling my business to grow. This was a win-win relationship.

One day I received a telephone call from the president of the Bank of Greer. He began the conversation saying, "Jack, one of our shareholders wants to sell a few shares. Are you interested?"

Without hesitation, I replied "yes" and purchased the shares offered me. Then little by little, the process of accumulating bank shares began.

Periodically I would receive a similar call from the president or the chairman of the board offering me a small number of shares that I would purchase. I became a ready market for as many shares as they would allot to me. Even so, how would I ever accumulate a significant holding at this pace?

In time, some of the employee shareholders, aware that I was a purchaser of Bank of Greer shares, began to contact me directly when they had shares for sale. This direct contact gave me the opportunity to purchase all the shares being offered. Management generally allocated the shares among several purchasers. Not every shareholder, especially those not employed by the bank, appreciated this arrangement—this market—for selling their shares.

Word began to circulate that I was an active purchaser of Bank of Greer stock, and many of these outside shareholders began to offer their shares directly to me. These shareholders wanted to negotiate the sale of their shares, some resenting the role of management in the process. Dealing directly with me, they accomplished their objective, and I was accumulating more and more shares in a very limited market.

It was now time to move to the next level. I began to study the shareholder list and make inquiries, especially to those with significant holdings, as to shares that they might be willing to sell. This approach led me to one of the founding families of the Bank of Greer. The resulting conversation challenged my creative deal-making skills. The process went like this:

Bank of Greer stock is the primary holding in my mother's estate, but the dividend is not adequate to support her. I proposed an arrangement that would significantly increase her income while enabling me to control a large block of shares. My proposal involved a financing arrangement where the seller would become the secured lender. I would pay interest on the note at the prime rate, greatly increasing her income. This agreement provided for the shares to be transferred to me, and I would assign them to her as collateral for the note. The plan was accepted and was a win-win accomplishment for each party. As part of this agreement, I also negotiated an option to purchase additional shares at a later date, and I did exercise the option.

This purchase put me on the bank's radar screen. I was now recognized as a player. The president inquired if I would consider an appointment to the bank board. Tongue in cheek, he commented: "The board wants you where they can watch you." The board of directors was a very closed group. I enthusiastically agreed to serve and became the only person outside the Greer community to be elected to the Bank of Greer board of directors.

I was no longer the stealth acquirer.

At this time, some of the larger shareholders began to look for a more organized, public market through which to offer shares for sale. Even then, local stockbrokers, aware of my interest in the Bank of Greer, would contact me as shares became available. Obviously I was not the only purchaser for these shares; however, I was now the most visible. I would be contacted by representatives of other estates with large Bank of Greer holdings, and I was able to successfully bid for many of these shares.

This was also a time when the banking landscape was changing. Banking regulations and laws began to be relaxed, creating the opportunity for branch banking and multi-bank holding companies. The era of single unit banking was coming to an end. What began as *intrastate banking* soon became *interstate banking*, creating unprecedented opportunities for those with vision as to the future of banking. I would evaluate these changes and reassess my goal to own or control a bank. I determined that I would develop a new personal investment strategy for the changing banking landscape.

Mergers and acquisitions were quickly becoming the vehicle for banking growth. It seemed that every bank, regardless of size, was now on some acquirer's screen. The Bank of Greer, though small in assets, possessed a significant market niche and was not overlooked. South Carolina's largest bank came calling. Their top executives requested a meeting with the Bank of Greer's board of directors. A meeting was scheduled, and an offer to purchase the Bank of Greer—for cash—was presented.

Some of the Bank of Greer's directors were caught off guard and did not know the protocol for dealing with this matter in their fiduciary role. Some moved to say no and slough it off without informing the shareholders. This was before the days of Sarbanes/Oxley, an attitude that certainly would not stand the scrutiny of this in-depth investigation. Conscious of my director's role, I requested the record show that I moved to present the details of the proposal to the shareholders.

Many non-bank shareholders in Greer assumed the Bank of Greer was *theirs* and published the following advertisement:

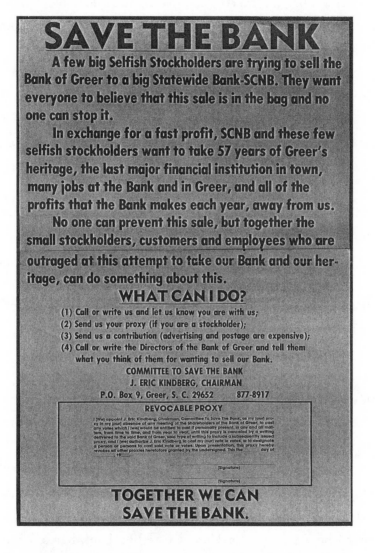

Even though this offer was rejected by the board, the pace of inquiries and proposals accelerated—some friendly, some unfriendly, even hostile.

The Bank of Greer directors developed a strategy for dealing with this new environment. And now as a bank director, I was involved in developing this strategy. The Bank of Greer was not for sale. Most of the directors did not want to consider offers to purchase the bank. Nevertheless, fearing the inevitable, a friendly, white knight, potential acquirer advised us of their interest should we decide to sell or merge.

Soon after the offer by South Carolina's largest bank was rejected, one of North Carolina's largest banks came calling. This scheduled meeting was unfriendly. The chairman of First Union presented an offer and an ultimatum. Assessing the ultimatum, our board realized it was time to negotiate with the white knight, and the First Union offer was rejected.

Like many other banks, the Bank of Greer was now on many acquirers' radar screens. It was now time to get serious with our "white knight" strategy. United Carolina Bankshares appeared to be a "cultural fit"—a term used by public relations agencies for most mergers. Nevertheless, it did prove to be a good fit for the Bank of Greer, and the due diligence process began culminating in a merger with United Carolina Bank.

Local civic leaders and some shareholders continued to voice their disapproval at losing "their" bank. Nevertheless, the benefits of the merger began to be realized, making the shareholders a lot of money.

At the time of the merger in 1986, the Bank of Greer had assets of $138,069,000. United Carolina Bankshares had assets of $1,400,851,000. The Greer community became the South Carolina headquarters for United Carolina Bankshares. Through this merger the Bank of Greer shareholders received:

- 2.39 times the number of shares they held.
- 2.39 times the dividend Bank of Greer was paying.
- A broader, more orderly, liquid market for trading shares.

The merger process continued to accelerate, and UCB became an acquisition target of the larger regional bank holding companies. When they would come calling, UCB's corporate response was: "We plan to remain independent and grow the bank." That line was the strategy of management and the board.

Nevertheless, Southern National Bank (now BB&T) would keep calling. Southern National's reputation was that of a friendly suitor. However, John Allison, the chairman of Southern National, being a skilled negotiator, was insistent and compelling. The time came for United Carolina Bank to consider Southern National's proposal. I was selected as one of United Carolina's outside directors to participate in the discussions leading to the merger.

Merging banks is a process—not an act—much like a period of courtship prior to marriage. At this level and in an accelerating merger and acquisition environment for banks, bank directors became more aware of their fiduciary role to all of the shareholders and were not as cavalier as some of the Bank of Greer directors had been in the early days leading up to banks merging.

I would be elected to serve on what would become BB&T's corporate board of directors. This combination began with assets of $22,000,000,000 and recently surpassed $136,000,000,000 in assets.

See what "little by little" can amount to when you're willing to work at it?

8

LIGHT FOR THE JOURNEY

Finding the Right Path

The road to success on the journey *for* life is discernible and open to all who desire to travel thereon. Travel will not be guided by a global positioning satellite (GPS). It is a journey of faith. You will not have an advanced look at the route, nor will you see it detailed or highlighted on the finest globe, maps, or the most up-to-date atlas. Instructions for travel on the journey *for* life are recorded in the Bible.

Even though there is no GPS, each traveler has a guidance system more exact than the most technologically advanced GPS system available. This guidance is provided by the indwelling Holy Spirit as was promised by Jesus prior to His leaving the earth. The Holy Spirit's presence and guidance are promised 24/7 without interruption. Hebrews 13:5 records Jesus' promise in these words: "I will never leave you or forsake you."

Fuel for the Journey

Travel on the journey *for* life is fueled by good books, beginning with the Bible. My exposure to the Scriptures began early in life, and I have found its truth to be foundational for all of life.

As a boy, I began reading, studying, and memorizing Bible verses. Today I draw upon its truth and principles to guide me in life and in business. On the journey, Jesus assured success when He said, "Seek ye first the kingdom of God, and his righteousness; and all these things shall be added unto you" (Matt. 6:33 KJV).

Notice He exhorts us to *seek first*—to know God as the foundation for life and of life—not to *seek only*. You will never find the way of life without knowing God.

Unbelievable Faith

I encourage you to take a step of faith by beginning to read and study the message of the Bible for yourself without any preconceived ideas or conclusions. The Bible tells us that "faith cometh by hearing and hearing by the word of God" (Rom. 10:17 KJV). This faith will lead you to success on the journey *for* life.

Own a Bible! I suggest you own several translations of the Bible.

Study your Bible! God speaks directly to the heart and mind of the person who meditates upon His word. Even though the Bible was written many years ago, it is as applicable to the issues of life today as it was centuries ago. The Bible is the Book of life. Know it and live.

My desire is that you know and experience the power of Bible truth in your life. Jesus said, "If you remain in Me and My words remain in you, ask whatever you want and it will be done for you" (John 15:7).

Paul's instructions to Timothy mirror my desire: "Be diligent to present yourself approved to God, a worker who doesn't need to be ashamed, correctly teaching the word of truth" (2 Tim. 2:15).

When you read, allow the Bible to speak to you. On my journey *for* life, when I don't have an answer and have exhausted my human resources and I still don't know which way to turn, I follow the instructions given in James 1:5: "If any of you lacks wisdom, he should ask God, who gives to all generously and without criticizing, and it will be given to him."

Believe what the Bible says. Sometimes we over-interpret the Word of God, but most often we *under*-interpret it, and as a result receive less in life than God has promised us.

What Did the Creator Have in Mind for Us?

Everything God planned for us is contained in the Bible. Therefore, through our knowledge of the Scripture, we have access to everything we need for life. The Bible is not to be skimmed as a novel. The Bible is to be studied. Ponder it, master it—line by line, little by little—and live.

The promises God gave Moses and Joshua for travel on the journey *for* life have not been depleted, diminished, or retracted. The Bible's great and precious promises are given so that we may escape "the corruption that is in the world because of evil desires" as we transition from the journey *of* life to the journey *for* life. On this journey *for* life, knowledge of the Bible will enable you to be effective and productive.

Since the Bible's truths have been preserved and passed on to us, we should commit its truths to memory and pass it on. In life, truth is more caught than taught. Believe this and begin to pass it on.

My approach to Bible study is to begin by prayerfully inviting the Holy Spirit to open God's message to my mind and heart and to enlighten its truth and apply it to me as I read and meditate systematically its pages. As you begin reading and studying the Bible, remember that the God who inspired the sacred writings looks over your shoulder as you read His Word.

On occasions as I study and meditate, challenging and inspiring words have leaped from its pages conveying much needed guidance and direction to me on my journey *for* life. One of the foundational verses I learned and memorized early is Joshua 1:8: "Do not let this Book of the Law depart from your mouth; meditate on it day and night, so that you may be careful to do everything written in it. Then you will be prosperous and successful" (NIV).

Another of my foundational faith-building verses is recorded in John 15:7—"If you remain in Me and My words remain in you, ask whatever you want and it will be done for you."

From these verses we see that success on the journey *for* life depends upon our obedience to the commands of the Bible. King David wrote:

> The instruction of the Lord is perfect, reviving the soul; the testimony of the Lord is trustworthy, making the inexperienced wise. The precepts of the Lord are right, making the heart glad; the commandment of the Lord is radiant, making the eyes light up. The fear of the Lord is pure, enduring forever; the ordinances of the Lord are reliable and altogether righteous. They are more desirable than gold—than an abundance of pure gold; and sweeter than honey— than honey dripping from the comb. In addition, Your

servant is warned by them; there is great reward in
keeping them. (Ps. 19:7–11)

Another verse that captured my attention forever is recorded
in Acts 1:11: "Ye men of Galilee, why stand ye gazing up into
heaven?" (KJV). This was a challenge to action given by heaven's
angels to those who had followed Jesus, as they watched Him
ascending into heaven. Jesus was no longer on earth and there
was no time to waste in obeying His commands. I am a person of
action, and since these words in boxcar-sized letters leaped from
its pages into my spirit, I have never been the same. I knew at that
moment that I must follow these instructions as mine—"Why
stand ye?"—as I continued to travel the journey *for* life.

In much the same way while reading Exodus 23, the words
"little by little" came alive in my spirit—seeing success as a life
journey, not an instantaneous happening.

The Manufacturer's Handbook

The Bible is the Guidebook on the journey *for* life. It is the
Manufacturer's Handbook.

The Bible is a message about salvation. However, if you take
away the message of salvation that is threaded through its pages,
those who would choose to put into practice the Bible's principles
and concepts about life would have a system of values that would
differentiate them—even on the journey *of* life—in attitude and
relationships. Someone added, "Absent salvation, you would still
have the finest 'How to Live and Succeed' manual available."

The Bible is not an outdated Book without meaning in today's
complex society as some maintain. The Bible is an *endless* Book.
Its values will never be extinguished nor will its truth become

irrelevant. Jane and our daughter Deborah often re-read novels and watch videos again and again, even though they know the outcome.

This reminds me of two avid John Wayne fans leaving a movie. The conversation went like this:

"I can't believe that hombre knocked John Wayne off his horse."

"I don't believe it either. Let's go back and see it again, and I'll bet you five dollars he can't do it again." He took the bet, and in they went.

The Bible may be read every day of the year, for all the years of the longest life, and the reader will continue to find more nuggets of truth. How delightful these newly-discovered truths from the Bible will be! Absent the Bible, there is no authoritative guide to challenge and focus a person on the meaning of life and give guidance on the journey *for* life.

If I believe the Bible is the greatest Book ever—and I do—then I must study and learn from its pages the foundational blocks of knowledge, wisdom, and truth which, when followed, will guide every honest inquirer from the journey *of* life to the journey *for* life.

Notables Guided by the Book

As the Bible is read and applied, the lives of those who read and believe its truths are radically changed. *Halley's Bible Handbook* records these notable sayings about the Bible:[5]

- Abraham Lincoln: "I believe the Bible is the best gift God has ever given to man. All the good from the Saviour of the world is communicated to us through this book."

- W. E. Gladstone: "I have known ninety-five of the world's great men in my time, and of these eighty-seven were followers of the Bible. The Bible is stamped with a Specialty of Origin, and an immeasurable distance separates it from all competitors."
- George Washington: "It is impossible to rightly govern the world without God and the Bible."
- Napoleon: "The Bible is no mere book, but a Living Creature, with a power that conquers all that oppose it."
- Daniel Webster: "If there is anything in my thoughts or style to commend, the credit is due to my parents for instilling in me an early love of the Scriptures. If we abide by the principles taught in the Bible, our country will go on prospering and to prosper; but if we and our posterity neglect its instructions and authority, no man can tell how sudden a catastrophe may overwhelm us and bury all our glory in profound obscurity."
- Thomas Carlyle: "The Bible is the truest utterance that ever came by alphabetic letters from the soul of man, through which, as through a window divinely opened, all men can look into the stillness of eternity, and discern in glimpses their far-distant, long-forgotten home."
- John Ruskin: "Whatever merit there is in anything that I have written is simply due to the fact that when I was a child my mother daily read me a part of the Bible and daily made me learn a part of it by heart."
- Thomas Huxley: "The Bible has been the Magna Charta of the poor and oppressed. The human race is not in a position to dispense with it."

- W. H. Seward: "The whole hope of human progress is suspended on the ever growing influence of the Bible."
- Patrick Henry: "The Bible is worth all other books which have ever been printed."
- U. S. Grant: "The Bible is the sheet-anchor of our liberties."
- Horace Greeley: "It is impossible to enslave mentally or socially a Bible-reading people. The principles of the Bible are the ground-work of human freedom."
- Andrew Jackson: "That book, sir, is the rock on which our republic rests."
- Robert E. Lee: "In all my perplexities and distresses, the Bible has never failed to give me light and strength."
- Lord Tennyson: "Bible reading is an education in itself."
- John Quincy Adams: "So great is my veneration for the Bible that the earlier my children begin to read it the more confident will be my hope that they will prove useful citizens of their country and respectable members of society. I have for many years made it a practice to read through the Bible once every year."
- Immanuel Kant: "The existence of the Bible, as a book for the people, is the greatest benefit which the human race has ever experienced. Every attempt to belittle it is a crime against humanity."
- Charles Dickens: "The New Testament is the very best book that ever was or ever will be known in the world."
- Sir William Herschel: "All human discoveries seem to be made only for the purpose of confirming more and more strongly the truths contained in the Sacred Scriptures."

- Sir Isaac Newton: "There are more sure marks of authenticity in the Bible than in any profane history."
- Goethe: "Let mental culture go on advancing, let the natural sciences progress in ever greater extent and depth, and the human mind widen itself as much as it desires; beyond the elevation and moral culture of Christianity, as it shines forth in the gospels, it will not go."
- Henry Van Dyke: "Born in the East and clothed in Oriental form and imagery, the Bible walks the ways of all the world with familiar feet and enters land after land to find its own everywhere. It has learned to speak in hundreds of languages to the heart of man. Children listen to its stories with wonder and delight, and wise men ponder them as parables of life. The wicked and the proud tremble at its warnings, but to the wounded and penitent it has a mother's voice. It has woven itself into our dearest dreams, so that Love, Friendship, Sympathy, Devotion, Memory, Hope, put on the beautiful garments of its treasured speech. No man is poor or desolate who has this treasure for his own. When the landscape darkens, and the trembling pilgrim comes to the Valley of the Shadow, he is not afraid to enter; he takes the rod and staff of Scripture in his hand; he says to friend and comrade, 'Goodbye; We Shall Meet Again'; and, confronted by that support, he goes toward the lonely pass as one who walks through darkness into light."

Author of the Handbook

I am not a scholar of the Bible; I am rather a student of the Bible. I have learned to sit at the feet of its Author and to learn as much as I can from Him.

Bible study is most profitable when you know its Author and are in relationship with Him. Jesus said, "You pore over the Scriptures because you think you have eternal life in them, yet they testify about Me. And you are not willing to come to Me that you may have life" (John 5:39–40).

To further understand the possibilities of this relationship, Jesus said, as quoted earlier, "If you remain in Me and My words remain in you, ask whatever you want and it will be done for you" (John 15:7).

Paul the apostle was in relationship with Jesus and wrote, "I know whom I have believed and am persuaded that He is able to guard what has been entrusted to me until that day" (2 Tim. 1:12).

Jesus is no stranger on the journey *for* life. He is a fellow traveler. The writer of Hebrews reminds us that Jesus said, "I will never leave you or forsake you" (Heb. 13:5). In Proverbs 16:9, it is recorded that "a man's heart plans his way, but the LORD determines his steps."

You may ask, "Why do you have such a passion for the message of the Bible?" Without passion, compassion, and commitment, how will those without knowledge and understanding know? Paul expressed it like this: "If our gospel be hid, it is hid to them that are lost" (2 Cor. 4:3 KJV).

No One Should Ever Be Lost!

An invitation to the journey *for* life is extended to everyone. These words are recorded in John 6:37—"Everyone the Father gives Me will come to Me, and the one who comes to Me I will never cast out." Where are you on your journey? Are you merely traveling the journey *of* life, or experiencing the journey *for* life?

I encourage you to explore for yourself the Bible truth concerning the journey *for* life. Make honest inquiry. Don't prejudge until all the facts are before you. Set aside the thoughts, ideas, and suggestions of others who do not know the way or those who have misconceptions about the way.

God's love message to man is revealed exclusively in the Bible. You will never experience this truth by reading books, articles, and commentaries *about* the Bible. The Holy Spirit reveals God's message to those who spend time in the pages of the Bible. In the Bible we understand where we came from, why we are here, and where we are going.

The allurements and enticements on the journey *of* life are seasonal. They won't last. Moses understood this. The writer of the book of Hebrews said that he "chose to suffer with the people of God rather than to enjoy the short-lived pleasure of sin" (Heb.11:25).

God's Word is more true than any feeling, thought, experience, opinion, newspaper, magazine, teacher, preacher, church, law, legal document, or any other authority. All wisdom and knowledge is not resident in man. However, all wisdom and knowledge is available to the person who seeks it in open, honest inquiry without bias or preconceived ideas.

I believe it would be beneficial for all travelers on the journey *of* life to be well read in the books of James and Proverbs, and for those on the journey *for* life, this applied knowledge can be the equivalent of a spiritual MBA and PhD.

God gave Moses His Word in order to instruct the children of Israel. The Torah was to be taught, perpetuated, and repeated often. It was to be presented as simple, uncomplicated truth that would lead to life.

Man was made *by* God and *for* God, and man's satisfaction will only be realized through a personal knowledge of God's Word that, when followed, will lead to a personal encounter and relationship with God. In every human being is that universal longing for something, for someone that can bring satisfaction for this longing. Search the world over for such peace and satisfaction, and it will only be found in God!

A friend of mine, Bob Crawford, while visiting a mutual friend who was dying, shared with me words from our friend: "Bob, I've spent my life chasing the wrong thing." Thankfully for him, there was still time to make amends, and he did.

There is an abundance of the Scriptures referenced on these pages giving guidance for the journey. Study them. Memorize them. Absorb them into your heart and spirit. The psalmist wrote: "Thy word is a lamp unto my feet, and a light unto my path" (Ps. 119:105 KJV).

Without apology I take my stand of faith upon the Bible, the Word of God. The Bible has greatly influenced me on my journey *for* life.

9

GUIDANCE FOR THE WAY

Connecting with God in Prayer

*I*n the context of the journey *for* life, to pray is to make a humble, sincere request to God. As we have noted, one of the guiding lights leading to success on the journey *for* life is recorded in Matthew 6:33—"Seek first the kingdom of God and His righteousness, and all these things will be provided for you." God promises to bless the totality of life for the person who prays. Who else could make such a promise?

Effective prayer is not a monologue; prayer is a dialogue. Prayer is conversation with God. This means that there should be frequent timeouts to listen.

Things changed when Adam disobeyed God. Adam hid, but can a person really hide from God? The important consideration is that God did not hide from Adam.

God's desire is to talk with man. It has always been that way. He is not some impersonal recluse. God desired fellowship with

Adam in the Garden of Eden and sought him out "in the cool of the day" (Gen. 3:8 KJV).

How can a person know God today? Well, how do we know a spouse, a friend, or an associate? We spend time with them. We talk with them. These are special people, and the better we know them, the more we trust them.

On the journey *for* life, our complete trust must be in God. How can we know God and trust Him without often being in conversation with Him? In Hebrews 11:6, these words are recorded: "Without faith it is impossible to please God, for the one who draws near to Him must believe that He exists and rewards those who seek Him." Those closest to Jesus were so moved by His power in prayer—His intimacy with God—that they wanted to be like Him in prayer. They believed that if they could learn to pray, they would likewise have the key to communion and power with God.

His disciple's requested, "Lord, teach us to pray" (Luke 11:1). In response to their request, Jesus taught them what has become known as the Model Prayer:

> And he said unto them, When ye pray, say, Our Father which art in heaven, Hallowed be thy name. Thy kingdom come. Thy will be done, as in heaven, so in earth. Give us day by day our daily bread. And forgive us our sins; for we also forgive every one that is indebted to us. And lead us not into temptation; but deliver us from evil." (Luke 11:2–4 KJV).

To pray effectively, we must not only know *how* to pray. We must actively pray. Prayer is the breath of spiritual life. Prayer is as essential to our spiritual life as breathing is to our physical life.

Who may have power with God in prayer? James wrote: "The effectual fervent prayer of a righteous man availeth much" (James 5:16 KJV).

Who will *not* have power with God in prayer? The psalmist said, "If I regard iniquity in my heart, the Lord will not hear me" (Ps. 66:18 KJV).

To be effective in prayer, a person must come to God in the spirit of the repentant tax collector who prayed, "God be merciful to me a sinner" (Luke 18:13 KJV).

Confession of sin is the key that opens the door to the heart of God. What could be more simple than following Jesus' instructions for results? "Ask, and it shall be given to you; seek, and ye shall find; knock, and it shall be opened unto you. For every one that asketh receiveth; and he that seeketh findeth; and to him that knocketh it shall be opened" (Luke 11:9–10 KJV).

Prayer is a means of hearing and receiving from God. Effective praying is followed by our prayers being answered. Develop the listening aspect of prayer and then . . . *listen!* Listen to God's Word, the Bible. Listen to others. There are many faith-building testimonies affirming that God answers prayer. Powerful encouragement to prayer was spoken through His prophet Jeremiah saying, "Call to Me and I will answer you and tell you great and wondrous things you do not know" (Jer. 33:3).

What does Jesus offer us in prayer? Dr. Charles Allen viewed prayer as Jesus handing us a blank check on God's account, saying to fill it in for anything we desire and it will be honored. Think about the magnitude of this promise: no restrictions, no limitations, for everyone—including you!

When a soldier under the command of Alexander the Great was told by Alexander to ask what he would of him, the soldier did not ask stintingly after the nature of his own merits, but he made such a heavy demand that the royal treasurer refused to pay it and put the case to Alexander. Alexander replied, "He knows how great Alexander is, and he has asked as from a king; let him have what he requests."

When you pray, ask as the child of a King—the King of kings—who said, "If you then, who are evil, know how to give good gifts to your children, how much more will your Father in heaven give good things to those who ask Him!" (Matt. 7:11).

We could shelter ourselves from many of life's troubles and conflicts if we would follow Jesus' admonition to pray about everything. Yes, *everything*—your physical needs, temporal needs, professional needs, and relationships. As believers, pray about these needs with the same expectancy and assurance you have when you pray concerning spiritual matters. Our God is *Jehovah–jireh*, the God who supplies.

The greatest resource on the journey *for* life—including your career, your vocation, and your business—is prayer.

It is in this arena that I have often needed to pray. My business and investment portfolio would not be what it is without prayer. Grannie was my intercessor. I pray about everything, and that includes all aspects of business, including those I am associated with. In prayer we are able to avail ourselves of His wisdom, guidance, and blessings.

To pray about everything was quite a departure from the religious culture in Honea Path when Grannie was a young Christian and when Mother and Dad were a young couple. They were taught that God was only interested in the soul's welfare, the spiritual life. Jesus expanded this concept when He said, "With men this is impossible, but with God all things are possible" (Matt. 19:26). In Mark 9:23, speaking to a father whose son had an evil spirit, Jesus added the ingredient of faith when He said, "Everything is possible to the one who believes."

Even in Honea Path, some were beginning to believe these promises, upsetting the narrow cultural applecart of belief. But in the controlling religious culture of that time, how much leverage would these people be allowed? Remember, in this culture, there was no tolerance when challenged. How far could they go from tradition and be allowed continued fellowship in the local church? Yes, it was just that real.

Yet all my life I have been exposed to prayer. My Dad told me, "Son, you were prayed for before you were born, and God has given to you a wonderful mind that He wants you to use for Him. If you will try with all that is in you to develop what God has given you and to please Him, the blessings of your life will be many, and many others will be blessed because of you. It is worth everything to give your best to the master."

What a heritage I have! From my earliest recollection, the personal prayers that have been offered for me have greatly influenced me on my journey *for* life.

As a child I was taught to pray:

> Now I lay me down to sleep,
> I pray the Lord my soul to keep.
> If I should die before I wake,
> I pray the Lord my soul to take.

Prayer is so much more than this simple childhood expression seeking the assurance of heaven. Even at a later stage in life, this simple prayer may be the only prayer a person knows. Yes, on the journey *for* life, we each have the hope of heaven. But in life, prayer is so much more than hope. Throughout the Bible we are encouraged to pray, and prayer is a vital function of life now.

Don't tell me prayer is not effective on the journey *for* life. I have experienced the power of prayer in every area of my life and find prayer effective and sufficient. In order to pray effectively, it is essential that you be in relationship with the One to whom you are praying.

Remember, life is not compartmentalized on the journey *for* life. For the Christian there is *one* life, not a sacred life and a secular life. Pray about every aspect, and in *everything* give thanks to God.

Abundant life is God's provision for us, yet we miss so much of what God wants us to experience in life because we fail to express our thankfulness to Him. Our thanksgiving is one gauge to measure the extent to which our prayers are answered.

Prayer is a limitless resource; however, it is a resource too often neglected on the journey *for* life. Most of us are proficient in asking but deficient in receiving. In James 4:2, it is recorded, "You do not have because you do not ask." What are your expectations when you pray?

For travel, whether it be on land, sea, in the air, or in space, there must be a constant source of energy. Most vehicles are powered by an exhaustible source of energy. There is global concern about how long the supply will last. Research is continuous for alternate energy sources.

What will be energy's ultimate price? In my years, I have observed prices for gasoline as low as seventeen cents per gallon and more recently over four dollars a gallon. But for those who travel on the journey *for* life, prayer is the inexhaustible energy source, and its price does not fluctuate. Paul wrote in Philippians 4:19, "My God will supply all your needs according to His riches in glory in Christ Jesus."

On the journey *for* life, there will be no circumstances or conditions where the answer will not be found through prayer. Nevertheless, prayer is not a substitute for anything.

Is prayer your steering wheel, or your spare tire?

Is prayer your first resort, or a last resort?

Use your knowledge and skills as you pray. Always do what you know to do—what you are capable of doing—even while you pray. Don't just pray when trouble visits or after you have exhausted your resources. God encourages us to be always in prayer.

Let's cut to the chase: If you don't pray because your trust is in yourself, others, your possessions, or anything else, know that all these will fail you. Realizing our human limitations should cause us to turn to the limitless God who promises to hear and answer prayer.

On the journey *for* life, prayer will always be our inexhaustible energy resource, and prayer is available to everyone. Isaiah wrote:

"Come, everyone who is thirsty, come to the waters; and you without money, come, buy, and eat! Come, buy wine and milk without money and without cost!" (Isa. 55:1). You will not travel successfully through life without becoming a person of prayer.

A person of prayer cannot be a selfish person. To be effective in prayer you must be a *surrendered* person. Jesus gave us the example as He was facing the cross, when He surrendered His will to God's purpose for Him, saying, "My Father! If it is possible, let this cup pass from Me. Yet not as I will, but as You will" (Matt. 26:39).

A young boy getting ready for bed interrupted a family gathering in the living room as follows: "I'm going up to say my prayers now; anybody want anything?" We smile at the faith of the boy; and yet, in reality, this is how we all should pray. No wonder Jesus Christ was so conscious of children.

Prayer Expands Our Horizons

Prayer focuses our concern beyond the "me and my" attitude to others. Prayer is personal, but the scope of our prayers must include others. Prayer is global, not national. The reach of prayer encompasses all the world. God is One, and He is One for all.

Grannie's growing, intimate relationship with Jesus enabled her to become a powerful force in prayer. She was known as a praying woman. For Grannie, a journey of faith had begun that has blessed her family for generations and has impacted countless others who observed her and were influenced by her godly life.

Temporal Needs

Grannie had to pray! She did not have earthly resources. There was no surplus for her. Every day was a new day. Daily needs had to be met, and Grannie prayed for her daily needs. She was a widow. In her humble way, she took every need to God in prayer. She was small in stature—a little lady—but she was a dynamo in prayer. Her prayers were so effective that others often requested that she pray for their particular needs.

There is a biblical basis for this kind of prayer. Moses wrote, "Worship the LORD your God, and He will bless your bread and your water" (Exod. 23:25). Nothing was too small or insignificant for Grannie to present to God in prayer. The idea that God was only concerned with spiritual needs never caught on with her. Grannie knew her limitations, but she was in relationship with One who is limitless.

You may ask, "Does God really care about my material needs?" I can assure you that when a person comes to the end of himself, God cares. The psalmist wrote: "God is our refuge and strength, a helper who is always found in times of trouble" (Ps. 46:1). I've been there many times and have experienced His care.

Study, train, and exhibit all your skills. Use your resources and you will still be deficient; you will still need God. And when you need Him, He will be as near as the whisper of His name. Why neglect such a ready resource?

Physical Needs

Grannie believed that physical healing was provided for believers in the atonement of Christ. Many times I heard her testify to God's healing power. In Exodus 15:26, God had said through Moses, "I am the Lord that healeth thee" (KJV).

For some in the culture of that small mill village community, doctors and medicines were forbidden. Not so with Grannie. She believed that whatever the delivery system God might choose, all healing comes from Him. Grannie never ceased praying for her physical needs and the needs of others.

The miracle of modern medicine is a blessing from God that all believers should avail themselves of. Nevertheless, part of the redemptive package for the sick is to follow the admonition of James 5:14–15: "Is anyone among you sick? He should call for the elders of the church, and they should pray over him after anointing him with olive oil in the name of the Lord. The prayer of faith will save the sick person, and the Lord will raise him up; and if he has committed sins, he will be forgiven."

But when you pray, always remember that man is not in control. God is the giver and sustainer of life, and He is always in control.

Spiritual Needs

Perhaps this is where we are most deficient. Why do we neglect this aspect of prayer? When it comes to spiritual need, so many see themselves as unworthy. Not so with God. He sees us through Jesus' eyes.

Grannie had given her life to God and, like Joshua, her resolve became, "As for me and my family, we will worship the LORD" (Josh. 24:15). You may try some other way, like many others, but there is only one way. Using the analogy of a shepherd, Jesus said, "I assure you: Anyone who doesn't enter the sheep pen by the door but climbs in some other way, is a thief and a robber" (John 10:1). Grannie knew that only the work of God's Holy Spirit would bring salvation to her family. She prayed for her family members one by one, and God saved them.

One special prayer concern of Grannie's for many years was that her sons-in-law would be saved. The stigma of being a Christian was not for them. The church crowd was not their crowd. For years she carried a special burden and often prayed for them—by name—pleading before God to save them.

"Running from God," is an expression often heard about those who want no part of the Christian life. You may run from God, but you can't hide. Remember, Adam and Eve tried to hide from God, but God came down and said, "Adam, where are you?" Sooner or later every person has a scheduled appointment with God. You may run long and hard, but you will never be able to get away from the prayers of a saintly person, the influence of a godly life, and the convicting call of God's Spirit.

Ansel was Dad's sister Irene's husband. He stopped running from God the day Grannie died. The reality of the moment caught up with him, and he quietly slipped into Grannie's living room. On his knees before God, he invited Jesus Christ to be his Lord and Savior.

Grannie had prayed for Ansel while she lived, and God answered her prayer on the very day she met the Lord of her life face to face in heaven.

In life, we will each have our moments of hopelessness and helplessness. We ultimately come to the end of ourselves. Nevertheless, you are not left on your own. You may have great understanding and ability, but you can only go so far in your self-sufficiency. How will you face these times? In this world you will experience conflict and trouble, and only by reliance upon God will you prevail.

Grannie's with Jesus now, but she continues to influence my life. Observing her made me want to love Jesus. Jesus may not have lived at Grannie's house, but He visited there often, and on occasions—when Jane and I would draw near her door for a visit—she could be overheard in conversation with Someone we could not see. What an example of prayer! How could I not love Jesus—Grannie's best friend?

Grannie often said to me, "Son, I want to go home." She's home now, but even so, God continues to answer the prayers Grannie prayed while she was on earth. This is what I call prayer.

Prayer: The Key to Success

I miss Grannie. I guess I miss her most because she's not here to pray with me. Nevertheless, it is comforting to know that she is with Jesus who is our intercessor at God's right hand. But even though Grannie's gone, I am not alone in prayer. God did not leave me without an intercessory prayer partner.

Every traveler on the journey *for* life needs a prayer partner. Do you have a prayer mentor or partner? If you don't have one, *call me!* I will pray with you and for you.

Corporate prayer is powerful prayer. Jane and I established our home on our knees in prayer. Our family has always prayed together. Jane is my partner in life and my partner in prayer. Oh, by the way, Jane's 911 hotline is a cell phone.

Jane prays for me. We pray for each other. We pray together. I have found that I cannot be successful in my calling, my business, or my personal and professional relationships without prayer.

Prayer may not influence outcomes; however, I believe it does. Nevertheless, through prayer, I am prepared for the outcome— whatever it is. Winging it on my own won't cut it. There are many wrecks on the journey *of* life, as well as the journey *for* life, simply because the resource of prayer is neglected.

Don't be concerned about bothering God or invading His privacy when you pray. The door is open, and His invitation is extended to all: "Come to Me" (Matt. 11:28) and "The one who comes to Me I will never cast out" (John 6:37). Why neglect the Holy Spirit who is our promised guide and counselor for life?

Paul summed it up with these words: "My God will supply all your needs" (Phil. 4:19).

Prayer was not conceived as a crutch for a 911 happening. God does answer 911 prayers, but don't bank your praying on the red-button hotline.

In life's emergencies, don't neglect prayer. Prayer is an instant resource available to you in Jesus' name.

Has the memory of September 11 changed your understanding of God's protection? Does Jehovah God really listen when we pray for protection? Is God a personal God who cares about individuals, or is He only a generic God of the nations?

Since September 11, Americans have a new understanding of being in harm's way. As you contemplate this, have your thoughts caused you to become fearful, or faithful? Pray for protection.

For times like these I offer you Psalm 91:

> The one who lives under the protection of the Most High dwells in the shadow of the Almighty. I will say to the LORD, "My refuge and my fortress, my God, in whom I trust."
>
> He Himself will deliver you from the hunter's net, from the destructive plague. He will cover you with His feathers; you will take refuge under His wings. His faithfulness will be a protective shield. You will not fear the terror of the night, the arrow that flies by day, the plague that stalks in darkness, or the pestilence that ravages at noon. Though a thousand fall at your side and ten thousand at your right hand, the pestilence will not reach you. You will only see it with your eyes and witness the punishment of the wicked.
>
> Because you have made the Lord—my refuge, the Most High—your dwelling place, no harm will come

to you; no plague will come near your tent. For He will give His angels orders concerning you, to protect you in all your ways. They will support you with their hands so that you will not strike your foot against a stone. You will tread on the lion and the cobra; you will trample the young lion and the serpent.

Because he is lovingly devoted to Me, I will deliver him; I will exalt him because he knows My name. When he calls out to Me, I will answer him; I will be with him in trouble. I will rescue him and give him honor. I will satisfy him with a long life and show him My salvation.

In every life there will be occasional 911 emergencies, circumstances that border on panic. Where will you turn? Do you have a panic button—a panic line you can use?

David wrote in Psalm 3:6, "I am not afraid of the thousands of people who have taken their stand against me on every side." In 1 John 4:4 we read, "You are from God, little children, and you have conquered them, because the One who is in you is greater than the one who is in the world."

Grannie's telephone number was my 911 line. Only God could have been more ready to receive my call. I would often call her, share my anxious moments and my pressing needs with her, and ask her to pray for me. Often her reply would be, "Why, son, let's just pray right now." And when Grannie prayed, I knew the answer was on the way.

There are no insurmountable problems in life for the person who prays.

Peter was walking on the water to Jesus, but when he saw the waves and began to sink, he prayed a 911 prayer. As long as there is life, there is always time to pray a 911 prayer.

When Jesus was on the cross dying, a malefactor on an adjacent cross sent his 911 call to Jesus, saying, "'Jesus, remember me when You come into Your kingdom!' And He said to him, 'I assure you: Today you will be with Me in paradise'" (Luke 23:42–43).

I've had some anxious moments when I had to pray a 911 prayer. I was driving along US 123 near Easley, South Carolina, on my way toward home in Greenville, when suddenly I entered a violent summer storm. As my car transitioned from the dry pavement to the instantly flooded pavement, I lost control of the car. Sliding hopelessly, crossing traffic lanes, approaching an embankment that could take me out, I heard myself desperately praying: "Jesus! Jesus! Jesus!" Urgent prayer does not always have the luxury of time to petition for help.

My situation was much like that of Peter in the storm walking on the water toward Jesus. Suddenly Peter began to sink. (I think he got his eyes off Jesus and on the waves) and all he could do was pray, "Lord, save me!"

I've always heard that Jesus is as near as the "whisper of His name." This time it was more than a whisper for me, and I'm sure it was for Peter also.

Jesus heard my desperate heart cry. By His help I was able to guide the car back to the right side of the road where I purposely brought the car to a complete stop on the road shoulder. There bowing my head, I expressed my grateful heart to my very real, on-the-scene, prayer-answering God.

I realize that not all outcomes will always be like this one. It was not so for Jesus. Having been arrested and standing before Pilate as an accused felon, Jesus stated, "I was born for this, and I have come into the world for this: to testify to the truth" (John 18:37).

Troubled in spirit while facing life's most difficult moment, Jesus prayed, "My Father! If it is possible, let this cup pass from Me," but in trust and surrender, Jesus continued praying, "Yet not as I will, but as You will" (Matt. 26:39).

Life's most difficult moment may be in surrendering to God, but life's greatest triumph will be realized in being obedient to God. Prayer must not be conditional. Prayer must always be in surrender to God's will because in life, we each face overwhelming waves as Peter did.

Ted Turner, founder of Cable News Network (CNN) and one of the wealthiest men in the United States, once said Christianity is for losers. He later apologized for the statement. He said he was saved seven or eight times as a youth. He went to Sunday school and church and attended a Christian school where he was required to take religion classes and attend chapel. Turner said he started losing his faith when his sister died after a long illness despite his prayers. "If God is love and all-powerful, why does He allow these things to happen?" Turner asked. His faith was conditional. If God would answer his prayers and heal his sister, Turner suggested he would have believed.

What are your "waves"?

Reversals in business? Failed relationships? Health issues? Jesus' waves led Him to prayer. He had a solitary place where He often prayed (see Mark 1:35). Facing life's most difficult moments, Jesus went apart from those closest to Him to pray.

> Do you pray?
> Do you consider yourself a person of prayer?
> Have you ever been disappointed in prayer?
> Do others consider you a person of prayer?
> Do others ask you to pray for their needs and concerns?

The prayer attitude of some is that certain things are too menial to bother God with. In prayer, do you think you have disappointed God more by asking too much, or by asking too little of Him? My personal disappointment is that I have not spent more time in prayer.

> When needs surface, pray.
> Pray first.
> Pray for yourself.

Jesus prayed for Himself. He knew what He was going to face. He knew His mission. "God is our refuge and strength, a helper who is always found in times of trouble" (Ps. 46:1).

Why neglect prayer? Have a prayer place—your private prayer closet. And visit your prayer place regularly. Visits there set a person apart in God's eyes and will pave the way for God's answers to flow to you. It is in this special place you will get to know and experience God. Plan your prayer time so that time spent in prayer will be priority time, not wasted time. Have a well-thought-out prayer agenda. Prayer is not just a "want list" to the Almighty.

Real prayer has several components, and prayer is not complete without each of these:

- Faith—belief in your heart that "God is."
- Adoration
- Praise—for who He is.
- Thanksgiving—for health, love, friends, fun, home, work, and rest.
- Acknowledge answered prayer.
- Petition God—for protection, as in Psalm 91.
- Meditate on His goodness.

Pastor Tommy Barnett shares this true-life story from their church's community Christmas outreach:

> A little boy had told his mother he wanted a train set for Christmas and that he was praying for it. She knew in her heart she could not afford that gift— nor any gift—for there was no extra money in their household.
>
> This family attended one of our church Christmas parties where a gift was given to every boy and girl. As the little boy waited in line, he hoped for his train, but he was excited just to know he was getting something. His mother watched in the crowd and was just as happy as her son, knowing he would get at least one gift for Christmas.
>
> When they got home, the little boy unwrapped his present. To her amazement and wonder, it was a train! No one knew the boy had wanted or prayed for this. No one knew what was in the presents. The person just felt led to buy a train.

God answers prayer! Even though I was aware that my Grannie had prayed for me all my life, "little by little" I have grown in my prayer life.

When You Pray

Jesus said, "I assure you: If two of you on earth agree about any matter that you pray for, it will be done for you by My Father in heaven. For where two or three are gathered together in My name, I am there among them" (Matt. 18:19–20).

God is the focus of meaningful prayer. Without prayer, life's focus is limited by what *I* can do. *In* prayer, I become focused on

God and His promises and what *He* can do. Jesus said, "You can do nothing without Me" (John 15:5).

There are no underpinnings for those who don't pray. Become a person of prayer!

When we are physically ill, we look for symptoms, we take our temperature, we visit our doctor for a check up. What is your spiritual temperature? Spiritual temperature is easily measured by the thermometer of prayer.

> What is the condition of your prayer life?
> Do you have discipline in your prayer life?
> How is a disciplined prayer life measured?
> How much time do you spend in prayer?

President George W. Bush said, "I pray all the time. You don't need a chapel to pray. I just do." Whoever you are—wherever you are—prayer is essential for success on the journey *for* life.

Before a major speech, President Reagan requested Vice President Bush to give him the last few minutes to talk with "the Man upstairs." Remember, prayer is God's idea! He said about the praying person, "When he calls out to Me, I will answer him; I will be with him in trouble. I will rescue him and give him honor" (Ps. 91:15).

Jesus knows each of us by name, and He prays for us as individuals. Jesus prayed for Peter by name when He knew the danger he was in, even when Peter could not comprehend it. Luke recorded it like this: "Simon, Simon, look out! Satan has asked to sift you like wheat. But I have prayed for you that your faith may not fail" (Luke 22:31–32). To those who know Jesus, John records these words of His: "My sheep hear my voice" (John 10:27).

It is amazing that if someone calls our name in a crowded place, we hear it. For those who know Him, who listen for His voice calling your name it may be in the crowded mall, the excitement of a sporting event, or in the place of solitude that you have retreated for escape. But one thing is certain: we will never be absent from the presence of God.

Where would such a place be? He is omnipresent.

It is one thing to be aware of God; it is quite another thing to be in conversation with God. Why do we hesitate? Why do we carry our burdens when He has invited us to cast our burdens on Him, for He cares for us (see 1 Pet. 5:7).

Often, the only place God can get the attention of an individual is at the end of self. As long as man thinks he is in control, he does not need God. However, man's resources are limited at best. They cannot buy health, happiness, hope, security, and peace.

Tony Fontane traveled the journey *of* life apparently in total disregard to the prayers of his godly parents and the faith in which he was raised. Leaving it all behind, Tony made it! He had money. He had acclaim. He was recognized as one of the world's great voices.

At the pinnacle of his career, he was the victim of a tragic automobile accident. Attended by the best medical professionals available, Tony lay in a coma for thirty days. Success, fame, and fortune could not help him. Tony had rebelled against God and his family. To him, God was for the weak and the old.

When Tony could not help himself, his wife, Kerry, gave the doctors attending her famed husband a signed, blank check only to hear the reply: "Kerry, there's not a check big enough."

Up to now she had no need for God. It was different now: wealth, fame, and fortune had failed her in her greatest need.

Hearing these words, Kerry—for the first time in her life—realized she needed God and on her knees she prayed: "God,

I need you now." Bargaining with God, she continued her prayer: "Please bring Tony back, and I'll live for you."

The transition was made. Prayer and commitment to Jesus secured for Kerry the passage from the journey *of* life to the journey *for* life.

Some thirty days later, as Tony rallied from his coma, Kerry told him what she had done. Having been raised in a rescue mission operated by his parents, Tony mentally ran to Jesus, joining Kerry on the journey *for* life. What a dramatic change!

I met Tony while he was on crutches, recovering from the accident. In his new life he was singing different songs before different audiences: songs of redemption:

"I'd Rather Have Jesus."
"No One Ever Cared for Me Like Jesus."
"No One Understands Like Jesus."
"Amazing Grace."

His rebellious past was over. Now all things were new. For his remaining years, Tony sang for a new Master. On the Hollywood Christian scene and around the world, he began to sing Stuart Hamblin's song, "It Is No Secret."

Believing prayer had worked again. It is our connection to God on the journey *for* life.

$$\boxed{10}$$

FAITH

The Energy That Makes the Journey Possible

*Y*ou've got to have faith."

"You've got to believe."

These are statements of encouragement frequently heard from others when a person faces the challenges and difficulties of life. Too often, however, the most authoritative voice on matters of faith is the one without experience but strong on opinion. We are all familiar with the person who is often wrong but never without an opinion.

What is faith? Faith seems intangible, illusive. In the context of the journey *of* life, faith is:

- Anything believed.
- Allegiance to some person or thing.
- Pollyanna-ish—faith in faith.

To illustrate this, I share a story: "As I understand it, doctor, if I believe I am well, I'll be well. Is that the idea?"

"It is."

"Then, if you believe you are paid, I suppose you will be paid."

"Not necessarily."

"But why shouldn't faith work as well in one case as in the other?"

"Why, you see, there is considerable difference between having faith in Providence and having faith in you."

On the journey *of* life, is life a gamble? There is always the chance of loss. Is risk necessary? Does risk create opportunity? Do you have to hedge your bet in order to achieve a degree of success? Is insurance against loss available if you bet wrong? Let's think about it.

The journey *of* life can be approached in three ways:

The way of faith—a positive, optimistic outlook of expectancy. On the journey *of* life, faith is unquestioning belief in God, but not necessarily the Judeo/Christian God.

The way of doubt—a very limited outlook, never certain, always questioning and afraid.

The way of presumption—presumption represents something that is not factual. We have all experienced the presumptive person. He not only takes others for granted; the presumptive person often acts as though he were God and others are subject to him.

On the journey *of* life, man is guided by his senses—by what he sees and what he feels. On this journey, a person's faith is in himself. No one will accomplish much without a personal belief that "it can be done" and "I can do it."

A positive mental attitude, often referred to by the acronym PMA, should not provoke a negative connotation. Belief is essential to accomplishment. Nevertheless, just because you believe, success is not assured. Accomplishment is accompanied by risk, and the degree of risk a person takes often determines the outcome.

In life there is always the element of doubt. Doubt is characteristic of the journey *of* life. Satan introduced doubt into our world. The Bible tells us in minute detail how Satan deceived Adam and Eve. Satan's cunning and deceptive ways convinced Adam and Eve to question God and to ultimately disobey God. Sin and doubt always lead to disobedience of God's way, and disobedience is that which separates man and God.

Man's doubt birthed sin into the human heart, and at that moment, paradise was lost and the journey *of* life began. This life of doubt, pain, and suffering was not a part of God's creative plan for man, however. Faith and fear cannot walk hand in hand.

Sin was man's choice, not God's. Nevertheless, just because a person sins does not mean that God gives up on him. Quite the contrary, man's sin revealed God's heart of love for man by showing that even in the face of death, there is hope.

On the journey *for* life, however, faith is guided by the pure Word of God. Powerful promises of God's blessing are only received when you believe. Redemption from the quagmire of the journey *of* life to the infinite possibilities available by faith on the journey *for* life is God's plan. In the Bible, He told us how this would take place and how God's Word can be depended upon. God's Word is forever true.

"Faith comes from what is heard, and what is heard comes through the message about Christ" (Rom. 10:17). What doubt and disobedience lost for man in the Garden of Eden can be fully restored through faith in God and His Word.

On the journey *for* life, travelers are not immune to conflicts, struggles, and strife. Don't be misled. In stressful times—and they will come—your comfort and security on the journey *for* life will be found beyond human resources. Everything else will fail.

Even though we presently live in a world of increasing terror and fear and are constantly troubled by the unknown, we can be comforted by the assurance that Jesus has told us what to expect in life, and nothing—absolutely nothing—can get to us or harm us without first getting past God.

As we have noted, Paul wrote: "I am persuaded that neither death nor life, nor angels nor rulers, nor things present, nor things to come, nor powers, nor height, nor depth, nor any other created thing will have the power to separate us from the love of God that is in Christ Jesus our Lord!" (Rom. 8:38–39).

Personal faith will be tested many times and in various ways on the journey *for* life. I've often been fearful when facing life's challenges, wondering if I could pull it off, wondering if I had enough faith to get started, while at the same time thinking, "What in the world have I gotten myself into?" However, I have learned that it is not *fear* that makes saints. *Faith* makes saints. And true faith will always be vindicated.

Today, Satan continues his charade as the winner in the battle of the ages. He takes many forms and plays many roles. Peter depicts him as follows: "Your adversary the Devil is prowling around like a roaring lion, looking for anyone he can devour" (1 Pet. 5:8). At other times, Satan masquerades as an angel of light, and through false apostles and deceitful workers he attempts to distort God's Word. This is just a continuation of the serpent role in Genesis 3—subtle, cunning, and beguiling.

Don't be alarmed. The outcome is known. We have read the last chapter. Satan is a defeated foe. His continuing performance reminds me of Saddam Hussein's appearance in the Hall of

Justice introducing himself as the president of Iraq. Who was he kidding?

Fellow travelers on the journey *for* life, our sufficiency is in God. Our trust also must be in Him. Even in life's adversities, when all human resources have been exhausted—when you feel desperate and all alone, when you have eaten the last food in the house, when a friend or loved one has died—whatever the circumstances, be they physical, financial, psychological, or spiritual—God is aware of you and the burdens you bear. Even in your need, He knows where you are.

Listen to His comforting words in Matthew 11:28—"Come to Me, all of you who are weary and burdened, and I will give you rest." Acknowledge Him. Call out to Him. Your sincere cry of faith will bring Him near.

Even on the journey *for* life, however, some only seek God in the extremities of life, living on the periphery of faith, with little of faith's foundation to support them. According to Paul, that foundation of God's love is "wide and long and high and deep."

Cliff Barrows, associate evangelist with the Billy Graham Association, a former resident of Greenville, South Carolina, and a personal friend for many years, shared this story in a sermon a few years ago. It is a true story as told by Ken Gaub.

> "God, sometimes I wonder if You really know where I am," I mused to myself. A melancholy cloud of self-pity enshrouded my mind as I tried to concentrate on driving. "God, even a preacher needs for You to let him know once in a while that You are aware of him," I mentally implored.
>
> "Hey, Dad, let's get some pizza." The voice of my son Dan snapped me out of my self-induced cocoon of despondency. The voices of my wife, Barbara, and

my daughter Becki chimed in agreement with Dan. It had been a long day of driving and it was way past time to eat.

"Okay," I yelled back. Exiting from I-75, we turned onto Route 741 just south of Dayton, Ohio. Bright colorful signs advertising a wide variety of fast food restaurants welcomed us. Before I had fully parked, the kids were clamoring to get out. Barbara stepped to the bottom stair of our "home-on-wheels" and stopped.

"Aren't you coming, Ken?" she quizzed.

"Naw, I'm not really hungry," I replied. "You just go ahead with the kids. I need to stretch my legs and unwind a bit." I stepped outside, noticing a Dairy Queen down the street. I thought, "I am pretty thirsty." After purchasing a soft drink, I strolled slowly back to the RV, all the while musing about my feelings of God's apathy toward me. The sudden distinct ringing of a telephone somewhere up the street jarred me out of my doldrums. It was coming from a phone booth at the service station on the corner. I drew near and paused. I looked about to see if anyone was going to answer. The service station attendant seemed oblivious to the incessant ringing of the nearby phone. I started to walk on past, but curiosity overcame my indifference. I stepped inside the booth and picked up the phone. "Hello," I said casually.

The operator intoned nasally, "Person-to-person call for Ken Gaub." My eyes widened and I almost choked on a chunk of ice from my Coke.

Swallowing hard, I replied in astonishment, "You're crazy!" Realizing my rude remark, I added, "This can't be. I was just walking down the street, not bothering anyone, and this phone just started ringing."

The operator ignored my crude explanation and asked me once more, "Is Ken Gaub there, sir? I have a person-to-person call for him."

Searching for all possible explanations, I suddenly had the answer. "I know what this is. This is Candid Camera!" I reached up and quickly tried to smooth my hair, wanting to look my best for all those millions of television viewers watching me. I stepped out of the booth, looking in every direction. I nearly pulled the phone cord off stretching its limit.

I couldn't find a camera anywhere!

Impatiently, the operator interrupted again, "Sir, Ken Gaub—is he there, sir?"

Flustered, I half-laughingly replied, "As far as I know, I am he." To avoid any further disasters, I set my Coke down as I heard another voice interject.

"Yes, that's him, operator. I believe that's him!" I listened dumbfounded to a strange voice identify herself.

The caller blurted out, "I'm Millie from Harrisburg, Pennsylvania. You don't know me, but I'm desperate. Please help me."

She began weeping. I waited until she regained control of herself. She continued. "I'm about to commit suicide. I was finishing writing a note to let people know what I've done, when I prayed to God telling Him I really didn't want to do this. Suddenly, I remembered seeing you on television in Harrisburg. I thought if I could just talk to you, you could help me. I knew that was impossible because I didn't know how to reach you, nor did I know anyone that could help me find you. While I was writing, numbers began to come to my mind and I wrote them down."

While I was listening to her, I began to pray silently for wisdom from God to help her. She continued, "I looked at the number and thought, 'Wouldn't it be wonderful if I had a miracle from God and he gave me that preacher's number?'" I decided to have the operator call it. I figured it was worth a chance. It was! I can't believe I'm talking to you. Are you in your office?"

I replied, "Lady, my office is in Yakima, Washington."

A little surprised, she asked, "Really, then where are you?"

"Ma'am, you wouldn't believe this, but I'm in a phone booth in Dayton, Ohio!" Knowing this encounter could have been arranged only by God, I boldly counseled her, telling her of her need of Jesus. She shared her despair and frustration. In a matter of moments, she prayed the sinner's prayer and met the only Person who could lead her into new life—Jesus Christ.

I walked away from that telephone booth with an electrifying sense of our Heavenly Father's concern for each of His children. With all the millions of phones and innumerable combinations of numbers, only an all-knowing, all-caring God could have caused that woman to call that number in that phone booth at that time. Nearly bursting with joy and exhilaration, I jumped up to the RV. I wondered if my family would believe my story. "Barb, you won't believe this! God knows where I am!"

Faith is always tested in the extremes of life. I have faced some of life's extremes, and at the end of myself I have experienced God there, saying, "Don't worry about anything, but in everything, through prayer and petition with thanksgiving, let your requests be made known to God" (Phil. 4:6).

How important it is for us to often remind ourselves of the faithfulness of God. Never forget what God has done. Memory is a great tool of faith. When Jesus' disciples despaired, Jesus would inquire of them, "Do you not remember?"

When God seems distant, we can be reminded of God's faithfulness by these words of Benjamin Franklin.

> Have we now forgotten that powerful friend? Or do we no longer need His assistance? I have lived a long time; and the longer I live, the more convincing proofs I see of this truth: that God governs in the affairs of men. And if a sparrow cannot fall to the ground without His notice, it is not probable that an empire can rise without His aid.

Faith is an important ingredient on the journey *for* life. The faith attitude is: "I am able to do all things through Him who strengthens me" (Phil. 4:13). Hebrews 11 also reveals how faith makes all the difference.

On the journey *for* life, we will be faced with circumstances we have never encountered before. At times such as these, faith may be all we have. When it is, obedience is all we need. Faith is enough!

God's economy is not dependent on earth's depleting resources. Do your personal resources have to be exhausted before God's supply kicks in? Most of us act as if they do. What are your needs? Are you going to focus on the problem, or the solution?

But you say, "I don't want to bother a busy God." Peter wrote: "Humble yourselves therefore under the mighty hand of God, so that He may exalt you in due time, casting all your care upon Him, because He cares about you" (1 Pet. 5:6–7).

Now, what areas of life have you committed to God? Paul wrote with confidence: "I know whom I have believed and am persuaded that He is able to guard what has been entrusted to me until that day" (2 Tim. 1:12).

With the ravages of depression times evident everywhere, President Franklin Delano Roosevelt rallied America, saying, "The only limit to our realization of tomorrow will be our doubts of today." He also said, "There is nothing to fear but fear itself."

In fear, freedom to live productively is lost. Doubt blinds. Faith sees.

Where is faith when we don't receive the answer we pray for? Jesus gave us faith's answer to this question when He prayed, "Nevertheless." Faith does not always remove the pain; however, faith will enable one to endure the pain and realize God's purpose in allowing it.

Noah obeyed God and built an ark to save his family. When God tested Abraham, he responded by faith and obedience to God. "He considered God to be able even to raise someone from the dead, from which he also got him back as an illustration" (Heb. 11:19). By faith the people passed through the Red Sea "as though they were on dry land. When the Egyptians attempted to do this, they were drowned" (Heb. 11:29).

On the journey *for* life, faith consists of a series of little steps, each building upon the other, evidencing a growing faith. God had promised the Israelites "a land flowing with milk and honey," but they could only possess it "little by little" as they journeyed. Faith, like life, often appears to be a slow process. When will we see the results of faith? "Little by little" often seems like trying to watch grass grow or paint dry.

But trust me, life is not that slow.

When I was young it seemed that slow. Now that I am older, life seems to be in an accelerated pace. There is so much that I haven't done, so much that I want to do, so little time!

Doubt and unbelief are also evident on the journey *for* life; nevertheless, man's doubts do not diminish the power of God. Doubt just limits faith's impact in our lives. Matthew wrote, speaking of Jesus' ministry in His hometown, "He did not do many miracles there because of their unbelief" (Matt. 13:58).

When our needs and concerns bring us before our king's throne of grace, we are encouraged to ask largely, remembering, "He is able to do exceedingly, abundantly above all we are able to think or ask." Our Lord gives us unlimited credit at the Bank of Faith. Our "faith account" is quite different than that of the lady who overdrew her bank account. Receiving an "NSF" notice from the bank, she went to the teller at Wachovia Bank in Winston-Salem, North Carolina, inquired about the amount of the overdraft, and proceeded to write a check on that account to cover it.

How different with God. Our faith account is bottomless.

Faith is a way of life on the journey *for* life. The words, "The just shall live by faith" are recorded four times in the Bible (Hab. 2:4, Rom. 1:17, Gal. 3:11, and Heb. 10:38). Faith requires action. Faith may not make things easy, but faith makes "all things possible." No doors are barred to faith.

What Is Faith?

Faith is belief, but not *just* belief. Belief is a powerful force when it is properly focused—not *on* but *in*. Luke wrote in Acts 16:31: "Believe in the Lord Jesus, and you will be saved" (NIV). On the journey *for* life, faith is not a formula to follow. Faith is not speaking a spiritually correct series of words. Hebrews 11 is known as the "faith chapter" of the journey *for* life. It begins, "Now faith is . . ."

Faith is paradoxical.

Faith goes beyond reason.

Faith believes without understanding why.

Faith is a journey to travel. But you must be equipped for the journey. At times the journey will be adversarial. For these periods, Paul wrote in Ephesians 6: "Put on the full armor of God" (Eph. 6:11). This includes:

- The belt of truth
- The breastplate of righteousness
- Shoes representing the gospel of peace
- The shield of faith
- The helmet of salvation
- The Bible as our sword

With the armor of God, we are "more than conquerors." The importance of faith is evident since:

- We cannot know God without faith.
- We cannot live in victory without faith.
- We cannot please God without faith.
- We cannot pray effectively without faith.
- Peace with God is dependent on faith.

Everyone has faith, but it is important to learn how to focus faith. To be effective, faith must be directed toward a desired goal. Faith is measurable. Jesus' measuring scale was:

- "No faith"
- "Lack of faith"

- "Little faith"
- "Great faith"

Wherever you are in faith, your faith can grow. Jesus' disciples petitioned Him to "increase our faith."

Growing faith is a process. It comes "little by little" as we are ready. As the children of Israel were prepared to possess the Promised Land "little by little," faith is also to be acquired "little by little."

All the blessings of God are devised so that they increase. Peter wrote: "But grow in the grace and knowledge of our Lord and Savior Jesus Christ" (2 Pet. 3:18).

Mustard seed faith can move mountains. There is no end to God's resources and the possibilities of faith. In John 1:16, we read: "We have all received grace after grace from His fullness," so that—as Paul wrote—"in the coming ages He might display the immeasurable riches of His grace in His kindness to us in Christ Jesus" (Eph. 2:7).

Learn and follow this faith principle: Faith operates in the present tense. "Tomorrow" faith never shows up.

As faith is practiced on the journey *for* life, exploits of faith will be observable. Through faith in God you become superior to circumstances and triumph over the evil forces that seek to destroy travelers on the journey.

Real Faith Is "Now" Faith

Yesterday is gone, and tomorrow is not certain. The most important consideration of faith is not the *degree* of faith but the *direction* of faith. In your faith walk, appreciate and appropriate the faith you have in this "now" moment, not the great faith you desire and hope for. The faith of others may inspire us, but our personal faith is that which sustains us and leads us to success on the journey *for* life. However inspired we may be by the faith of others, Jesus—"the author and finisher of our faith"—must be our example.

Like Jesus, our faith will be tried and tested many times, in many ways, but faith will always be vindicated. He has made our faith victory possible. *Believe it!*

Travelers on the journey *of* life live by their own self-sufficiency, but on the journey *for* life, "the just live by their faith."

Effective faith is often compared to that of a child: "Whosoever shall not receive the kingdom of God as a little child, he shall not enter therein" (Mark 10:15 KJV).

Dick Van Dyke illustrates it like this: "Children's prayers have an amazing intimacy and directness. One child, told by his mother that he might go on a picnic she had previously vetoed, sighed, 'It's too late, Mom. I've already prayed for rain.'"[6]

Faith is not idealism or utopia. Rather, in real life situations, faith sees the better, fuller, more useful way. Faith expects the best and sees good in what is allowed to happen. Paul wrote in Romans 8:28: "We know that all things work together for the good of those who love God: those who are called according to His purpose."

It is not a common attitude to see good in everything; nevertheless, there is that special something that manifests itself in those who have determined not to be satisfied with the commonplace in life. Faith does not *make* things happen; faith *causes* things to happen.

Henry Ward Beecher wrote, "Every tomorrow has two handles. We can take hold by the handle of anxiety or by the handle of faith."

Faith in my life has been "little by little," a step-by-step unfolding of a continuing dream. From the humble beginning that I still remember, I know the power of positive faith to see fulfillment of my dream: to be, to do, to live a life of purpose, passion, and significance—a dream of desire placed in my heart by a good, caring, loving God.

Faith knows the difference between the journey *of* life and the journey *for* life. For me, faith was manifest when I accepted God's personal plan of redemption. In that moment, a new life began for me. The old life was changed. In fact, as we have noted before, Paul wrote: "Old things are passed away; behold, all things are become new" (2 Cor. 5:17 KJV).

Since that moment, I have never doubted that God had a plan and purpose for my life, and His plan and purpose continue to unfold today. Faith opens my spiritual eyes to things the natural eye cannot see and gives evidence of the things we do not see.

Ronald Reagan's faith attitude and optimism always inspired me. Jack Kemp, speaking of Ronald Reagan, said, "It wasn't an ostentatious or self-absorbed faith that manifested itself in rigid certainty about matters of this earth; it was a deep, abiding knowledge that we are all playing bit parts, albeit eternally important parts on this earthly stage and being directed by a higher power. It was that certainty of faith that freed Reagan of hubris to be humble . . . in the decisions he made as President."

Nancy Reagan put it this way: "Ronnie has always been a very religious man. He has always believed that God has a plan for each of us and that while we might not understand His plan now, eventually we will."

Faith is an attitude and a confident knowing.

Faith Is Believing the Instruments

As an airplane pilot, I learned that faith is believing the instruments. Most vehicles and instruments operate according to an owner's and operator's manual. This is especially true regarding aviation. Airplanes are manufactured to exacting standards. Instruments are installed in order to safely provide guidance and control, even in adverse weather conditions.

A common occurrence in conditions like this is for a person's physical senses to betray him, for him to experience vertigo. The dictionary defines vertigo as "a disordered state in which the individual or his surroundings seem to whirl dizzily"—a dizzy confused state of mind when, regardless of feeling and sensation, the pilot must believe the instruments. The instruments relate the real attitude of the aircraft and, regardless of the pilot's feelings and sensations, a safe flight and landing is dependent upon the pilot believing the instruments over what he feels and sees.

Much instrument training is required for those who would be instrument rated and qualified to pilot in IFR conditions. The appropriately rated pilot is a tried and tested individual even in extreme conditions.

Man is a creation of God, made in His own image. He is not a creature of chance; rather, man is a human being conceived in the mind of God and created to dwell in fellowship with God and man. However, it seems that adverse conditions of life sometimes eclipse man's vision of God. Man's senses cannot find God. Spiritual vertigo takes place, and man is in great danger of losing his course. Unless he is aware of and qualified to deal with these conditions, destruction is at hand.

How do we overcome spiritual vertigo? We must *believe the instruments*. As noted earlier, God has made available for each of us His Manufacturer's Handbook—the Bible. Through the Holy Spirit, we have God's guidance system enabling us to overcome the adverse conditions of life that the devil brings against us. It is simply by believing the instruments.

The walk of faith on the journey *for* life is not a walk by sight, feeling, or any other physical sense. Faith means trusting what God has said to be true.

How can a faith attitude be developed? Faith can only be attained and increased by spending much time studying the Bible. Faith is not based upon conditions, circumstances, or feelings. God's Word enables us to apply His truth to what we face in life and experience overcoming faith. An old friend gave me a faith lesson as follows:

- Faith minus works equals "nothing."
- Faith plus works, minus patience equals "confusion."
- Faith plus works, plus patience equals "inheritance" (see Heb. 10:36).

The journey *for* life is not problem free; at times it can be an obstacle course. Success on the journey *for* life becomes a process of solving problems and overcoming obstacles. Expect the challenges and be content. They are just part of the overcoming process for travel on the journey *for* life. As you overcome the challenges, you grow in faith and knowledge "little by little," and experience God guiding you and sustaining you. In the process, He enables you to realize purpose and significance. Success will not be an exact location on the journey *for* life. Success will be a sense of God's presence where you are at the moment.

The favor of God will not always mean a life void of conflict. Joseph went to prison. Paul was beaten and often in jail. Jesus was crucified.

It's a faith journey. You will not always understand God's ways and His purpose. The whys will be there, but stop questioning the why and begin to trust God's purpose.

A journey requires movement. The Lord said through Moses in Deuteronomy 1:6, "You have stayed at this mountain long enough." Most people become satisfied where they are. God called Abraham to move. And as Abraham's seed, we too are on a journey of faith. We may not always know where we are going, but we know our Guide and can follow Him with confidence.

Abraham could have stayed in his comfort zone with family and familiar surroundings, but he believed God and started the journey. He encountered problems and difficulties along the way. At times he questioned God. At other times he had to resolve family conflicts. Even though Abraham did not always obey God and follow His guidance, God did not give up on Abraham.

While others may doubt and compromise, I have chosen to follow the guidance of faith: God said it, I believe it, and that settles it. *Now!*

Success is the "now" moment where God has placed you. Success on the journey *for* life is up to you. Fulfill your purpose where you are. Give this "now" moment your best, and when you do, God will enable you to fulfill your purpose, become a person of significance, and succeed on the journey.

Be an example as you travel. Be all that you can be. Manifest who your Father is. How do you represent God in the routine of the mundane? Always maintain a goal of excellence.

You may not always realize the results of faith, but God is faithful. Results are God's part; He will make it happen. You are His child of promise. As you travel, your promised land is "flowing with milk and honey." Possess it!

Redeem the Time

Another important lesson of faith concerns *time*. Faith is not a product of time. Faith has no clock. Time does not determine the *degree* of faith. Faith is a "now" experience. When time has been exhausted, *faith is!* Time as we know it does not alter the certainty of God's promises.

The results of faith may not be evidenced by the natural senses; however, the end of faith is as certain as the reality of God. The seed must first be planted, then comes the fruit; so faith expressed will have like results—the fruit of reward. By faith we please God *now!*

The mind follows visible evidence toward conclusions:

> Food satisfies physical hunger;
> Musical tones satisfy the ear;
> Color pleases the eye.
> But faith touches the unseen realm.

However, these cannot be found by natural phenomena. Only by faith can we be certain of things spiritual. The satisfaction for the cravings of the soul of man is only achieved by faith. By faith we know, and by faith we experience the satisfaction for our soul's thirsts.

For more than thirty years, I have periodically recorded faith reflections and thoughts. Here are some of them:

- The one force more powerful than fear is faith.
- Faith cannot be denied.
- Faith is not fragile.
- Faith is able.
- Faith never disappoints.

- Faith engages in the battle, confident of victory.
- Faith's answer is always on time.
- Faith has no mirror.
- Faith knows the present but sees the future.
- Faith is not believing God can, faith is knowing God will.
- Have faith in God, not faith in faith.
- Faith does not reason, faith accepts.
- Faith's source is inexhaustible.
- Not every person is equal in faith. Faith is contagious.
- The faith of one person can inspire and ignite others toward a common goal.
- Faith is the key to successful living.

Paul wrote to the Corinthians about gifts and manifestations of the Holy Spirit of God. Among these is the gift of faith. This spiritual gift is a deeper dimension of faith, whereby on occasions a believer is especially gifted and in a time of special need he experiences a supernatural removal of doubt—a knowing of faith that makes it impossible to doubt.

On occasion, in times of personal need and in sharing the need of others, I have experienced this gift of faith. You can also!

There is much more to experience as we continue on the journey *for* life. Man has never tested faith to its fullest extent. Every resource of God's storehouse is available to the believer.

God's Plan for You Is Abundant Life

I don't want what I write to be only a shadow of reality. The faith I write about is more than positive thinking—a positive mental attitude, a positive outlook—even though faith embraces each of these. My purpose and passion is that you will come face to face with the essence of reality, and that this reality will be foundational as you explore truth.

I encourage honest inquiry. Unless you consider the claims of Jesus Christ, how can you be certain you are living for what really matters? Honest inquiry is an open-minded approach in which you are willing to consider other ways, willing to give audience to other prevalent viewpoints of the time.

Faith is a "risk or reward" venture. As Paul wrote in Romans 6:23: "The wages of sin is death, but the gift of God is eternal life in Christ Jesus our Lord."

Don't ever apologize for your faith. Faith's adversaries don't. They often demean faith, ridicule faith, mock faith, contest faith. But in the face of adversity, you must earnestly contend for the faith. Don't back off! Don't compromise!

Faith is our victory!

Faith does not motivate God to answer prayer. God is love, and His love for us is the basis for answering our prayers. Our faith enables us to believe and receive His promises. Faith, prompted by what God has done, enables us to know what God wants to do— what God *will* do. Faith is not just belief; faith has foundation.

When you transition from the journey *of* life to the journey *for* life, some things will not change. You will continue to experience struggles—perhaps even more so.

You will be challenged to "fight the good fight for the faith" (1 Tim. 6:12). At times you will be challenged to "walk worthy of the calling you have received" (Eph. 4:1). At other times you will be required to "run with endurance the race that lies before us" (Heb. 12:1). Whether it be a walk or a run, let us keep "our eyes on Jesus, the source and perfecter of our faith, who for the joy that lay before Him endured a cross and despised the shame, and has sat down at the right hand of God's throne. For consider Him who endured such hostility from sinners against Himself, so that you won't grow weary and lose heart" (Heb. 12:2–3).

Faith is trust in God, and the journey *for* life is a faith life. Sometimes faith is all we have; and when faith is all we have, faith is all we need. In Matthew 9:29, Jesus said, "Let it be done for you according to your faith!"

You can only go so far on your own. Success on the journey *for* life embraces faith in God, and as Jesus spoke to the centurion, "As you have believed, let it be done for you" (Matt. 8:13).

God is not bound by the normal, natural, explainable way to accomplish His purpose. God is in control of outcomes, and He is limited only by man's unbelief. If you believe God's Word, you will receive what God has promised.

┌─────┐
│ 11 │
└─────┘

GIVING

The Hilarious Living

Alifestyle of giving should distinguish those who travel the journey *for* life. Every individual begins the journey *of* life receiving. During this stage of life, others are responsible for our being here, our sustenance, our shelter and security. So very early in life, children tend to become selfish and satisfied. If memory serves me well, children are born saying:

> "It's mine."
> "I want that."
> "Gimme."

Possession is everything to a growing child, and on the journey *of* life many of us never get beyond the giving and receiving mentality of early childhood. Could it be that the failure to learn and practice the Golden Rule—"Do to others as you would have them do to you" (Luke 6:31 NIV)—is the seed for so much of the personal and corporate discord in relationships throughout the world today?

Giving—sharing—is an acquired grace. It does not develop instantaneously. It is a growing grace. It is developed much like life, "little by little," as it is practiced in life's experiences.

Let me share a story with you about a mother trying to teach her children this grace: As she was preparing pancakes for her young sons Kevin and Ryan, the boys began to argue over who would get the first pancake. Observing this behavior, she seized the opportunity to teach them a lesson. She said to Kevin and Ryan, "If Jesus were sitting here, He would say, 'Let my brother have the first pancake; I can wait.'" Kevin turned to his younger brother and said, "Ryan, you be Jesus."

Giving is not just a spiritual grace; however, grace giving is practical giving. A person cannot travel long on the journey *for* life without becoming sensitive to the need to practice grace giving. Even though it is undeserved and often requires personal sacrifice, this is the best expression of human love for another person. Grace giving is the shoe leather God often uses to meet the need of the one giving, as well as the need of the one receiving. When a person truly loves, he is motivated to give.

Many people ascribe to the popular contemporary pseudo-gospel message that "you give to get." Jesus did not teach this as a principal of giving. Conditional giving, like conditional love, is not "journey *for* life" giving.

A prosperity gospel appealing to man's greed may be a motive for giving on the journey *of* life, but this should never be the motive for giving on the journey *for* life. God is not influenced by man's wealth or by man's poverty. Affluence is not indicative of His approval, nor (as some believe) is poverty indicative of His disapproval. There is too much emphasis on gospel tangents as a route to health and prosperity. There is more—*much* more—in the gospel than "name it, claim it, and frame it."

God gave. The journey *for* life was made possible by God's grace gift. "For God so loved the world that he gave his one and only Son, that whoever believes in him shall not perish but have eternal life" (John 3:16 NIV).

Jesus gave. It is beyond human comprehension that Jesus thought enough of me to redeem me and give me as His grace gift to God.

Grace giving was God's way of assurance that everyone would have access to the journey *for* life. No one is excluded. Everyone is included. There is no way to deserve it. There is no way to earn it. Jesus is God's way to receive it.

Giving to others is one channel of service to God that will not go unnoticed or unrewarded by God. Jesus said, "Whoever gives you a cup of water to drink because of My name, since you belong to the Messiah—I assure you: He will never lose his reward" (Mark 9:41).

You may give a grace gift to God by sacrificially serving others in His name; however, you will never develop a lifestyle of giving that will enable you to outgive God!

I read about Dr. James H. Milby, chairman of one of the largest life insurance companies in America. "What is the key to your success as a businessman?" a friend asked.

He said, "The answer to that is very simple. Many years ago I made a contract with the Lord, claiming the promise: 'Them that honour me, I will honour' (1 Sam. 2:30 KJV). So I began tithing." He said he began tithing when he could not "afford" to tithe. But he kept his contract with the Lord, and God began blessing him as he went from one level of business to another. He said that he never envisioned the kind of prosperity that came, but he took God's promise seriously and God honored His part.

Tithing is a solution to every financial problem of the church, but it is also a benefit to the person who tithes. Everyone may not be at the top of management or the president of a giant corporation, but there are some plain promises that suggest you cannot outgive God—even in reference to material return. "He which soweth sparingly shall reap also sparingly; and he which soweth bountifully shall reap also bountifully" (2 Cor. 9:6 KJV).

> Bring ye all the tithes into the storehouse, that there may be meat in mine house, and prove me now herewith, saith the Lord of hosts, if I will not open you the windows of heaven, and pour you out a blessing, that there shall not be room enough to receive it. And I will rebuke the devourer for your sakes, and he shall not destroy the fruits of your ground; neither shall your vine cast her fruit before the time in the field, saith the Lord of hosts. (Mal. 3:10–11 KJV)

These promises point to a material return as one kind of blessing from the Lord. Obviously some will prosper more than others because of personal gifts, places of responsibility, or opportunity. But the bottom line of it all is that all believers who tithe will be honored, even at a material level, regardless of whether they receive more or less than others.

There are many who would testify that God has brought them out of financial stress because they tithe. They may not become a millionaire or drive a Rolls-Royce, but they live without the terror of constant financial adversity or destruction.

Again, you cannot outgive God! A person's giving does not obligate God to him; however, God has obligated Himself by His

Word, His promises, and His covenant. Nevertheless, this is not sufficient for many today. Just as in Jesus' time on earth, people want a sign. Their acceptance of Him is based upon seeing Him perform another miracle.

What about you? If you don't believe, what would it take for you to believe?

God is not man's servant; however, He is a caring benefactor to man. His relationship to man, and man's relationship to God, is a love relationship. And God's love for man is not measured by the contemporary message of some as to *where* we give or *how much* we give to have our needs (more likely, our *wants*) satisfied.

A Lifestyle of Giving

There are many organizations and ministries worthy of our gifts, and on the journey *for* life we will be greatly blessed by adhering to a lifestyle of giving—a lifestyle that includes not only our financial resources but also our love, time, and concern.

On occasions, all that is necessary to portray a lifestyle of giving to others is just *being there.* How can you develop a lifestyle of giving? Read on!

Giving as a lifestyle is revolutionary. Giving means to let go of—to completely abandon—the ownership of the gift. Our gifts, totally abandoned and surrendered in service to God, are the only things that we can be sure will endure.

As a young boy, I was taught at home and at church the importance of giving. One thing was certain—whether or not it was practiced by its members—the church taught and preached the necessity of giving.

A lesson I learned later in life is expressed by Philip Gibbs: "It is better to give than to lend, and it costs about the same."

A person's attitude about giving becomes an expression of who that person is and of the things that are important to him. In personal relationships, I have observed the following traits of the *givers* and *takers*:

Cheerful givers are courteous, radiate joy, and are content and successful.

As for takers, they never have enough, are routinely miserable, and are often cynical, missing the significance of life because in their greed they become isolated from others and all that is meaningful. As recorded in Proverbs 11:24—"One person gives freely, yet gains more; another withholds what is right, only to become poor."

Also, a person's attitude about God affects his attitude about others and giving. Jesus illustrated this by the parable of the talents, recorded in Matthew 25.

> It is just like a man going on a journey. He called his own slaves and turned over his possessions to them. To one he gave five talents; to another, two; and to another, one—to each according to his own ability. Then he went on a journey. Immediately the man who had received five talents went, put them to work, and earned five more. In the same way the man with two earned two more. But the man who had received one talent went off, dug a hole in the ground, and hid his master's money. (vv. 14–18)

What is the lesson of this parable? Be good stewards of the gifts that you have because you are responsible for them, and you will be rewarded accordingly. Remember, each was given responsibility according to his ability.

The one with five talents and the one with two talents received this commendation, "Well done, good and faithful servant. I will put you in charge of many things" (vv. 21, 23). The man with one talent reported to his master, "You're a difficult man, reaping where you haven't sown and gathering where you haven't scattered seed. So I was afraid and went off and hid your talent in the ground. Look, you have what is yours" (vv. 24–25). All the things this servant knew about his master should have aroused faith rather than fear in his heart; therefore, the master replied, "You wicked, lazy servant" (v. 26 NIV), and gave his talent to the servant with ten talents. This servant was deemed worthless and was cast into darkness.

Beth Moore, Bible teacher and author, has been called "a woman of purpose, preparation, prayer, and passion." She is the founder of Living Proof Ministries. On the matter of giving, I heard her say, "The more we have, often, the less we are willing to risk."

I read somewhere that when it comes to giving, "Some people are tighter than the bark on a tree."

Another has said, "If you cling tightly to what you have instead of opening up to share with others, your heart is like a clenched fist, holding everything for yourself. But with a clinched fist, you can't receive anything else. You are closed to other good things that may come your way. But if you walk through life with an open-handed attitude, ready to share generously who you are and what you have, you're in a great position to receive and enjoy even more. Don't let a miserly heart rob you of all that life has to offer. Open up, share generously, and begin enjoying life."[7]

When it comes to giving, the keepers and takers have clenched, arthritic hands that will only be set free by the frequent exercise of being opened and extended, sharing with others. Get out of selfishness into the lifestyle of giving.

Love gives. Love shares. Those who never learn to give will always be wanting, like the keepers and takers described above.

Examine your lifestyle. Are you a giver, or a taker?

Perhaps you have items in your possession—in your house, your attic, your basement, your closets, or your pantry—that have accumulated through the years. You no longer use them and will never use them again. You can initiate a lifestyle of giving by letting these things go. Stop thinking in terms of what is "mine" and begin visualizing how sharing these things will benefit others. When you do, you will begin "little by little" to experience a constant stream of God's blessing flowing to you.

The real measure on the journey *for* life is that the personal satisfaction received by giving is more gratifying than the ego satisfaction of accumulating "my" things. "Journey *for* life" giving is not measured by how much you give but by what you have left.

Bob Pierce, founder of Samaritan's Purse and mentor to Franklin Graham, would say, "A good day is when the purse is empty." Radical thinking? Yes. But that's the difference between a person who's merely on the journey *of* life, and those who are choosing to travel the journey *for* life. Think about it.

How to Begin a Lifestyle of Giving

I encourage you to begin giving at some level. Any level. Select an entry point into the lifestyle of giving at a level you feel comfortable. (On second thought, even if you are not comfortable, begin by giving something meaningful regardless of how you feel.)

In the lifestyle of giving, everyone can give. Jesus expressed it this way:

> He looked up and saw the rich dropping their offerings into the temple treasury. He also saw a poor

widow dropping in two tiny coins. "I tell you the truth," He said. "This poor widow has put in more than all of them. For all these people have put in gifts out of their surplus, but she out of her poverty has put in all she had to live on. (Luke 21:1–4)

David expressed it this way: "I have been young and now I am old, yet I have not seen the righteous abandoned or his children begging bread" (Ps. 37:25).

As already mentioned, the prophet Malachi put forth God's challenge concerning giving: "'Test Me in this way,' says the Lord of Hosts. 'See if I will not open the floodgates of heaven and pour out a blessing for you without measure'" (Mal. 3:10).

Someone has said, "The person who lives in fear of giving away too much often finds that what he has kept for himself is too little to live upon." So hear these words recorded in Deuteronomy 15:10—"Give to him, and don't have a stingy heart when you give, and because of this the Lord your God will bless you in all your work and in everything you do."

A Bible-based giving attitude develops a Bible-based receiving attitude. Jesus said, in some of His only words recorded outside the Gospels, "It is more blessed to give than to receive" (Acts 20:35). Unfortunately, too many people in our world know only how to receive. Again, a prevalent teaching in some circles is that you "give to get." You can learn much about a person by examining his motives and expectations concerning personal giving.

The joy of giving comes when you learn how to give, and this joy can be tested. But you have the ability to take the test now and experience unspeakable joy. "Each person should do as he has decided in his heart—not out of regret or out of necessity, for God loves a cheerful giver" (2 Cor. 9:7).

Late one evening Jane and I were watching a guest appearance of Bill Wilson on a Christian television channel. As I often do at this hour, I drifted off to sleep while Jane continued to watch. Some time later Jane observed that I had awakened, and she really got my attention with these words: "Guess what! We just bought a bus!"

Quickly I was wide awake for what was a priceless moment. Jane's excitement in giving—her passion for what this bus represented—was contagious. You see, no one has a heart for the street kids of New York City like Bill Wilson. This vehicle would be used to share with the less fortunate the love and care of Jesus. Just thinking about it, our joy was exploding! Now *that's* hilarious giving and living.

John Wesley, founder of the Methodist movement, a forerunner of the United Methodist Church, exhibited a lifestyle of giving. Bishop Kenneth L. Carder said of him, "Sharing material goods was a cornerstone of his Christian faith."

I read about John Wesley's model for giving. He established for himself a modest standard of living; then he would give away everything else. Bishop Carder also said, "When Wesley was young, he earned 30 pounds (about $4.00) a year, but found he needed only 28 on which to live. So he gave away 2 pounds. As his earnings increased, he continued to live on 28 pounds"—giving away the rest.

Now, *that* is "journey *for* life" giving!

This is not some impersonal exercise or formula to be followed, like paying the rent or mortgage payment and other monthly bills. This is an authentic lifestyle motivated by a person's love for God, prompted by the needs of others, and having the knowledge that in a lifestyle of giving you cannot outgive God.

Tommy Barnett, pastor of one of America's great churches, sold his retirement dream property in Flagstaff, Arizona, and gifted the proceeds to start the Los Angeles Dream Center. This center has become an incubator for multiple life-enhancing "Dream Centers" across America. In my mind, that's not retiring; that's refiring.

But don't try to emulate a lifestyle that is a contradiction to the life you live. It should be an extension of your heart and growing character, not an artificial add-on meant primarily to draw attention to yourself.

In the early church, Luke wrote about a lifestyle of giving: "No one said that any of his possessions was his own, but instead they held everything in common. For there was not a needy person among them, because all those who owned lands or houses sold them, brought the proceeds of the things that were sold, and laid them at the apostles' feet. This was then distributed to each person as anyone had a need" (Acts 4:32, 34–35).

Caught up in the emotion of the time, a man named Ananias, together with his wife Sapphira, sold a piece of property. But "he kept back part of the proceeds with his wife's knowledge, and brought a portion of it and laid it at the apostles' feet" (Acts 5:2). This lie to God and fellow Christians cost Ananias and Sapphira their lives.

High-profile giving is characteristic of the journey *of* life. The focus is often upon the philanthropy of the donor and the amount or nature of the gift rather than the worthiness of the cause. But God has a different test: a test of obedience and faithfulness to His command.

I was taught that the biblical directive for giving is to give a tithe. I have learned, however, that this is only the first step of stewardship.

Giving a tithe to God is a way of saying that all we call ours is a gift and trust from God. On the journey *for* life, the point is not that 10 percent is God's and 90 percent is ours. *Everything* belongs to God! By following the lifestyle of giving, when a person gives a tithe, it is a token, a testimony, that we also commit the 90 percent to Him.

I personally experience the results that come from "journey *for* life" giving, and I like that part of the equation. But even this satisfaction pales in comparison to the joy of giving. In the lifestyle of giving, we are managers of His resources, and our perspective about that role must be properly assessed. The basic principle of stewardship is that all things belong to God. David wrote, "The earth is the Lord's, and the fullness thereof" (Ps. 24:1 KJV). Giving is one attribute of God that man receives because he is created in the image of God.

Good stewards follow God's commands and prioritize their giving. The Bible teaches "firstfruits" giving, which means giving off the top, first to God.

Nido Qubein's life exemplifies the lifestyle of giving. What a story! Nido came to the United States as a teenager with little knowledge of English, about fifty dollars in his pocket, and a praying Mom left behind. This intrepid immigrant has now received the highest awards in professional speaking, and Nido is founder and chairman emeritus of the National Speakers Association Foundation.

Nido says, "What matters most in my life is stewardship." A life example of his stewardship occurred recently when he accepted the appointment as president of High Point University. This personal choice—at the peak of his career—raised many questions, but decisions like this are the seeds of success on the journey *for* life.

Nido is my friend. I served with him on the board of directors of BB&T Corporation, a Fortune 500 financial corporation exceeding $120 billion in assets. I am inspired by his philanthropy and dwarfed by his many accomplishments. Nido not only exemplifies the lifestyle of giving, but his example also challenges and inspires others to give. I am challenged by his lifestyle of giving.

Nido says, "You give not because you have to, not because you owe it, but rather out of a heart of gratitude. God is not pleased with people who simply give back. People who view their stewardship as a role in giving back miss the point. Significance focuses on giving, Period. Not giving back. Not giving as payment. It's not that giving back is in itself a bad thing, but it's when you graduate from *giving back* to *giving* that you arrive at the zenith of true pleasure."

William Barclay, the Scottish theologian said something about giving: "Always give without remembering. Always receive without forgetting."

Nido shares his formula for how he spends his time: "I invest one-third of my life in earning; you have to earn resources if you want to be able to give resources. I invest one-third of my life in learning; I read thirty or forty periodicals and at least a few books every week. And I invest one-third of my life in giving and serving. My point here is not to brag but to illustrate that giving has to be a pattern, not just an event. It has to be a way of life."

God is not a 10 percent God. We must be very careful in teaching tithing and be sure that we are reminded that we are stewards of all, the nine-tenths as well as the one-tenth. How we handle money shows whether we are controlled by self or Christ. Lest we get hung up on money, stewardship involves more than the money we give.

A woman asked her husband, "Would you give me a little money?" He replied, "How little?" As we grow in stewardship on the journey *for* life, our promptings will be not *how little* but *how much* we can give.

Firstfruits giving—giving off the top—will more than meet "all our needs." Accept God's challenge. Be bold in giving. And prove God now. To do so is not a lack of faith.

A serious look at the cost of Calvary should cause any greed in the human heart to evaporate, enabling a vision of the true heart of God. On the cross He was 100 percent God. There "He died for all so that those who live should no longer live for themselves, but for the One who died for them and was raised" (2 Cor. 5:15).

I read that one out of every six verses in the Gospels deals with our possessions. The lifestyle of giving on the journey *for* life embraces more than money and possessions. It embraces all of life.

Give Time

How do you tithe your time? Work is necessary, sleep is essential. But how do we use our two and a half days of free time per week? William James said, "The great use of life is to spend it for something that will outlast it."

Focused giving is not always giving money. Often, our best gift to God or another person is the gift of time. Dr. Jimmy Harley, associate pastor of Taylors First Baptist Church in Taylors, South Carolina, shared the following example with me:

Vince Cervera is an effective evangelist in Greenville, South Carolina. Many years ago he told how as a young preacher he did not give serious attention to the invitation to accept Christ at the conclusion of his message. However, his attitude changed quickly. One night after a service, a young man came to him and said, "Mr. Cervera, I am lost and was planning to come forward on the second stanza, but you stopped the invitation after one stanza."

Then the young man said, "Mr. Cervera, will you tell me right now how to be saved?" Vince said he patted him on the shoulder and said, "Come back tomorrow night, and maybe the Holy Spirit will speak to you." The young man turned, walked out the front door, down the steps, got on a motorcycle, and started home. He ran under a logging truck, and his life was taken instantly. Vince said he then realized the urgency of what he was doing, and since that time he has always said to a congregation, "*You* will determine when we close the invitation. As long as someone is coming, we will sing. Our work is urgent."

Take time to listen. Time is necessary to really listen, to really hear the heart of someone. Develop this gift. A hearing heart is a caring heart. Your gift of time will enable you to be God's hands extended, meeting the need of many on the journey *of* life and of fellow travelers in need on the journey *for* life. Also, it may take time for the intended recipient to get beyond his pride and sense the sincerity of your heart in order to receive God's grace gift sent through you. That's the full circle of "journey *for* life" giving.

This is not meant to be high-profile giving. "Journey *for* life" giving is not yielding to pressure tactics of skilled solicitors. My friend, the late John Noseworthy, was a gifted fund-raiser. I heard him address a group as follows: "How many of you believe in the hereafter?" Everyone lifted their hand. John replied: "I'm *here after* your money."

Consider the pastor who addressed his congregation as follows: "I have some good news and bad news. The good news is, we have enough money to pay for our new building project. The bad news is, it's still in your pockets."

Characteristics of Giving

- "Journey *for* life" giving enables a person to say "no" gracefully to some requests, and be as spiritual in God's eyes as when on other occasions he or she is prompted by God to say "yes."
- "Journey *for* life" giving involves an inner knowing, a witness within that is not easy to resist.
- "Journey *for* life" giving is not motivated by what others give. Competing with others is not the measure.
- "Journey *for* life" giving does not first consider the tax benefits or consequences of giving.
- "Journey *for* life" giving does not let "your left hand know what your right hand is doing, so that your giving may be in secret" (Matt. 6:3–4).
- "Journey *for* life" giving is sacrificial.
- "Journey *for* life" giving is "now" giving. Samuel Johnson said, "He who waits to do a great deal at once will never do anything."
- "Journey *for* life" giving is prompted by God—in God's time, in God's way, for God's purpose.
- "Journey *for* life" giving is one of God's ways to support the downtrodden, the poor, and the needy; however, it will never be the most publicized gift you could make. The accolades may be few, but the personal satisfaction gained will be most gratifying. John Bunyan in *The Pilgrim's Progress* wrote: "You have not lived until you have done something for someone who cannot pay you back."

How many needy people are forgotten because no public campaign includes their needs? "The least of one of these" is still an object of God's care and concern. Where would the Salvation Army be, for example, without "journey *for* life" giving?

Allow God to speak to you about your giving. As you follow His guidance, you will have that inner knowing and peace about your gifts to God and experience joy unspeakable and hilarious living.

On the journey *for* life, the Holy Spirit will enable you to be aware of life's hurts, despair, grief, and conflicts that inflict others. Given this awareness, you will find fulfillment as you are challenged to creatively make a difference in another person's life. Where you are right now, you may be at the point of someone's urgent need. Reach out where it really counts and be God's hand extended to meet someone's need.

Are we accountable for our stewardship giving? Some slough it off by saying, "I am not responsible after the gift leaves my hand." Yes you are! Research before giving—before you release your gift. Know where your gift is going. Due diligence is a necessary component of good stewardship.

"Journey *for* life" giving is sacrificial giving. "Give until it hurts" is not what it's about. You give until it feels good. Jesus said, "Give, and it will be given to you; a good measure—pressed down, shaken together, and running over—will be poured into your lap. For with the measure you use, it will be measured back to you" (Luke 6:38).

I am convinced that strategic, focused giving by those who travel on the journey *for* life can impact the world and make a difference. It will happen as each one of us becomes a faithful steward in our assigned role. In 1 Corinthians 3:6, Paul wrote: "I planted, Apollos watered, but God gave the growth." You will never know how to *live* until you know how to *give*. In receiving, a person is never to be a reservoir but a channel, much like a public water system—not static, but always flowing.

Water is essential to life. Sometimes the distance from the source to the recipient covers many miles, but as it flows it continues to meet the needs of life. All God's blessings that we receive are given to enable us to meet the need of others in His name.

Giving is one evidence of God's grace at work in our lives. It is characteristic of all that God is, and it should be characteristic of His people are as we represent Him.

"Journey *for* life" giving should also be stress-free. Jesus said, "Freely ye have received, freely give" (Matt. 10:8 KJV).

A physician, vacationing in the sparsely inhabited Cumberland Mountains, stopped at a humble cabin to request a drink of water. He was greeted by a young girl who, handing him a glass asked, "Wouldn't you like to have a glass of cold milk?" It was an appealing offer the doctor could not turn down. He drank the refreshing milk, and not wanting to appear ungrateful, offered to pay for it. The radiant young girl replied, "No, we like to share."

Two years later this young girl, dangerously ill, was admitted to Johns Hopkins Hospital in Baltimore, Maryland, for a very difficult operation. After the surgery her parents, being quite poor, worried over the prospective bill. Upon preparing to leave the hospital, the girl was handed a statement for the surgery with a note written across it: "Paid by a glass of cold milk."

An anonymous poet wrote:

> I do not know how long I'll live
> But while I live, Lord, let me give
> Some comfort to someone in need
> By smile or nod, kind word or deed

And let me do what else I can
To ease things for my fellow man.
I want naught but to do my part
To lift a tired or weary heart,
To change folks' frowns to smiles again
Then I will not have lived in vain
And I'll not care how long I'll live
If I can give—and give—and give.

How blessed we are to be able to give. How blessed we are when we give.

As Americans, materialism is ingrained in our minds almost from birth. Eternal values are often neglected while we spend our time making money to satisfy our temporal appetites. Jesus illustrated this in a story of a young ruler. You and I may not be challenged to "sell our goods," but we often need to be reminded of Jesus' admonition: "Where your treasure is, there your heart will be also" (Matt. 6:21).

The way out of fear and doubt is through giving. The blessings promised by God to those who are obedient in stewardship are more credit worthy and secure than a U.S. Government-backed FDIC Insured Account. "Heaven and earth will pass away" before His word fails.

Circumstances and conditions are never attached to God's promises—only obedience. Nevertheless, our giving is one way to be assured of receiving what God has promised. In Matthew 6:19–20, Jesus said, "Don't collect for yourselves treasures on earth, where moth and rust destroy and where thieves break in and steal. But collect for yourselves treasures in heaven, where neither moth nor rust destroys, and where thieves don't break in and steal."

What have you wanted to do for Christ and others that you have not yet done?

> It's not what you'd do with millions
> If riches should e'er be your lot
> But what are you doing at present
> With the dollar and quarter you've got?

Julian LeGrande, one of the richest merchants that Paris ever knew, hit on hard times during one of the great depressions in France. His big stores were in need of $100,000 in cash. Julian went out to borrow it, but neither the banks nor his friends had any money. All day long he looked in vain, and he came back thinking, "Have I been in business for forty years, have I built up a chain of great stores, and now cannot even borrow $100,000, and the business may go under for the lack of this small sum, when we've taken in millions of dollars in a single year?" But there is more to this story.

Julian LeGrande said, "I was sitting in my office at sundown when a knock came on my door, and without lifting my head, I called, 'Come in.' The door opened, and a very striking, handsome man stood there. He was faultlessly attired, and he said, 'Julian LeGrande?'

"I answered, 'Yes, sir, but you have the advantage of me.'

"He said, 'You probably would not know my name, but I'll tell you in a moment or two what it is. I understand that you need some money.'

"'Yes, sir, I do.'"

"'How much do you need?'"

"'I need a hundred thousand dollars.'"

"'Well,' he said, 'if you will write your note for a hundred thousand dollars for a year with no interest, I'll give you my check for it. You can get the money from the bank tomorrow morning.' I got up slowly, my mouth hanging open, and I said, 'My friend, who in the world are you, and why do you do this?'

"He answered, 'Mr. LeGrande, my name is _____. I live in America now, but there was a time when I lived here, and I went to school here. You were Commissioner of Education, and you came to hear the final examination of our graduating class, and you helped give us our marks on our last speeches before the assembly. I was ragged, for I was of a very poor family. There were some rich boys, and I thought surely you would talk to some of them and commend them, but when I had finished, and the exercises were over, you came and laid your hand on my head and tilted it back so you could look into my face. You said, "Young man, you have something that the world needs. You can do better than you did today. It's in you. You can do better. You can do most anything you want to do if you set your heart on it. Now, make a man of yourself." You wouldn't remember those words, but every time I topped some achievement—and I'm very wealthy now—I've said, "Thank you, Mr. Julian LeGrande." And this day I have the pleasure of giving you a check for a hundred thousand dollars, just a tiny interest payment on what you have meant to me.'"

"Apples of gold in baskets of silver"—what wonderful words of encouragement—as are these words from Henry Wadsworth Longfellow:

The Arrow and the Song
I shot an arrow into the air,
It fell to earth, I knew not where.
But long years after, in the heart of an oak,
I found my arrow still unbroken.

I breathed a song into the air,
It fell to earth, I knew not where.
But long years after, in the heart of a friend,
I found my song from beginning to end.

While we should never be thinking of the dividends that come to us from our words of encouragement and appreciation to others, God thinks of them, and He who sees in secret rewards us openly. Life will be so much happier and better for those around us if we will just think and take time to say the nice, cheery things to the people who need them. Where is the man who has not hugged some compliment to his heart and brought it out in the dark hours to let it light his way? Someone has said, "We will cross over a busy street just to pass and speak to someone who has said something nice about us, but we will walk around the block to miss coming face-to-face with someone who has criticized us."

Distinguish yourself by your lifestyle of giving.

The God of the Inexhaustible Supply

Many experiences of life as chronicled in the Bible illustrate this truth. On the journey *for* life, no traveler is promised that he will never experience the extremes of life. Trust me, there will be perplexities and troubles. Not even Jesus was exempt from them. "For we do not have a high priest who is unable to sympathize with our weaknesses, but One who has been tested in every way as we are, yet without sin" (Heb. 4:15). John 16:33 says, "I have told you these things so that in Me you may have peace. You will have suffering in this world. Be courageous! I have conquered the world."

Throughout time, God's servants have witnessed God's deliverance from life's direst circumstances. Life, including spiritual life, has its highs and lows. Often the valley experience is encountered on the heels of a mountaintop experience. It doesn't take long for life's storms to develop; nevertheless, you need not fear. God has promised to be with us wherever life takes us. Our God is *Jehovah-jireh*—the God who supplies.

Consider Elijah. His life abounds with supernatural provision from God's inexhaustible supply. Elijah delivered God's word of a coming drought and famine, and because of his faithfulness to God, his life was threatened by godless King Ahab.

In that extreme period, Elijah's obedience to God was the key that accessed God's protection and inexhaustible supply. When the famine came that Elijah had foretold and the rest of the world was parched with drought, he was led by an angel to his own private water source. While there, God directed the ravens to bring him bread and meat in the morning, and bread and meat in the evening. But some time later, the brook dried up.

What would Elijah do? What would God do?

God would tell Elijah what to do, and Elijah would obey. The brook may have dried up, but not God's resources. This time, God's inexhaustible supply would come through a widow in Zerephath. All she had was an obedient heart, a handful of flour in a jar, and a little oil in a jug, which she intended to prepare for her and her son. Elijah said to her:

> Don't be afraid; go and do as you have said. Only make me a small loaf from it and bring it out to me. Afterwards, you may make some for yourself and your son, for this is what the LORD God of Israel says: "The flour jar will not become empty and the oil jug will not run dry until the day the LORD sends rain on the surface of the land." (1 Kings 17:13–14)

Obedience to God's Word and His guidance—even when the cupboard is bare—transcends the natural order and opens the supernatural flow of God's inexhaustible supply for the totality of man's need. This widow gave out of her need. From her last meal she gave first, and "the flour jar did not become empty, and the oil jug did not run dry" (1 Kings 17:16).

Many times the only way God manifests Himself is at man's extreme need. Too often, that is the only time man calls upon God.

Are you at such a place in your life? Are you experiencing the empty cupboard? If so, trust Him. God will supply your need even though it may not be through what others think is the normal way. Remember, it was the ravens that fed Elijah. When your brook dries up, God still has His source. In Psalm 9:10, David wrote: "Those who know Your name trust in You because You have not abandoned those who seek You, LORD."

But you reply, "Those were Bible times." Even so, God did not die when the Old Testament canon was completed. Yes, there was a long period of silence but never a time of His absence. Even then, the reason for His silence was man's disregard for God rather than a lack of concern by God.

God Is Always Aware of Human Need

Peter and others of the disciples had fished all night without catching anything. Early in the morning, Jesus called out to them, "You don't have any fish, do you?"

"No," they answered.

"Cast the net on the right side of the boat," He told them, "and you'll find some" (John 21:5–6). When they did, they had such a large catch that they were unable to haul the net in—a net-tearing, boat-sinking load.

How many of us approach life on the wrong side of our boat? We become discouraged. We give up too soon, and we are too soon satisfied.

Many of the travelers to the Promised Land wanted to settle before arriving there. Is that not like many of us traveling on the journey *for* life?

How many times have you heard someone say: "I've never had it this good" and then became satisfied and useless? I often ask a friend, "How are things?" He replies, "Better than I deserve." Listen, how good you have it is not the measure for success on the journey *for* life. The measure is God's Word, God's promises, and your obedience.

On the other hand, life is not adequate for those who lack personal commitment, thinking the world owes them the best of life and demand more. They presume on life. Often they are proponents of a self-gratifying prosperity gospel. That is not the gospel that placed Jesus on a cross. The gospel for which Jesus gave His life is an all-sufficient provision for the totality of life's need. Most Christians live below the provision line—the need line—God has established.

This is the message to which we are called. Those who travel on the journey *for* life are the called, the anointed. They are the conduit, the pipeline, the delivery vessel to those God blesses and prospers in His sovereignty.

In my life's adversities, when others didn't understand or care—this is the God I have called upon.

Objections are often voiced here: "That's not what God does. Why bother Him?"

But when did God ever hint that His provision for man is limited only to man's spiritual need? Man cannot function in fulfilling God's call limited only to the spiritual realm. Man is a trinity—body, mind, and spirit. David speaks to this matter in the twenty-third Psalm: "The Lord is my shepherd; I shall not want" (Ps. 23:1 NKJV). I am intrigued by the following interpretation: "The Lord is my shepherd; what else could I want?"

On the journey *for* life—even at life's extremity—the Lord God of the universe is only a petition and prayer away. Prove it! Call on Him now! Solomon wrote: "Trust in the LORD with all your heart, and do not rely on your own understanding; think about Him in all your ways, and He will guide you on the right paths" (Prov. 3:5–6).

I have often experienced God at the point of personal need. You, too, can trust God to meet your need, whether it be life's daily need or some extreme need. God's promise is sufficient.

You may ask, "Where is God today? All the happenings are so distant. What about me, my need?" Don't trust in what you can see. Don't put your hope in wealth, which is so uncertain. Trust the God who supplies. God is in control. He can be trusted.

> What is it you want from God?
> What is it you want to do for God?

Don't expect God to release His guidance or resources to you when you are not in relationship with Him. It is in that relationship you find joy beyond reason and a hilarious life.

It is easy to get ahead of God in business ventures. Because of my haste, I've prayed more to God about getting me through (or out of) deals more than I have prayed about getting into deals. Take time to inquire: Is God in it? Does God want me in this deal?

There are deals that may be good but not best for me. I've had to learn the hard way that I can't participate in every good deal.

Pray about it. Does God want you to do it? Make decisions only after praying about them. Praying time is not wasted time. Remember, you are praying to the Almighty God whose store-houses are full. God's best often comes to those who wait.

Due diligence is essential—even when you risk losing the deal. Don't venture into areas outside your area of expertise unless you are called there. Another good strategy to learn early: Don't keep feeding a dead horse.

God's provision will enable you to accomplish all He has called you to do, and He will enable you to do all that is in your heart as you stay surrendered to Him.

Never stop giving!

"CAN YOU HEAR ME NOW?"

Lessons in Communication

*W*e are all familiar with the TV commercial that begins with the question: "Can You Hear Me Now?" Our culture is entertained and propagandized by clever media advertising seeking a listening moment.

However, there is a difference between hearing and listening. To hear is to perceive or to sense sound. To listen is to make a conscious effort to hear. You can hear without listening. We should learn the art of good listening.

What a person hears is not always what has been spoken. According to Peter F. Drucker, the most important thing in communication is to hear what *isn't* being said. As someone has said, "Home is where you can say anything you like, because nobody listens to you anyway."

Our listening filters are not always appropriately tuned to facilitate good hearing. I've heard someone wisecrack, "My wife says I never listen to her. At least I think that's what she said."

To listen well, a person must focus and pay attention to the person speaking. The message to be conveyed is not always in a boisterous, commanding voice. Sometimes the message is given in deliberately soft tones—"a still small voice," as referenced in 1 Kings 19:12 (KJV).

Did you hear about the minister's outline notes? On the side margin he had written: "Raise voice—weak point." The strong points usually come in a whisper.

We have all heard, "Stop, look, and listen." Stopping and looking may be relatively easy, but listening is definitely difficult. This has forever been the challenge of God's people. The prophets often wrote, "Hear the word of the Lord." We are often challenged to hear words of wisdom from parents, teachers, friends, and people of authority. I have learned more with my mouth shut and my ears open than any other way. Learning to listen is high on my list of "Things I Wish I Had Learned Sooner."

By the way, I read that women like silent men. They think they are listening.

How to Become a Better Listener

One leadership expert says, "A good listener tries to understand thoroughly what the other person is saying. In the end he may disagree sharply, but before he disagrees, he wants to know exactly what it is he is disagreeing with."[8]

Epictetus, a Greek philosopher around AD 50, is often quoted as being the one who said: "We have one tongue and two ears that we may hear twice as much as we speak." Another consideration might be that we have two ears because God knew that listening was twice as hard as speaking.

James wrote: "Everyone must be quick to hear, slow to speak, and slow to anger" (James 1:19). We are taught how to speak, and we learn well. However, we are deficient in our ability to listen.

Talking is not nearly the skill that listening is. Calvin Coolidge said, "No man ever listened himself out of a job." Observe the many talk shows on radio and TV. We need to develop appropriate listening filters, especially in that arena, to filter out all the garbage being spoken. But critics retort, "Free speech is our constitutional right." So, likewise, we can exercise our constitutional right to use the OFF control.

I'm constantly trying to improve my listening skills. A person cannot become an effective listener by impatiently opening his mouth, trying to help another person finish conveying his thought or comment. If you feel you must interrupt someone speaking, *don't!* It is much more courteous to take notes for later comment as you listen. And sometimes it is important to recognize that people need an ear more than a word.

Developing *listening* skills and becoming an effective listener are acquired skills. These skills should be taught and developed early in life, and they should be honed as an essential skill for personal development and growth. Elementary school teachers struggle for ways to challenge and teach the minds of the young and restless when they are inattentive. From these early lessons, a major accomplishment in the growth process is observed as children grow out of childhood into a selfless servant role of concern for others. What a challenging and necessary vocation is teaching.

The human brain works about four times as fast as the mouth. This is why the dictionary characterizes listening as an art. Work at developing the lost art of listening. Listening is vital to success.

Listening should be considered as a tool. Just as an artist develops and improves his skill with a brush, a musician with his bow, and a craftsman with the tools of his trade, the art of listening is developed and enhanced by practice. One of life's greatest accomplishments is to become an effective listener. Often the greatest need of a person is for someone just to be there and listen to them. Most prolific talkers are focused on themselves. When a person listens attentively, the focus is on others.

Allow me to share a laugh with you: Did you hear about the man who had not spoken to his wife in eighteen months? He didn't want to interrupt her.

The late Dr. Bill Bright, founder of Campus Crusade, told a story that goes something like this: "Don't ask him how he feels, or he'll tell you and you'll be late for supper."

On the way home with Jane after teaching our Sunday school class, I told her of the many favorable comments from class members concerning the lesson. Jane's reply was: "Yes, but *they* haven't been listening to you all week."

Tongue control is the first step in developing effective listening skills. According to M. Scott Peck, "You cannot truly listen to anyone and do anything else at the same time."

Pollsters tell us that the average American has about thirty conversations per day and spends twenty percent of his or her life talking. (I'm not sure the pollsters took into account some people I know very well.) We are told that the annual conversations of most individuals would fill about sixty-six books of eight hundred pages each.

From the moment we begin talking coherently, we learn quickly that our tongue can get us in a lot of trouble. Nevertheless, some people go through life without learning this lesson. As the saying goes, "Men who know little say much; men who know much say little."

Learn to control your tongue. Have you ever said something to another person that you wish you had not said? Perhaps at the time you knew it was something you should not say. A good rule to follow if you must write that letter or send that e-mail is to follow the rule of "overnight settling." Write it if you must, but sleep on it before you actually mail the letter or push the send button. Larry Estridge, an outstanding attorney in Greenville, shared a personal story that illustrates the value of following this rule:

> E-mails to your partners and associates can be very misleading and can create unnecessary ill feelings. I learned this lesson in a vivid way shortly after learning to use the intra-office e-mail system in my former law firm.
>
> Late one afternoon, I received a message from one of my partners. He was asking us to allow him the flexibility to make a career change but to keep the door open for a return if things did not work out to his satisfaction. He had been through a similar cycle a couple of times in the past.
>
> I quickly typed a response which reflected my initial frustration with his request. I accused him of being selfish and callous to the welfare of the firm and his partners. I pushed the infamous "SEND" button and left the office.
>
> On my way home, I reflected on my response. I realized that I had been influenced by an impulsive, negative reaction to his written request. I would never have said to him in person exactly what I said to him in writing. I had made a mistake! The next morning I got to the office early and planted myself outside his door. When he arrived at the office, I confessed to

him that I had responded to his e-mail without giving the matter adequate consideration. I also told him that this was not the type of dialogue I wanted to have with my own partners through electronic means. At my request, we went into his office together so that he could delete my response without reading it. Over a cup of coffee, we had a face-to-face dialogue in which I expressed my feelings in a constructive manner, received his feedback, and completed our discussion with no damage to our personal friendship.

Following that meeting, I adopted a policy about e-mails which has served me well over the years. If I have anything negative to say about my partners, business associates, or clients, I will first endeavor to express my feelings in a person-to-person meeting. If that is not possible and the circumstances call for a more immediate, electronic response, I compose a message on my computer. However, I "sleep on it" one full night before deciding whether or not to send it. When I come back into the office the next morning, I re-read the message and then make a decision as to whether to send it. More often than not, the original message is substantially modified or deleted in its entirety.

In a recent *New York Times* article entitled "E-mail Is Easy to Write (and to Misread)," the author expressed quite eloquently one of the limitations with e-mail: "In contrast to a phone call or talking in person, e-mail can be emotionally impoverished when it comes to nonverbal messages that add nuance and valence to our words. The typed words are denuded of the rich emotional contest we convey in person or over the phone."[9]

Who Is in Control of Your Tongue?

How many times have I wished I could take back hurtful words I had spoken? In time, broken bones and bruises heal, but there is no perfect healing to the spirit of the one to whom callous and insensitive words were spoken. Even though words spoken cannot be retracted, restitution and reconciliation should be attempted.

In Proverbs 12:15, the wise man said, "A fool's way is right in his own eyes, but whoever listens to counsel is wise." How many times have I opened my mouth and closed my ears. Nothing is opened more by mistake than the mouth.

In Proverbs 17:28 we read, "Even a fool is considered wise when he keeps silent, discerning, when he seals his lips."

My nature has been to butt in too often when someone else is speaking. Someone had it right when he said, "Some people just keep on talking while I am trying to interrupt." It is extremely important to learn the negative message this sends to others. It says, "I'm not really interested in what you are saying. Something more important has my attention."

Tongue control can only come about by being responsive to the Holy Spirit. If men would just control their tongues, great good would come to our world. In James 3, we are reminded that we all stumble at times. Friends—even Christian friends—can allow spoken words to create hard feelings causing separation. James says:

> Now when we put bits into the mouths of horses to make them obey us, we also guide the whole animal. And consider ships: though very large and driven by fierce winds, they are guided by a very small rudder wherever the will of the pilot directs. So too, though the tongue is a small part of the body, it boasts

great things. Consider how large a forest a small fire ignites. And the tongue is a fire. The tongue, a world of unrighteousness, is placed among the parts of our bodies; it pollutes the whole body, sets the course of life on fire, and is set on fire by hell. (James 3:3–6)

The greatest obstacle we face in life's relationships and in advancing in our careers is our tongue. Success on the journey *for* life will be proportionate to how adept you become as an effective listener. Mark Twain wrote: "When I was a boy of fourteen, my father was so ignorant I could hardly stand to have the old man around. But when I got to be twenty-one, I was astonished at how much the old man had learned in seven years."

Obviously, it took Mark Twain seven years to acquire the art of effective listening. Charles Wadsworth said, "By the time a man realizes his father was right, he usually has a son who thinks he's wrong." It never ceases to amaze me how much I learn when I listen.

Come Near

When your ears are sensitive to a beaconing, inviting voice, listen. Be alert and move in the direction of the person speaking. On the journey *for* life, always be sensitive for the voice of God. When prompted, move in His direction. James wrote: "Draw near to God, and He will draw near to you" (James 4:8).

What must a speaker do to capture the attention of an audience? A casual observation of almost any audience or classroom, regardless of the number of people, is very revealing of America's developing culture. Our ever-present communication devices challenge our attention. Fingers fly across the keyboards of laptops. Thumbs chase the letters on the Blackberrys. Text messaging never ends on the variety of PDAs available. E-mails are sent and received.

Even in a one-on-one setting, take a quick glance toward your partner or associate and you will often observe him checking his Blackberry. In route from one meeting to the next, whether walking or in a taxi, fingers fly or the Bluetooth connection keeps hands free for other activities. For those less challenged to communicate, Gameboys are in hand to pass the time.

When it is required that all devices be shut down in an upscale restaurant or upon entering the grounds of a prestigious golf club, the trauma is comparable to a withdrawal experience.

With all the technological advances that keep us globally in touch, why gather in conferences, conventions and other arenas? Are we so *in touch* that we are *out of touch*? Are we so dependent and traumatized that we no longer have any attention span for pure, wholesome, intimate, interpersonal relationships? More and more, we are becoming a people whose intimacy is with our devices. We are human, but we act as if we are zombies and robots. Our devices link us to humans or to objects that represent them—provided we have the access addresses, numbers, or codes.

In our homes, children spend hours text messaging on their cells. Parents do e-mail while talking with their children or while having dinner. They talk on the cell phone while driving them to a game or event.

Wake up! Hear me! Where have our priorities gone? It seems that our interpersonal skills have gone down at a greater speed than our technological communication advances have accelerated—and this at the cost of taking us away from our real self. Paul wrote to the Romans: "It is already the hour for you to wake up from sleep" (Rom. 13:11).

This is not directed to those on the journey *of* life, even though it applies there. This is a challenge to those of us on the journey *for* life. The journey *for* life is a way of relational life. We give lip service to it, but do we believe it? Are we practicing it?

It is time we recommit, reconnect, and get in touch.

First, retire to a quiet place with all distractions and obstructions closed out. You will never hear God clearly in the clutter of the routine. To hear God clearly, turn off the radio, the television, the DVD. Find a private place where you can be alone and get in touch with yourself. Initially, this may be a painful and traumatic experience; nevertheless, it is out of silence that we will realize the urgency to reconnect. An African proverb may be applicable here: "Much silence makes a powerful noise."

Next, reconnect with our relational God.

Then, reconnect with those closest to you. This will require courage and resolve. Courage is the attitude of facing anything dangerous, difficult, or painful instead of withdrawing from it. Winston Churchill said, "Courage is what it takes to stand up and speak; courage is also what it takes to sit down and listen."

We get in touch and reconnect by listening. Begin the process "cold turkey"—without your cell phone, PDA, or laptop. This will get the attention of those closest to you. There may be unlimited time available to you on your devices, but at what cost? Transfer this time to the account of relationships that really matter.

What have we missed by becoming so relationally starved?

- The inspiration of others.
- The challenge to open up one on one.
- The contagion of the passion of others.
- The ability to be doers, not just hearers.

We have also lost the reality that life is not a machine. A machine will never inspire a person to the ultimate reality of the great hope in Jesus Christ.

In order to succeed on the journey *for* life, you must listen to God. Sometimes God speaks by promptings—an impression in your mind, your heart, your spirit. Do you often feel or sense something you ought to do or say or somewhere you ought to be? Practice listening for these kinds of promptings by God's Spirit. Often God prompts a person to share his or her experience. Write these promptings down. Remind yourself often of how God spoke to you as you transitioned from the journey *of* life to the journey *for* life.

Listen to God as you read the Bible. My practice is to quietly invite the Holy Spirit who inspired the Scriptures to illumine my mind and spirit to listen to what God is saying as I read. God will speak to you as you read the Bible. God speaks through His Word, not psychics or horoscopes.

Most of us speak to God; however, few of us listen to God. God listens to us when we pray, and we should listen to God in prayer. When you pray, pray as if someone is listening, because Someone is! God listens to our prayers. Prayer is not complete until we reciprocate.

We listen to God by allowing the Holy Spirit who resides in a believer to "teach you all things and remind you of everything I have told you" (John 14:26).

He is real—listen to Him.

Observe Circumstances

We listen to God by observing circumstances. There are providential occurrences in life. Observe them. What is God saying to you?

We listen to God by becoming familiar with His voice. Jesus said, "I know My own sheep, and they know Me" (John 10:14). Still referring to Himself as the Good Shepherd, He said, "He calls his own sheep by name and leads them out" (John 10:3).

The psalmist wrote: "I love the LORD because He has heard my appeal for mercy. Because He has turned His ear to me, I will call out to Him as long as I live" (Ps. 116:1–2).

You can hear God by listening to others. Listen to others and test what they speak by what the Bible says. *You can hear God by listening to yourself.* In your quiet time, make notes of the thoughts and impressions you receive. Your heart speaks to you, even when your head tells you not to listen. The head may be the *hardware*, but the heart is the *software* for effective listening. A person receives from his heart the *program* for the control of his speech and his mind. Learn how to listen to your heart.

How We Listen to Others

Work at the art of listening.

- Give your undivided attention to the person speaking.
- Make eye contact with him; this will challenge him.
- Don't interrupt. Give the speaker time to complete his thought.
- Keep your mind focused.
- Pay attention to a speaker's questions. They are a clue that he is about to say something important. Since the speaker already knows the answer, his purpose is for *you* to know.
- Ask questions if you don't understand.

During his interim pastorate at First Presbyterian Church in Greenville, South Carolina, Dr. Walter A. Ray shared the following story concerning his mother:

> My mother lived till she was ninety-two, and died seven years ago. I always knew my mother loved me, and I always loved her. But we still had many fights. She would often say, "Walter, you are the most stubborn person I know!" We each had a lot of little things that seemed to irritate the other. Of course, I always thought she did more things to irritate me than I did to her. We had so many heated discussions that I had drawn up my boundaries for our relationship.
>
> Then something happened seventeen years ago that significantly altered those boundaries. My mother was 82 years old when this took place. My Mom and I were shopping at the mall. She loved to go shopping. We stopped for a Coke. And she told me about an incident that occurred when she was about nine years old. Her mother was having a party that evening. My mom had a sister Renee, who was one year older. My grandmother told my mother, "I am having some guests over for dinner. Your sister Renee can come out in the living room because she is pretty, but I don't want you to come out. I want you to stay in your room!"
>
> It must have been very difficult for my mother to grow up with a mother who would say that to her. This had a profound effect upon me. She had never told me anything this personal about her childhood. I don't know what prompted her that day, at the age of eighty-two, to tell me that story about her childhood, but I was glad she told me that. No wonder she might be a little overly sensitive and sometimes hard to get along with. If her mother had said that to her

on one occasion, I thought there were probably many other things like that her mother said to her. She had grown up wounded by her mother. I found myself softened toward my mother. It changed the way I dealt with her. I found myself treating my mother with more grace and forgiveness.

Maybe there is someone in your life you are having trouble getting along with: a spouse, son, daughter, parent, someone at work, another student at school. Maybe they have experienced something very difficult and painful in their life, something you do not know about, and maybe you could treat them with more grace. Is there anyone in your life that you could begin to treat with more grace? Ask God to help you treat that person with more grace, so that we can fulfill what our Lord taught us to pray: "Father, forgive us our debts, as we also have forgiven our debtors."

Listen. And be an encourager.

What is the reward of effective listening? Effective listening encourages a speaker to open up so that you can receive his best. "Wisdom is the reward you get for a lifetime of listening when you'd have preferred to talk."

Why Should I Become an Effective Listener?

There are many reasons to develop good listening skills. A good listener is often assumed to know more than he does, when an open mouth might remove all doubt.

Professionally, our careers are advanced when we master the art of effective listening. Proverbs 1:5 says, "A wise man will listen and increase his learning." By effective listening, you earn the right to be heard.

The most beneficial and lasting lessons in life come through personal experience. When you listen well, you come to better, more discerning conclusions. Therefore, listening is a first step toward success in life. To listen is not only courteous and respectful to others but can also be an effective tool for gaining knowledge and valuable information.

When I transitioned into commercial real estate, my knowledge was limited and my best learning tool became my ears. Develop the art of listening. Don't interrupt. When purchasing, you'll come out ahead. When selling, you'll leave less on the table.

Success in sales is not dependent on how fast you talk. Success just might come from how well you listen. Listen to the one you are trying to engage. Whatever your career path, the art of listening will enhance relationships and pay dividends on the journey. It just might be more important than talking.

Listening may not be in the college curriculum of an enterprising entrepreneur, but when properly developed, listening has the potential to positively impact the bottom line of any business enterprise. And you don't have to add personnel to the payroll to effect it!

I learned the importance of acquiring and developing listening skills early in my professional career, and even now continue to develop this asset. In the era of "The House that Jack Built," I had a significant niche in the Greenville, South Carolina, residential market. Jack E. Shaw Builders, Inc. (now Shaw Resources) was not only a builder of houses but also a developer of residential subdivisions. Today, Shaw Resources is a multi-faceted enterprise.

During the early years I developed a pretty good pipeline to executives being transferred to corporate headquarters in the upstate area of South Carolina. I had an early opportunity to introduce quite a number of those being transferred to the local real estate market and "The House that Jack Built."

One opportunity and challenge I especially remember was my introduction to Robert C. "Bob" Crawford, plant manager for Fiber Industries, Inc. On the day our meeting was scheduled, Bob, his wife, Louise, and I conferenced to discuss their housing needs. I listened well and confidently assured them, "I know the house you will buy."

Listening was the key.

Bob replied, "Let's go look." I drove Bob and Louise a short distance to our development and walked them through the house that I had concluded would meet the housing need for their family. Bob was impressed, but he softly resisted saying, "I'm not going to buy the first house I look at. Let's look at some others."

I obliged, and after visiting two or three other available "houses that Jack built," Bob said, "Why waste time? I've already seen the house we are going to buy. Let's go back there." Arriving there, the negotiations were brief, the completion details were agreed to, and the deal was sealed. I had listened to their needs, and this gave me the information I needed to find them a perfect match.

Sometime later, the mortgage loan officer asked me if Bob got a good deal on the house. My comment was: "He thought he did."

Needless to say, my friend, the loan officer, became a friend of Bob's, and he often repeated that comment to Bob. This event still brings a smile when we are reminded of it. (Incidentally, this was not the only house that Bob and Louise bought from Jack E. Shaw Builders, Inc.) Bob not only became a good resource for me, but also in the process we became great friends and business partners in several ventures. Louise has since passed away and Bob is now married to Mary Frances Barlow, whose first husband had also passed on. However, something must have been right with Bob and me. I think the relationship is strong because we respect and listen to each other. I was asked to be the "best man" at his wedding, yet today he still thinks he's the "best man."

As Oliver Wendell Holmes said, "It is the province of knowledge to speak, and it is the privilege of wisdom to listen."

Learn the fine art of listening. It will serve you well on the journey *for* life.

13

STRATEGIES THAT LEAD TO FREEDOM FROM CONFLICT

*L*ife on earth begins and ends with documents. Birth is acknowledged by the filing of a birth certificate. It is this document that establishes individual identity throughout life. When life is over, death is documented by a person of authority attesting as to the time and cause of death by filing a death certificate.

Between birth and death, life is governed by documents dealing with the issues of life and relationships. Where there is no law, chaos reigns. Think of how chaotic your life would be without established rules of law and order.

God the Creator is a covenant God. His covenant with man is recorded in the Bible. In the Garden of Eden, guidelines for living were established by God, and these guidelines have not been extinguished by time.

As time moved on and humankind increased, God continued to speak through prophets and inspired writers about how people should live in relationships on the journey *for* life. In Exodus 34:27, Moses wrote this command of God: "Write down these words, for I have made a covenant with you and with Israel based on these words."

The first document was therefore created.

God continues to communicate with man today. The New Testament writer in the book of Hebrews wrote: "Long ago God spoke to the fathers by the prophets at different times and in different ways. In these last days, He has spoken to us by His Son, whom He has appointed heir of all things and through whom He made the universe" (Heb. 1:1–2).

Following in chapter 2, he wrote: "We must therefore pay even more attention to what we have heard, so that we will not drift away. For if the message spoken through angels was legally binding, and every transgression and disobedience received a just punishment, how will we escape if we neglect such a great salvation?" (Heb. 2:1–3).

God is the God of documents. He documented His love for man in the Bible, where He said, "God is love" (1 John 4:16).

Documents and Relationships

What does it mean to *document?* The dictionary says: "to gather and report the details of relationships and understandings. A document is anything printed, written, etc., that contains information or is relied upon to record or prove something." Documents are foundational to establish laws and procedures for relational interaction in society.

Meaningful personal relationships often provide the basis for working together as partners or associates in life and in business, but—however well-intended the parties may be—an undocumented understanding of the terms of a working agreement has caused much misunderstanding, resulting in the demise of many friendships, partnerships, and professional associations.

In a bygone era, integrity counted. A man's word was his bond, and often a binding agreement was sealed by a handshake.

Integrity still counts. However, not everyone has integrity. Documents executed by a person of devious intent often cause devastating results.

Trusting relationships are important on the journey *of* life and are *essential* for travelers on the journey *for* life. One way trustworthy individuals can manifest their integrity is by following the steps and procedures necessary to formally and legally document their word and commitments to their partners and associates. Even then, conflicts may arise, and in such a situation documents can establish a starting point for resolving conflicts.

In God's eye, a handshake is as binding as an executed document. Many ventures get started via a handshake understanding prior to documents being formulated. Regardless of the status of formal documentation, in life—whether on the journey *of* life or the journey *for* life—"Your word is your bond." Guard it at all costs.

Due diligence should always precede the preparation of documents. Documentation should not be delayed. If documentation is delayed for some reason, contributions by the partners, members, or shareholders should be held up or placed in trust subject to specific guidelines and controls prior to being released to the venture.

It does not matter how good a deal you negotiate. You only have the deal you document. I offer this word of caution because circumstances can change for better or worse, causing other participants to want to renegotiate or reinterpret the terms and conditions of the relationship. Even among friends and acquaintances—people you know well and trust—conflicts can arise. When a conflict relates to money, authority, and control, it is only accentuated.

A joint venture partner of mine in several real estate developments informed me, "I can't do any more; give it back to the banks." This was not an anticipated outcome. As Christian brothers we had come together with desire and passion to advance the kingdom of God through a business partnership. In the beginning of the partnership, we could not acquire *enough* real estate. The bankers accommodated our enthusiasm and leveraged our personal resources significantly. What happened?

The financial markets changed. One thing is certain when you invest in real estate: do it for the long term. Financial markets are cyclical, and in what seemed overnight, the cycle changed. A good decision at one point in a credit cycle might become a bad decision at another point in the cycle.

The financial stress that this relationship would experience is not uncommon. We would experience a down cycle that would challenge our endurance. Loans must be serviced, even in a down cycle. Loan documents are drafted to protect a lender from loss. Each of us had executed the loan documents and were honor bound to perform according to these documents. To walk away was no option for me. We had committed to God, each other, and the projects, and we were obligated to the banks. What would we do?

I had been in workout situations before and, given time and cooperation, a good result was achieved. Performance in markets like these had established trust and integrity in the marketplace for me. Nevertheless, in a challenging market cycle, reality sets in. Pledged personal resources are at the mercy of the banks and subject to loss, and the emotions of the moment do not always follow the original script.

In the beginning, a partnership understanding had been agreed to and formulated, but we had failed to formalize it into an executed document. Agreements and documents should attempt to cover every eventuality detailing the commitments to each other. Likewise, there should be defined, enforceable penalties if either partner defaults. In this relationship and others I would experience along my journey, I would learn a valuable lesson. When considering investing with anyone, whether friends, family, or confidants, "Document or don't deal!"

For my partner, "I can't do any more; give it back to the banks," was a well thought-out plan by him and his financial advisor. They were aware of the impact that this strategy would have on me, my career, and my banking relationships, and they privately concluded that I could not follow such a plan. The moment I would surrender a property to a bank, I would effectively be out of business. For me to give less than my best effort in order to perform, I would first have bankrupted my integrity. This proposal, if followed, would be an escape route for my joint venture partner and a bear trap for me. This was not what we had agreed to when the ventures were planned and initiated, and at this juncture was unacceptable.

Contribution has its value, whether it be in the form of cash, property, labor, creativity, loans, or personal guarantees. Fairness dictates that the value of contributions be established and documented. In the process of developing, establishing, and growing a venture or business, whatever the circumstances that create the need for additional contributions—such as economic changes (positive or negative), a windfall order, or misjudgment in planning—you are honor bound to document contributions when you accept them, even if it means dilution of equity or control.

Contributions to business ventures may be in various forms, including experience, ideas, capital infusion, or sweat equity, and the economic value of each participant's contribution must be established and documented by the parties, keeping in mind that a legal document, though not perfect, is a "best effort" to record understandings and agreements between parties.

The initial documentation should include a compensation plan for services to be provided by the parties. The documents should also provide details as to the ownership and the distribution of profits and tax effects.

Anyone seeking venture capital should familiarize himself with the process and the cost. It is not inexpensive because in the early stages, it is high-risk capital. Depending upon the current status of the venture, what the owners must surrender is negotiated and documented. Without additional contribution, the venture may not make it or at least the process will be prolonged. Be objective.

What is best: a big piece of a stagnant or failing company, or a lesser piece of a vibrant company? Which has more value? More is less, or less is more. You can't have it both ways.

The commitment of venture capital is a compliment to those whose dream is on the line. Many wealth-building success stories follow the surrendering of equity for a cash infusion. Usually the price is significant, but in the process, time is purchased and risk is transferred. Time has value, and "ready" funds keep the ship afloat. When value begins to be realized and success is in view, the entrepreneur who sought and accepted venture capital may think, in retrospect, that he surrendered too much.

Integrity Still Counts

Keep your word on the journey *for* life. There is no other option.

Suppose in the midst of an anxious moment, an advisor encourages you to write a letter that says, "I have been subsequently advised not to execute the documents to which I previously agreed." Hear me as a Christian brother: it is *your* integrity that is on the line, *not* the integrity of your advisor.

Is your word not to be depended upon all of a sudden? Honor is valued on the journey *of* life, and it should be priceless on the journey *for* life. How can you have respect for someone who advises you to disavow your word? Advice is cheap from those who don't have "skin" in the game. Put yourself in the other person's shoes and follow the Golden Rule.

The Devil's greatest success was getting Adam and Eve to question God's Word. He used the same approach on Jesus in the wilderness experience, and the trustworthiness of God's Word sustained Him. God's Son trusted His Father's Word. Ask yourself this question: "Will your son trust your word?"

Document or Don't Deal

Even so, the undocumented word of an associate, friend, or stranger is not sufficient in good times and is inadequate in times of controversy. The arena can change rapidly. Misunderstandings and controversy often accompany even documented agreements, but they can be sure to surface and manifest themselves when there is no documented agreement. A perceived understanding between two parties is not an enforceable document.

Remember, more often than not, disagreements in life and in business surface about money, authority, and control.

A handshake is not enough in today's complex society of global, cross-cultural economies where others are often seeking an advantage. Whether on the local, regional, national, or international scene, complex laws govern. Being knowledgeable of these laws represents a significant cost of doing business. Good legal advice is almost always worth more than its price.

In the process of documentation, each party should insist that consideration for his contribution to the investment or venture is fully detailed and accounted for in the documents. If applicable, each participant's role and authority should be defined in the job description, operations agreement, or bylaws. The document should also deal with downside contingencies and the possibility of default.

A young friend got caught in the trap. He and a friend and brother in the church began a loosely documented business relationship, incurring substantial debt without developing a step-by-step operating plan. Value for contributions other than cash was not detailed, and far into a growing partnership, undocumented understandings quickly became misunderstandings. Being Christian brothers and desiring to maintain Christian unity, they decided to be guided by Matthew 18:15–17:

> If your brother sins against you, go and rebuke him in private. If he listens to you, you have won your brother. But if he won't listen, take one or two more with you, so that "by the testimony of two or three witnesses every fact may be established." If he pays no attention to them, tell the church. But if he doesn't pay attention even to the church, let him be like an unbeliever and a tax collector to you.

This is an appropriate forum for dealing with moral or spiritual failings of a brother, invoking the guidance of the Holy Spirit in the process.

In civil matters, there are established laws and procedures for resolving conflicts. God recognizes and instructs us to recognize civil authorities. Jesus said, "Give back to Caesar the things that are Caesar's, and to God the things that are God's" (Matt. 22:21).

Church brothers are not equipped to handle the complexities of the delicate, intrinsic nature of corporate and civil issues. Matthew 18:15–17 assumes the guilt of the one accused. But in civil and corporate matters, it is never wise to prejudge. Too often, the spiritual brothers are conflicted because of friendships or personal loyalties within the fellowship and the just outcome is not achieved.

Prudence calls for those engaged in commerce or business—even Christian brothers—to have the agreed understandings reviewed and documented by an independent source. Too many bad outcomes result when civil matters involving church members are placed before church leadership for resolution.

Again, a good word for everyone on the journey *of* life—and especially for those traveling on the journey *for* life—is "Document or don't deal!"

Before initiating any partnership, LLC, joint venture, or corporate enterprise . . .

- Stop
- Look
- Document

Make Sure You Understand the Documents

Professionals with established credentials and experience in the area of your need should be engaged to draft and circulate for approval the necessary and required documents. Even so, don't be so naïve that you leave the process solely to the professionals. Be diligent, stay involved in the process, and *make sure you understand the documents*. After all, it is your business. Always understand that the most talented professionals are not infallible. No document is foolproof. A client's directive may be to detail every eventuality, but there are not enough "whereas's" and "wherefore's" to document away all potential controversy.

Attorneys can only draft agreements based upon existing laws and the details provided by the parties to the agreements and the guidance they provide. Remember, documents are subject to interpretation by others and may not always accomplish the results intended.

When controversy arises, parties to agreements often become plaintiffs and defendants in courts of law. What started out with promise becomes adversarial, and resolution of the conflict will be based upon some independent third party's interpretation of the contents of documents. This may not necessarily be what you intended or what the other party thought.

As a rule in documentation, always have your own counsel. Don't fall into the conflict of interest trap of believing these words: "My attorney is familiar with this property, this transaction. Let's use him and save the venture some costs on preparation of the documents." I have experienced the tragic results of this scenario. Avoid conflicts of interest at all cost. How can you be sure you will be the one saving money when you yield your independence in the process of documentation to one whose loyalty rests with his client? When conflicts occur, you can bet on which one this professional will be advising and representing.

A recognized Christian leader, the son of a renowned international evangelist, introduced to me his cousin, a nephew of the evangelist. He was represented as a knowledgeable and successful real estate entrepreneur. In the introductory process I was told of others who had invested profitably with him. As I recall, each reference in some way was connected with the family or the organization led by this evangelist's son. At the time, I was one of the board members of the son's ministry.

With other members and associates of this board, a day was scheduled for us to meet with the cousin to look at available, undeveloped tracts of land. He described to me his preferred way to structure land deals: "I acquire the land in my name, add a small (say, five percent) markup and *if* the deal is profitable—and that is entirely up to you—I will participate (say, ten percent) on the back side of the deal, depending on how profitable it is. You can trust me to be fair, with my last name being _____. I could not chance it being otherwise."

Being in the real estate business and a real estate investor, this sounded fair and reasonable to me. On this basis (although detailed and documented rather loosely, primarily by a handshake), I purchased four substantial tracts of unimproved land. He explained his reasons for acquiring the land in his name. He was not a broker, and this allowed him to do tax-free exchanges, forestalling income tax payments.

In later discussions with an individual who had previously optioned one of the properties and subsequently sold the option to the nephew, I was made aware of the "real deal." My eyes were opened as to why the properties were acquired in his name and why he had suggested, "Let's use my attorney. He's familiar with these properties, and it will save us money." That's because if controversy occurs, this professional either represents his client's interest or removes himself from the process because of a potential "conflict of interest."

Mutual or multiple party representations are not recommended. Arm's-length independence is essential for those who provide professional services when more than one party is involved. *Document!* Never engage a professional to represent both parties. A good lawyer will not agree to represent both sides.

Belatedly, my son Donnie and I visited a county courthouse in North Carolina to research previous transfers related to one particular property. How quickly my eyes were opened! My partner and his attorney were in collaboration to distort the public record as to the true consideration applicable to his purchase: "The law states that transfer stamps affixed to deeds are to represent the true consideration of the conveyance." On *his* acquisition deed, additional stamps had been purchased and affixed, reflecting a false consideration in excess of $300,000 over the actual purchase price.

This manipulated value was represented as his cost basis for transferring the property to me. Of course, the five percent markup for his overhead and expenses was added to the inflated price when the property was transferred to me.

I was devastated by this maneuver and subsequent revelations as the processes relating to this and the other properties unfolded.

I had been had!

In the process of my seeking retribution from the "cousin," it was suggested by the "son" (who was chairman of the board that his cousin and I both served on) that I take a sabbatical until these matters were resolved. I inquired, "Is your cousin also going to take a sabbatical?"

"Oh, no, he's family. I can't ask him to do that. His father is on my father's board."

I knew what he meant by those words. Earlier at his request, as a lay member of his board, he had requested that I write his father a personal letter to dispel rumor and innuendo as to his business acumen and his qualities of leadership. I did, and it was well received and acknowledged by his father. Having served his purpose—and not being family—I was now expendable.

I now knew what his agenda was, and since the sabbatical request was only applicable to me, I replied: "I'll do you one better—I resign!" I had been a faithful board member, but I no longer fit into his personal agenda. He needed the votes of members of the "other" board to further his personal ambition.

I requested that my letter of resignation be presented to the board. But I never received any acknowledgment or response to my request, and I doubt if it became a part of the official ministry record since it could have raised more questions than answers.

I have shared the tone and backdrop of a long story for illustrative purposes. I won't bore you with the details. After all, it's not about me; it's about Him. God keeps the only record that matters, and He has greatly blessed me as I have been associated in leadership roles in my denomination and other ministries.

Trust but Verify

Another trap to avoid is the, "you don't trust me" trap. Don't allow yourself to be subjected to a guilt trip by this devious maneuver. Don't condemn yourself for your mistakes or the mistakes of others. This is the *modus operandi* used by many seeking unfair advantage.

In romance there is courtship, marriage, and the honeymoon, followed by real-life experiences. Also in business relationships there is courtship, marriage, and the honeymoon, followed by real-life experiences. Whether in romance or in business, the initial phase always begins by putting the best foot forward. But "trust and verify" was good enough for President Reagan in his dealings with President Gorbachev during the Cold War, and this is also good advice in professional relationships.

- Trust
- Verify
- Document

Do Your Due Diligence

Due diligence is essential. If there is not enough time to properly understand and document the details, be willing to miss the "opportunity." If it's too good to be true, it probably is *not* true. Don't rush! If something about a deal doesn't sound right or feel right, take time to conduct the "smell test." Your intuition is most likely right. Feel good about it or don't deal.

Not every deal works. The economy is cyclical and fickle, and it's too late in the game to try to document after conflict arises. That's when the "blame game" begins, and those experienced in this game can blame others for everything except the common cold and original sin. At this advanced stage, reason seldom prevails.

"But you said—"

"Too late. That was *then;* this is *now.*"

"I thought the deal would stand on its own."

"What do you mean 'Capital Call?' 'Guarantee?'"

Your word against the accusation of an associate or partner has little weight when it comes to undocumented understandings. Unfortunately, afterward is too late to plead ignorance or innocence.

Resource Documents Professionally

In business, life is guided by documents. So when you're documenting, seek independent, professional advice. In fact, there is available to us a resource of great documents to enable us to experience success on the journey *for* life. Some of these are:

- The Bible
- The Constitution
- The Bill of Rights

Familiarize yourself with these, beginning with the Bible. God gave Moses the Law to guide the children of Israel. As long as they were obedient to God's law, it worked for them. Likewise, God has given His Word to whoever will accept it. Obedience is the key to experiencing God's blessings, and disobedience triggers the promised curse for those who don't obey it.

For over three hundred years, life in the USA has been guided by the greatest governing documents the mind of man has ever conceived. Even so, the Constitution was not approved on the first draft. It took seven years after the Declaration of Independence to ratify the Constitution—America's prized document. Documents like these—proclaiming "all men are created equal" and "freedom for all"—set America apart. These foundational and time-honored documents that evolved "little by little" have stood the test of time, even when they have been assaulted from without and within.

Not everyone respects our beginnings and our history as a nation. Never has our freedom and liberty been so under attack as from those whose social agenda and influence in the courts of America continue to have success in interpreting our founding documents in the light of a social agenda that has not been enacted through the legislative process.

Those who love freedom must stand up. If we allow this process to continue to erode our freedom—America will not stand. America is diverse! That is her unique quality.

What Is Freedom?

Freedom is liberty from the control of some other person or some arbitrary power. It is the freedom to be able to act, move, and use without hindrance or restraint.

The opportunities of freedom deserve loyalty. For those of us on the journey *for* life and citizens of the United States of America, our lives should unashamedly honor freedom. A good place to begin is with the Pledge of Allegiance:

> I pledge allegiance to the flag of the United States of America and to the republic for which it stands—one nation under God, indivisible, with liberty and justice for all.

Buy into America's great future by pledging the following, as captured by Kelly King, president of BB&T Corporation: "If it is to be, it's up to me."

As a citizen of the United States of America, I am bound by the laws of my country, and obedience to the law is essential if order is to be maintained on both the journey *of* life and the journey *for* life.

As Pilate inquired, you may also inquire, "What is truth?" Jesus had already answered this question by proclaiming, "I am the way, the truth, and the life" (John 14:6).

In His sojourn on earth, Jesus referred to the Document, the Word of God, in His wilderness experience with the Devil. The Word was Jesus' weapon of defense. On four occasions as recorded in Matthew 4, Jesus reminded Satan (who was also knowledgeable of God's Word)—"It is written . . ."

My choice to travel on the journey *for* life is documented and sealed by the sacrifice of Jesus Christ on a cross. In my life, the Document has stood the tests of doubt, ridicule, assault, and time.

You see, travel on the journey *for* life is not without conflict. Just as Satan was righteous Job's accuser, Satan is my accuser—and yours. He will either *control* you or *accuse* you, depending on whether you travel on the journey *of* life or the journey *for* life.

On Job's journey *for* life, every fiber of his being was tested. Job cried in distress, "Oh, how I wish that God would speak" (Job 11:5 NIV). "Oh, that I had someone to hear me!" (31:35 NIV). But even when he did not understand, Job's confidence was in God.

Job's wife had lost faith in God and said to Job, "Curse God and die" (Job 2:9). But Job would later say, "Even if He kills me, I will hope in Him" (13:15). Job believed the covenant and, like him, I have had periods when faith was all I had. I did not understand God's plan or God's doings. The only place I could stand was on faith.

After the times of testing I can now say, as Job expressed, "I know that You can do anything and no plan of Yours can be thwarted. I had heard rumors about You, but now my eyes have seen You. Therefore I take back my words and repent in dust and ashes" (Job 42:2, 5–6).

As for Job's journey *for* life, it was fully expressed in this way: "The Lord blessed the latter part of Job's life more than the earlier. He owned 14,000 sheep, 6,000 camels, 1,000 yoke of oxen, and 1,000 female donkeys. Then Job died, old and full of days" (Job 42:12, 17).

Job knew success on the journey *for* life.

I know what it is to be attacked by Satan. I've been tempted. I've been tested. But I've been blessed, and I *am* blessed. I still believe the covenant revealed in the Bible.

How did I come to this assurance? I have put God's Word to the test in real-life experiences and have found the promises are true. Most important and personal among His promises are ones like these: "If we confess our sins, He is faithful and righteous to forgive us our sins and to cleanse us from all unrighteousness."

I remember when I transitioned from the journey *of* life to the journey *for* life.

I know *what* I believe.

I know *why* I believe it.

I know *when* I believed.

I know *how* what I believe has molded me into the person I am.

And my purpose and prayer is that *you* will know. You *can* know! I believe that without coercion any person can know and be positively influenced by truth.

As I have said before, I challenge you to put God's Word to the test of experience. Honest inquiry prompted by a desire to really know and experience new life will lead you to know. I have no fear trusting the outcome to Jesus, the One who said, "And I, if I be lifted up . . . will draw all men unto me" (John 12:32 KJV).

You can trust the document of God's Word, the Bible. "Heaven and earth will pass away, but My words will never pass away" (Matt. 24:35).

The journey *of* life is about *me*, who *I* am, what *I* have, what *I* have done, how *I* am perceived by others. Success on the self-centered journey of life blinds a person to the awesome possibilities of selfless living on the journey *for* life.

The journey *for* life is not about me; it is about *Him*, *His* way, *His* glory, and *His* promise of abundant living for those who travel this way. Jesus said, "If anyone wants to come with Me, he must deny himself, take up his cross daily, and follow Me" (Luke 9:23).

The hymnwriter B. B. McKinney wrote:

"Let Others See Jesus in You"

While passing thro' this world of sin,
And others your life shall view,
Be clean and pure without, within,
Let others see Jesus in you.
Your life's a book before their eyes,
They're reading it thro' and thro';
Say, does it point them to the skies,
Do others see Jesus in you?
What joy 'twill be at set of sun,
In mansions beyond the blue,
To find some souls that you have won;
Let others see Jesus in you.
Then live for Christ both day and night,
Be faithful, be brave and true,
And lead the lost to life and light;
Let others see Jesus in you.

Experience in the Trenches

What could be more devastating than the betrayal of a long-time friend in a trusting business venture? On this occasion, I had endorsed a note "in good faith" for my friend. We were in partnership on several properties, and from outward appearances things were going well.

But things were *not* going well!

The bank note was in default, and my friend had not been responsive or communicative with the bank's request for payment. Past due payment notices were followed by "Demand for Payment" followed by foreclosure proceedings being initiated. My partner effectively had become a recluse. The bank then demanded payment from me as guarantor.

Financial statements and signatures that were presented to the bank when making the loan may have been impressive. However, my partner, anticipating trouble, "protected" his personal assets through devious methods to avoid personal bankruptcy. The results were devastating to me.

What would I do? What *could* I do? I was in lonely and rarefied air. What had happened? I had never been in a situation like this before.

On a hunch, Jane and I made a visit to the county courthouse. My fears were confirmed. All my assets were at risk. All his personal assets had been transferred, effectively shielding them from risk. What good is a document when nothing is at risk?

I have always been a trusting person, especially in business relationships with friends. Unfortunately—and at significant cost—I have learned the fallacy of deals based only on friendship and undocumented or loosely documented professional relationships. This is something I wish I had known sooner.

I didn't.

But you can!

Undocumented details as to understandings and commitments made in good times are often subject to interpretation in bad times and become difficult to remember or easy to forget. Too late it becomes "But I thought you said . . ."

In the good times, you share the profits. In the bad times, you are subject to become responsible for all the loss.

So what did I do when I found myself in this situation? I went to my prayer place and on my face (literally) I reminded God that in public and in private, I had acknowledged that He was responsible for everything good that had occurred in my life. Then I told God that before I'd compromise my integrity, "I'll lose it all." Seeking God's guidance, I prayed, "If you will help me, I will do my best to work through this."

He did!

Documentation is not merely intended for protection against fraud or deceit. Documentation is essential when circumstances, illness, or death occur. Who can know the intent of the parties otherwise?

Conflict occurs on both the journey *of* life and the journey *for* life. Conflict in itself is not wrong. In fact, it is inevitable in business transactions. However, the way you deal with conflict may be wrong. Some ugly rumors and lies are often concocted that cause once beautiful relationships to be broken.

"But friends work things out," you say.

Not always.

"Christians always work things out."

Not necessarily. Restoration should be the goal, but it is not always achieved.

Dealing with Loss

My most significant, personal financial loss in business involved a corporate venture called Covenant Towers Retirement Center in Myrtle Beach, South Carolina.

I was one of five shareholders in this development, a limited care retirement center. In addition to each shareholder's proportionate, personal loan guarantee, each of the investing shareholders further agreed to contribute professional services to the venture as required, in his area of expertise.

The pro forma was reasonable. The lending bank accepted it as their basis for approving the required financing. The bank also agreed to what I considered to be a well drafted, limited liability document that was essential for me to participate in the venture.

Experience in the trenches had taught me the importance of limiting my personal financial exposure to a level that is proportionate to my equitable interest in a project with others. After consulting with my counsel, I proposed to the bank what I considered to be a "win-win" plan for the bank and the investor personal guarantees. In this plan, the guarantee shareholders offered the bank a 25 percent cushion to have a limited *pro rata* guarantee rather than joint and several guarantees. On the $10 million dollar loan commitment, this provided a cushion of $2.5 million dollars for the bank.

The second negotiated point relative to the personal guarantees of the shareholders was an agreement that in case of default, the bank would first look to the collateral for repayment and subsequently to each guarantor for his *pro rata* share of any deficiency.

With these approvals in place, the marketing process began.

Sometimes, even the "best efforts" at documentation cannot anticipate how the documents may be perceived or interpreted by other parties. In litigation, decisions as to what the documents mean are left to jurors who become further confused by the arguments of the plaintiff's and defendant's attorneys.

Unfortunately, the timing of Covenant Towers Retirement Center coincided with a financial market down cycle. Tight money accompanied by high interest rates had not been anticipated. Sales dried up and the project could not sustain itself. The other guarantor shareholders were either unwilling or unable to meet capital calls and they bailed out, some filing for personal bankruptcy protection when the bank demanded payment from the guarantors. The other guarantors, most of whom by then were insolvent, were not responsive.

As the process for collecting on the guarantees moved along, the collateral was foreclosed and sold by the court establishing a deficiency of $2 million.

Through legal maneuvers and a ruling by the courts that to this day I along with legal minds that I respect don't understand, the court ruled that each Guarantors Guaranty was 25 percent of the face amount of the note, not 25 percent of the deficiency or the amount owed when the collection process began, resulting in a judgment against me for the entire deficiency.

How can you owe what you never borrowed? Debt is not the face amount of a note. If I request a loan of twenty dollars from you and initially only want ten—ten is what I owe. But this was not the ruling on my guarantee. The judgment was based upon the face amount of the note, much of which had not been advanced.

I had been advised by what I considered to be the most qualified and respected law firm in Myrtle Beach and never thought this result possible. Yet this was the ruling of the court. It was not right. Throughout the process I had been assured by my counsel that rights essential for an appeal of an adverse ruling had been preserved. This assurance quickly evaporated when the court ruled otherwise. Bottom line, I became the only source for repayment.

Subsequently, the appeal process began and ultimately moved to the Supreme Court of South Carolina.

Even when you are right, the best outcome may be to settle and move on. A good outcome may not always be achievable. Your day in court may be your constitutional right, but a day in court is not likely to satisfactorily resolve a deal gone bad. In a courtroom, what appears to be a sure outcome is not a certain outcome. I've had legal battles in court that could have—should have—had a different outcome. We could have accepted a settlement that I thought I could not afford. Ultimately, I lost much more. I could have been 500 percent ahead, but standing on principle, what a price I paid! Yet in the school of experience and hard knocks, I gained much. What I learned from this experience has sheltered me from absorbing other potential losses.

Some of life's greatest success stories of past eras—as well as the world-changing, high-tech advances of the present era creating immense wealth for the partners—began as partnerships or joint ventures. Friends or associates with vision and talent have dazzled the high-tech world. Close to home, I have observed many successful enterprises in real estate, homebuilding, and general construction that began with a handshake partnership and became very successful.

One was Leslie and Shaw. This was a homebuilding and real estate developing company that began when two friends recognizing their complementing talents decided to combine their skills. Together their efforts multiplied, resulting in Leslie and Shaw which would become a household word in the Greenville, South Carolina, residential market. Jane and I observed this partnership "close up" because the partners became our fathers-in-law.

Even though success often occurs, multiple reasons suggest that all partnerships and joint ventures should be defined and documented. The caution I express herein is not an effort to demean partnerships but to enhance them.

Avoid the pitfalls. Dot your i's and cross your t's. My experiences are shared so that you won't have to say with regret later, "I wish I had known that sooner."

The real test for success on the journey *for* life will be what is recorded in a heavenly document called the Book of Life. The apostle Paul referenced his epitaph in 2 Timothy 4:7–8: "I have fought the good fight, I have finished the race, I have kept the faith. In the future, there is reserved for me the crown of righteousness, which the Lord, the righteous Judge, will give me on that day, and not only to me, but to all those who have loved His appearing."

What will be recorded in this document about you?

The Rules of Documentation

I close this chapter with a few practical pieces of advice gleaned over years of experience, some learned the hard way. As summarized here, you will be helped by these insights on your journey *for* life. You will often be tempted to break this one rule, and reason may appear to justify an exception, but I say again: "Document or don't deal!"

"His banker speaks so highly of him."
His banker is not your partner.
Document!

"He is a person of integrity."
A person of integrity won't mind acknowledging his word.
Document!

"He's a Christian brother."
You want him to continue to be your brother.
Document!

"A Christian brother introduced him to me."
Always insist on good references and weigh them.
Then *document!*

"It's a family deal."
Still, it's about money, authority, and control. Why risk dissension in family unity?
Document!

"My mother is my partner."

Jealousy is prevalent among siblings. Insist that your mother protects the integrity of the deal.

Document!

"My father is my partner.

I've been there, done that. A clear document is essential if father becomes incapacitated or dies.

Document!

"He's a longtime friend."

Don't chance losing his friendship.

Document!

"His uncle is a well-known, recognized, high-profile person."

His uncle will not be your partner. Name droppers seek an advantage they have not earned. Integrity is not in the bloodline.

Document!

"We have done other deals and never had a disagreement."

Make sure there is no basis for disagreement.

Document!

One probable exception to the Rule of Documentation would concern transactions between a husband and wife. In the biblical sense, they are "one." In the marriage relationship, unqualified trust between the couple is essential, and their oneness should be allowed to flourish. Even so, in this era, many couples opt for prenuptial agreements. Perhaps marriages would last longer if they were not viewed as a business transaction!

Documents often outlive those who execute them and become the basis for carrying out the intended purposes of the deceased.

Document!

If you don't document your wishes, think what you might be saddling others with if the unfortunate happens to you. *Document!*

Don't use generic documents. Detail your will for your heirs and associates who, if your wishes are not documented, might not have a clue.

It's that important!

14

NOW WHAT?

A Look into the Future

The ultimate test determining success on the journey *for* life will not be the accumulated good deeds achieved on the way. Success on the journey *for* life is determined by a person's obedience and faithfulness to God's Word. This verdict will be spoken after death when we stand before God.

We are each terminal.

Death is certain.

Everyone must face death.

At that moment, you will have accomplished all you can on earth. You will have made your mark on the journey *of* life. In retrospect, you may then review all the good you have done.

I applaud you. I congratulate you. Your accomplishments were many.

Now comes the moment to deposit it all—the accomplishments of time on the scales of eternity. No longer in retrospect but looking beyond this moment, looking beyond this life, you ask, "Is this all there is? It seems so hollow."

In the reality of this moment you can only conclude with King Solomon as expressed in Ecclesiastes 1:2: "'Meaningless! Meaningless!' says the teacher. 'Utterly meaningless! Everything is meaningless'" (NIV). Why? Because if you have disregarded God in this life, He says, "You have been weighed in the balance and found deficient" (Dan. 5:27).

Other than what we innately know, we humans are limited in knowledge, especially concerning the meaning of life and death. God, however, is not deficient at all. He is omnipotent and omniscient. In Matthew 28:18, Jesus said, "All authority has been given to Me in heaven and on earth."

On one of her television shows, Barbara Walters made this statement about death and the afterlife: "No one has ever come back to tell us for sure." I wanted to ask her, "Have you considered the claims of Jesus Christ?"

In order to really know and experience the meaning of life, you must make honest inquiry about the claims of Jesus Christ. In your inquiry, I challenge you to consider Him with the same intellectual honesty through which you consider the philosophies, religions, and claims of others.

The answer to Barbara Walters and every other inquirer is that One *has* come back from death, as He said He would. His name is Jesus, and He spoke with knowledge and authority about the afterlife. He proclaimed, "Because I live, you will live too" (John 14:19).

Relax and be open to dialogue. There is no coercion in honest inquiry. Be objective. Are you willing to risk eternity on what you have heard, on what someone told you?

Don't!

"For God did not send His Son into the world that He might judge the world, but that the world might be saved through Him" (John 3:17). Honest inquiry will overcome bias, controversy, prejudice and lead to truth.

Blaise Pascal (1623–1662) became one of France's leading scientists, inventors, and religious philosophers. He would not settle for the status quo. A religious conversion turned Pascal to a focused inquiry for God. In what is called Pascal's Wager, his probability analysis offered four possible outcomes. His choices included:

- "If I wager for and God is—infinite gain."
- "If I wager for and God is not—no loss."
- "If I wager against and God is—infinite loss."
- "If I wager against and God is not—neither loss or gain."

Pascal concluded God alone could provide answers as to the purpose and meaning of life. Belief in God is the only option that offers hope. Honest inquiry does not cost, and if it leads to life, it is priceless! What a successful conclusion that would be to your journey!

Where Are You in Your Search?

Before you resist or reject God's Word, give honest consideration to its claims. Historical proofs abound that what biblical prophets foretold has come to pass. What higher authority is there? *Listen!* God continues to speak through His words today. *Listen!* He knows you by name.

Where has your journey taken you? Have you realized your dreams and ambitions? Do you have understanding as to why you are here and the purpose of your life? Do you still have unanswered questions? God invites you to inquire of Him. His invitation is absolute: "Keep searching, and you will find" (Matt. 7:7).

The journey *for* life is a call to relationship. Jesus' personal invitation to you is: "Come to Me, all of you who are weary and burdened, and I will give you rest" (Matt. 11:28).

The journey *for* life is not a call to a religion, a temple, a mosque, a synagogue, or a church. The journey *for* life is a call of love—a call *to* love. "God is love" (1 John 4:8). And His love conquers all.

As the end of life approaches, many travelers on the journey *of* life face unexpected outcomes, prompting mental and intellectual challenges. The pages of history are replete with the last words of many who would not, did not believe.

- Voltaire—This famous eighteenth-century writer and unbeliever vowed to destroy single-handedly "the edifice it took twelve apostles to rear." His physician recorded Voltaire's last words: "I am abandoned by God and man. I will give you half of what I am worth if you will give me six months life. Then I shall go to hell; and you will go with me. O Christ. O Jesus Christ." Voltaire's nurse is recorded as saying, "For all the wealth in Europe, I would not see another infidel die."

- Thomas Paine—This early American author known for his anti-God rebellion throughout his life said in his last hours, "I would give worlds, if I had them, that *Age of Reason* had not been published. O Lord, help me. Christ, help me. O God, what have I done to suffer so much? But there is no God. But if there should be, what will become of me hereafter? Stay with me, for God's sake. Send even

a child to stay with me, for it is hell to be alone. If ever
the devil had an agent, I have been that one."

- Beethoven—"Too bad! It's too late."

The words before death are significant because often they
crystallize the actions of the individual's life. They can also reflect
the priorities of that person's life. How different the last words of
those who believed! What a contrast with those who travel on the
journey *for* life!

- Francis of Assisi—"Welcome, Sister Death."
- John Wesley—"The best part is God is with us."
- Woodrow Wilson—"I am ready."
- George Washington—The father of the United States
  of America and our first president knew the Lord
  Jesus. As he lay dying, he ordered that these words of
  Jesus in John 11:25 be inscribed over his tomb, "I am
  the resurrection, and the life: he that believeth in me,
  though he were dead, yet shall he live." His last words
  to his physician were, "Doctor, I have been dying a long
  time; my breath cannot last long, but I am not afraid to
  die."
- D. L. Moody—"I see earth receding, heaven is opening,
  God is calling me."

I want to say with Paul: "I am convinced that nothing can ever
separate us from his love. Death can't, and life can't. The angels
can't, and the demons can't. Our fears for today, our worries about
tomorrow, and even the powers of hell can't keep God's love away.
Whether we are high above the sky or in the deepest ocean, nothing
in all creation will ever be able to separate us from the love of God
that is revealed in Christ Jesus our Lord" (Rom. 8:38–39 NLT).

If the issue is to be resolved on your journey, you must respond to the prompting of God's Holy Spirit. He will not intrude. He will not invade your space. However, He will make Himself known to you. But you must invite Him to come in. In Revelation 3:20, Jesus says, "Listen! I stand at the door and knock. If anyone hears My voice and opens the door, I will come in to him and have dinner with him, and he with Me."

If you will respond to the call of love, you will experience a relationship that will bring peace, contentment, and fulfillment on your journey *for* life. It will not be measured by the number of years you may live. On this journey, it's *how* a person lives that makes all the difference.

In my life, I've had great examples to emulate. Jane's dad, Waldo Norman Leslie, lived an exemplary life. He had made his decision to journey *for* life years before. He was a man of exceptional business acumen whose professional wisdom and advice were sought by many. It was his pleasure—his gift—to share, to plant seeds that helped lead others to success. He was not a man of degrees and letters. He was a person of humble spirit, and his distinction was his personal integrity and the respect of all who knew him—a legacy that continues beyond his earthly life. He was inducted posthumously into the South Carolina Home Builders Association Hall of Fame. For forty-nine and one-half continuous years, he served on the board of the Salvation Army in Greenville, South Carolina. He now has his reward. His "Well done, thou good and faithful servant" has been spoken, and he is in God's presence.

Early on a Sunday morning, a few days before he died, Jane and I shared a memorable few minutes with him. The hallucinating effects of the morphine and other medicines surrendered to us for this moment the lucid, pragmatic person we had known and loved. It was the moment he had chosen to express to us his departing wishes. Speaking to Jane, he said, "Sister, get a pad and put this down."

Jane did, and through cloudy eyes she recorded his instructions. We assured him that we understood his wishes and would faithfully carry them out.

Overcome by emotion, Jane momentarily left the room. (I understood why). While Jane was out of the room, I placed my hand tenderly on my father-in-law's arm and spoke: "Mr. Leslie, I appreciate all you have done and made possible for Jane and me. I loved Jane when I married her, and I love her now."

Interrupting me, he spoke words etched in my memory forever: "Don't say nothing; your life has said it all." Recounting this to Jane later, she said, "You were the son he never had."

As overwhelming as this affirmation was, I anticipate a coming event we each must face. Paul wrote: "We will all stand before the judgment seat of God. . . . So then, each of us will give an account of himself to God" (Rom. 14:10, 12). On that day, may "our lives have said it all."

As a young man, I met Dr. R. G. Lee when he was pastor of Bellevue Baptist Church in Memphis, Tennessee. He was a powerful, poetic preacher. I heard him preach his legendary sermon, "Payday Someday." He seemed at his best when preaching on heaven, as his many publications attest.

I read that when Dr. Lee lay on his deathbed, with periods in and out of consciousness, he would say, "Oh, look. Look!" Returning briefly to consciousness, he told his nurse, "I wanted so badly to help people see heaven when I preached. But, oh, I never did it justice."

My father-in-law, Waldo Leslie, ravaged by cancer and at times hallucinating and incoherent because of debilitating drugs, would occasionally have lucid moments when reality was evident. He would open his eyes and reach up as though he was seeing something—someone Jane and I did not see. Even in the physical agony of dying, he was experiencing the reality of life in the presence of Jesus, comforted by the promise recorded in Hebrews 13:5— "I will never leave you or forsake you."

King David said it like this in Psalm 23: "Even though I walk through the valley of the shadow of death, I will fear no evil, for you are with me; your rod and your staff, they comfort me" (Ps. 23:4 NIV)

In January 2000, leaders in Charlotte, North Carolina, invited their favorite son, Billy Graham, to a luncheon in his honor. Billy initially hesitated to accept the invitation because he struggled with Parkinson's disease. But the Charlotte leaders said, "We don't expect a major address. Just come and let us honor you." So he agreed.

After wonderful things were said about him, Dr. Graham stepped to the rostrum, looked at the crowd, and said, "I'm reminded today of Albert Einstein, the great physicist who this month has been honored by *Time* magazine as the Man of the Century."

Einstein was once traveling from Princeton on a train when the conductor came down the aisle, punching the tickets of each passenger. When he came to Einstein, the scientist reached in his vest pocket. He couldn't find his ticket, so he reached in his other pocket. It wasn't there, so he looked in his briefcase but couldn't find it. Then he looked in the seat by him. He couldn't find it.

The conductor said, "Dr. Einstein, I know who you are. We all know who you are. I'm sure you bought a ticket. Don't worry about it." Einstein nodded appreciatively.

The conductor continued down the aisle punching tickets. As he was ready to move to the next car, he turned around and saw the great physicist down on his hands and knees looking under his seat for his ticket.

The conductor rushed back and said, "Dr. Einstein, Dr. Einstein, don't worry. I know who you are. No problem. You don't need a ticket. I'm sure you bought one."

Einstein looked at him and said, "Young man, I too know who I am. What I don't know is where I'm going."

Having said that, Billy Graham continued, "See the suit I'm wearing? It's a brand new suit. My wife, my children, and my grandchildren are telling me I've gotten a little slovenly in my old age. I used to be a bit more fastidious. So I went out and bought a new suit for this luncheon and one more occasion.

"You know what that occasion is? This is the suit in which I'll be buried. But when you hear I'm dead, I don't want you to immediately remember the suit I'm wearing. I want you to remember this: I not only know who I am, I also know where I'm going."

Stuart Hamblin experienced the transforming grace of God in an early Billy Graham campaign. With the journey *of* life behind him and now on the journey *for* life, he wrote many songs expressive of his faith in God, including such classics as "Until Then."

RCA recording artist Tony Fontane, who likewise has made the transition from the journey *of* life to the journey *for* life, often sang this song in praise to God for His great grace. By God's choosing, Tony became a great friend and Christian brother to me, and as he lay dying at the young age of forty-seven, Tony asked me to speak at his funeral service. Stuart sang "Until Then" and concluded by looking toward Tony's casket as he spoke: "Tony, you made it, boy."

My dad recently observed his ninety-third birthday, and at ninety-three he is not looking backward but forward. In a private conversation in my office, he said, "Son, I'm not here for long."

"Where are you going?"

"Heaven."

"Why are you anticipating Heaven so eagerly?"

"I hear it's a wonderful place."

"Who told you?"

"I read about it in the Bible."

> Do not let your hearts be troubled. Trust in God; trust also in me. In my Father's house are many rooms; if it were not so, I would have told you. I am going there to prepare a place for you. And if I go and prepare a place for you, I will come back and take you to be with me that you also may be where I am. You know the way to the place where I am going. (John 14:1–4 NIV)

Death for a Christian is the final step of arriving home. Grannie often told me, "Son, I want to go home." I was with her when she slipped away. As she was leaving, I whispered in her ear, "I love you, Grannie," and I heard a faint, fading whisper responding from what seemed to be some distant place, "I love you too, son."

These were her last words.

Now she was home.

Dr. John Lennox is a fellow in mathematics and the philosophy of science, as well as pastoral advisor at Green College, Oxford. He is also visiting fellow at the Mathematical Institute, Oxford University, and lectures on faith and science for the Oxford Centre for Evangelism and Apologetics. He has lectured at universities around the world and written many articles on Christian apologetics, particularly on the science-religion debate.

I heard Dr. Lennox lecture on a portion of the book of Revelation. Closing his lecture, he spoke of a fear resulting from a dream he'd had about heaven. Placing his arm around his wife, Sally, he said, "If I had known what it would be like, I would have invested more."

What hope! What assurance!

For each of us on the journey *for* life, God is in control and He is the author of the final chapter. Don't despair because of how things may appear.

I'm reminded of the story of a missionary couple returning home to England after forty years of service. They sent word ahead to their supporters that they were coming home. As they approached their country's coastline, the man anxiously said to his wife, "I wonder if anyone will be here to welcome us home?" Arriving at Plymouth Harbor, the couple stood on the deck of the ocean liner, holding hands and observing the throngs of people crowding the dock. The cheering crowd appeared to be pointing in their direction as a band played. Others were holding banners that read, "Welcome home! We're proud of you!"

"Isn't this wonderful?" the man spoke to his happy, laughing wife as they went below to claim their luggage. Emerging on the gangplank eager and full of anticipation, they saw the crowd was already dispersing. Then they realized the welcome was not for them but for a popular politician returning home.

No one was there to greet *them*.

The husband could not hide his disappointment. "After a lifetime of service, this isn't much of a welcome home."

Taking his arm, his wife said softly, "Come along, sweetheart, this is just England. We're not home yet."

Don't gamble your eternity on what others have said or on what you hope will be. I rest my concern for and challenge to you with the words of Jesus who said, "No man cometh unto the Father but by me," and "Him that cometh unto me, I will in no way cast out."

Time fades and the moment we take our last breath time is no more. "Then what?" you ask.

Don't chance it. You can know right now and begin to experience success on the journey *for* life.

15

PREPARATION FOR YOUR JOURNEY *FOR* LIFE

*Y*ou're not here by accident. Jesus loves you, and He wants you to have a personal relationship with Him. There is just one thing that separates you from God. That one thing is sin.

People tend to divide themselves into groups—good people and bad people. However, God says that every person that has ever lived is a sinner, and any sin separates us from God. That includes you and me. "For all have sinned and fall short of the glory of God" (Rom. 3:23).

According to man's rules, everyone should be punished or rewarded according to how good they are. Accordingly, it might be hard for you to understand how Jesus could love you when other people don't seem to. Nevertheless, I have great news for you! Jesus *does* love you! More than you can imagine! And there's nothing you can do to make Him stop loving you!

Are you thinking that you should make things right in your life before you come to Jesus? Many people feel that way, but that's not what God says! Paul wrote: "But God proves His own love for us in that while we were still sinners Christ died for us!" (Rom. 5:8).

For you to come to God, you must deal with your sin problem. However, God says that you can't make yourself righteous by being a better person. God wants to save you just because He loves you! "He saved us—not by works of righteousness that we had done, but according to His mercy, through the washing of regeneration and renewal by the Holy Spirit" (Titus 3:5).

It is only God's grace that allows you to come to Him—not your efforts to clean up your life or to work your way to Heaven. You can't earn it. It's a free gift. "For by grace you are saved through faith, and this is not from yourselves; it is God's gift—not from works, so that no one can boast" (Eph. 2:8–9).

For you to come to God, your sin must be paid for. God's gift to you is His Son, Jesus, who paid the debt for you. "For the wages of sin is death, but the gift of God is eternal life in Christ Jesus our Lord" (Rom. 6:23).

Jesus paid the price for your sin and mine by giving His life on Calvary's cross. God brought Jesus back from the dead and paved the way for you to have a personal relationship with Him through Jesus. All that's left for you to do is to accept the gift that Jesus is holding out for you right now. "If you confess with your mouth, 'Jesus is Lord,' and believe in your heart that God raised Him from the dead, you will be saved. With the heart one believes, resulting in righteousness, and with the mouth one confesses, resulting in salvation" (Rom. 10:9–10).

God says that if you believe in His Son, Jesus, you can live forever with Him in glory. "For God loved the world in this way: He gave His One and Only Son, so that everyone who believes in Him will not perish but have eternal life" (John 3:16).

Are you ready to accept the gift of eternal life that Jesus is offering you right now? If it is your sincere desire to ask Jesus to come into your heart as your personal Lord and Savior, then talk to God from your heart by praying the Seeker's Prayer.

Dear God,

I am where I am and don't know why. On my journey *of* life, I have searched for answers and found none. I have sought fulfillment only to find fleeting pleasure followed by loneliness and emptiness. In desperation and with honest inquiry, I now come to You seeking answers that have thus far evaded me as to the meaning and purpose of life.

Now I sincerely pray, forgive my sins and help me to know You. I believe that by the Holy Spirit, You have placed the desire in my heart to know You.

I acknowledge that according to the Bible, I am a sinner and need the Savior. In John 6:37, Jesus declared, "The one who comes to Me I will never cast out."

Jesus, I now come to you and I receive You as my personal Savior. Thank You for receiving me and for the gift of eternal life.

Now that You are my Savior, I surrender control of my life to You as I begin my pursuit of success on the journey *for* life. Amen.

Commitment Time

As you approach the end of this narrative, my prayer is that you have been challenged by one blessed life to begin your journey *for* life. Once more, may I point out the difference between the two—the journey *of* life and the journey *for* life. It has been recorded for us by David in Psalm 1—

> How happy is the man who does not follow the advice of the wicked, or take the path of sinners, or join a group of mockers! Instead, his delight is in the Lord's instruction, and he meditates on it day and night. He is like a tree planted beside streams of water that bears its fruit in season and whose leaf does not wither. Whatever he does prospers.
>
> The wicked are not like this; instead, they are like chaff that the wind blows away. Therefore the wicked will not survive the judgment, and sinners will not be in the community of the righteous. For the Lord watches over the way of the righteous, but the way of the wicked leads to ruin. (Ps. 1:1–6)

I have shared my journey *for* life on these pages with a prayer that you too will choose to travel the journey *for* life.

I welcome your inquiry. Let me hear from you—jackshaw. journeyforlife@yahoo.com.

All of us.

ACKNOWLEDGMENTS

Jane, the love of my life, whose constant encouragement, support, and suggestions gave me inspiration to write, rewrite, and keep writing.

Dr. Edna Ellison, author of many books including *Stronger Still* and *Deeper Still*. Edna is a popular women's conference speaker across America and other countries. Edna looked over my shoulder during this venture, prompting me and advising me that there is a ready market for *Little by Little.*

Sandy McAlister, my faithful assistant, who believed from the beginning and labored at the computer, never complaining "draft after draft" until the final version was presented to the publisher.

Robert C. "Bob" Crawford, president of Dan River Floor Covering and chairman of the board of Greenville Technical College for ten years, who laughed, cried, and critiqued the manuscript and encouraged me to complete the "journey." On several occasions he has told me, "I wish I had read this when I was younger."

Lawrence Kimbrough, B&H Publishing Group editor, who assured me I would continue to be involved through the editing and production process. His spiritual sensitivity, skillful insight, tweaking, and ability to flow with the inspiration that birthed *Little by Little* served only to clarify and enhance the message.

A special thanks to Jane, our children, and grandchildren, who allowed me to spend many hours of family vacation time working on the manuscript.

NOTES

1. Jim Cymbala, *The Promise of God's Power* (Grand Rapids: Inspirio, 2002).
2. C. S. Lewis, *Mere Christianity* (New York: Macmillanm 1943).
3. "Baptist Faith and Message," http://www.sbc.net/bfm/ bfm2000.asp#xviii.
4. Mark R. Douglas, *How to Make a Habit of Succeeding* (Grand Rapids: Zondervan, 1966), 115.
5. *Halley's Bible Handbook* (Grand Rapids: Zondervan, 1961).
6. Dick van Dyke, *Faith, Hope, and Hilarity* (New York: Doubleday and Co., 1970), 232.
7. Jerry Foster, *LifeFocus* (Grand Rapids: Fleming H. Revell, 2004), 199.
8. Kenneth A. Wells, *Guide to Good Leadership* (Chicago: Science Research Associates, 1953).
9. Daniel Goleman, "E-Mail Is Easy to Write (and to Misread)," *The New York Times*, October 7, 2007.

ABOUT JACK E. SHAW

*J*ack E. Shaw, from an obscure, humble beginning, is acknowledged by society's measure as a person of success and significance on the journey *of* life. Driven by faith and desire and guided by the principles of God's Word, he epitomizes "Success and Significance on the Journey *for* Life."

He has achieved a distinguished career as real estate developer, general contractor, and investor. Multiple residential subdivisions and commercial developments showcase:

"The House That Jack Built"
"The Apartments That Jack Built"
"The Shopping Center That Jack Built"

He describes his avocation as banking. Somewhat visionary, he abandoned his plan to own a bank and only participated in the evolving banking environment that allowed multiple bank holding companies and interstate banking franchises, leading to a frenzy of mergers and acquisitions. His banking journey began as director of the Bank of Greer and, via merger, was elected a director of United Carolina Bankshares. Through a subsequent merger he became a director of Branch Bank and Trust Company (BB&T).

Jack Shaw is more than his accomplishments through businesses and investments. Along the journey he was elected to the South Carolina General Assembly. He has served as trustee and chairman of the Greenville Hospital System University Medical Center Board of Trustees, member of the Clemson University Foundation Board, member of the Executive Committee of the Southern Baptist Convention, member of the Southern Baptist Foundation's Board of Trustees, the Greenville Community Foundation Board, and the Greenville Tech Foundation Entrepreneur's Forum, as well as chairman of the Emmanuel College Board of Trustees and on the Board of Regents of Oral Roberts University. He has also served on the Samaritan's Purse Board, the World Medical Missions Board, and Holmes Bible College Board of Trustees. He is an accomplished lay speaker, teacher, lecturer, and mentor to aspiring young entrepreneurs.

Mr. Shaw is a dedicated steward of the resources entrusted to him, guided by the principle that "to whom much is given, much is required." He is an "under the radar" philanthropist, focused primarily on educational institutions and student scholarship incentives.